AT EASE...PROFESSIONALLY
An Etiquette Guide
for the Business Arena

Hilka Klinkenberg

Bonus Books, Inc., Chicago

96   95   94   93   92   5   4   3   2   1

Library of Congress Catalog Card Number: 91-77018

International Standard Book Number: 0-929387-55-4

Bonus Books, Inc.
160 East Illinois Street
Chicago, Illinois 60611

Printed in the United States of America

To my sister, Kornelia Davidson, who was my fourth birthday present and has been a source of love, joy, wisdom, understanding and friendship ever since.

CONTENTS

PREFACE

Good manners are made up of petty sacrifices.

Ralph Waldo Emerson

In my international seminars, I stress that cultures are not right or wrong, simply different. And, in order to be effective, we must adjust our behavior to that of the person from the other culture. Sounds simple, but it is a great deal more difficult to put into practice than you might think. In fact, I'm always amazed at the amount of resistance to this concept, despite my awareness of the power of ethnocentricity.

Ethnocentric behavior sets up the culture we have learned, consciously and subconsciously, since birth, as the one correct standard of behavior. A fine concept if we all have the same cultural conditioning, but we don't. We need only witness world events on the front pages of the daily papers to see that neighboring countries don't get along with one another. Some countries such as Canada and Belgium even have different cultures within the same borders that conflict with one another.

The United States is a heterogeneous society with many regional, racial and cultural differences. So, how do we overcome these differences and get on with life? We learn to adjust! When playing in someone else's ballpark, we have to learn to play by the local rules rather than imposing our own.

In the 1980s, communicating and being understood became core concepts of interpersonal and business relationships. Therapists and trainers thrived on helping people get their message across. But, the 1980s was also the "me" decade and the decade of greed. We may have gotten our message across, but that is no guarantee we were effective.

To be effective, we must focus not on getting our message across, but on eliciting the desired response.

In advertising, the most brilliantly creative ad does not necessarily sell the product; it may simply be viewed as a creative ad. As such, it communicated and got a message across, but it did not elicit the desired response...to sell the product.

To put this into perspective, studies show our words only count for 7 percent of the initial impression we make in person and 35 percent of the impression we make over the telephone. The bulk of the impression we make is comprised of vocal quality and non-verbal communication: appearance, body language and behavior. A favorable impression is based on those silent indicators. What the other person thinks is what counts!

Etiquette is the manifestation of good behavior in any given society. *Webster's New Twentieth Century Unabridged Dictionary* defines it as "The forms, manners and ceremonies established by convention as acceptable or required in society, in a profession, or in official life. The rules for such forms, manners, and ceremonies."

A good working knowledge of business etiquette enables you to establish productive relationships by taking the focus off yourself and how you are being perceived. It also helps you to focus on the person with whom you are dealing. Once you start concentrating on other people you'll be able to better hear their expressed and implied needs. The person you're dealing with will give you all the clues you need to elicit the desired response. But first, you have to be comfortable with these forms, manners and ceremonies so that you won't be perceived as a boor.

Etiquette is nothing more than a combination of courtesy and common sense. It is the oil that greases the wheels of commerce and industry. By behaving in an acceptable manner, you don't put unnecessary obstacles in your way. Instead, you present an image of yourself and your organization as caring, canny and sophisticated. And, when you are perceived that way because of your manners, people tend to assume you're smart about other aspects of business, too, and want to deal with you.

Good manners really can be a matter of life or death in business. With them, you can be perceived as being much more able than you are. Without them, people will seldom give you full credit for your abilities; rather, the tendency will be to emphasize your negative qualities. No one is going to care whether your bad manners are based on ignorance, carelessness, selfishness, rudeness or hostility. They will only perceive you as someone they don't want to hire, work with or give their business. Even a strong economy is no cushion for negative behavior because economies are cyclical. The people you offend on the upswing are usually around to applaud, maybe even plot, your demise.

So, work smart. Maximize your potential by investing a bit of time in acquiring the most valuable business skill you can possess . . . etiquette, and you will feel at ease with anyone at any time in any situation.

Hilka Klinkenberg
March 1992

ACKNOWLEDGMENTS

No book is written without help. I would like to thank all the people who shared their knowledge, their experiences and their needs, all of which have found their way onto these pages.

Organizations and their staff like the Italian Wine & Food Institute, Ms. Natalia Bermejo at the Embassy of Spain's Commercial Office, the National Easter Seals Society, Richard Manley at the Westchester County Office for the Disabled, The Lighthouse, and my dear friend Sandy Silverman at Westchester Association for Retarded Citizens provided me with a great deal of information.

I would especially like to thank Dorothea Johnson for sharing so much of her knowledge with me over the years. Many thanks also to my friends and colleagues Nan Leaptrott, Robbie Patterson and Betty Ann Fisher who encouraged me and filled in the answers when my mind went blank.

Without Betsy Ryan, this book would have languished in "One of these days..." land. She has my thanks for this opportunity.

My editor, Traci Taghon, at Bonus Books has exhibited a great deal of patience with me and my schedule. I thank her for a masterful job.

A special thanks goes to my wonderful agent, negotiator and friend, Alice Orr, who has been my buffer this past summer.

I'm blessed with close friends like PR agent extraordinaire Robin Cohn who listened to me rant and rave daily, then made me laugh and told me stories when I stumbled, and Carolyn Gustafson, a savvy image consultant with impeccable grammar and good advice. I cannot thank them enough.

Other friends made major contributions, and I thank them. Margo Krasne taught me a great deal in her excellent and informative Presentation Skills workshops. My editor at *Agenda New York,* Pam Von Nostitz, has helped hone my writing skills.

Janice Brewster checked my French, Mercedes Menocal helped me avoid a few embarrassing faux pas in Spanish and Joy Braverman typed them all up.

My fellow dog parents listened to my anxieties and got me revved up every morning during our walks in Central Park or on the beach. Their four-legged charges exhausted our magnificent monster mutt, Cleo, so that she slept most of the day and allowed me to work in peace. I owe a rousing thank you to Jason and Beau, Peter and Joe, Susan, Ron and Buster, Marcus with Bianca, Bella and BeeBee, Katarina and Vincent and Carol and Zeke.

A thank you, also, to all my other friends who understood that deadlines and etiquette are not always compatible, much as we would like them to be, and forgave me late birthdays, missed lunches and dinners, and cancelled weekends, and still assured me they'd be around when I finished.

Most of all, I would like to thank my family. My mother and father have always been a wellspring of support in everything I've done. My brother-in-law David sacrificed his time in my sister's hectic schedule so that she could help me. Hilary and, most of all, my beloved Bernie deserve a medal of valor for having their lives thrown into upheaval these last four months, even if they do say so themselves. They all have my love.

THE BUSINESS ARENA

If you're going to play the game properly, you'd better know every rule.

Barbara Jordan

Politeness is the hallmark of the gentle-man and the gentle-woman. No characteristic will so help one to advance, whether in business or society, as politeness. Competition is so keen today, there is so much standardized merchandise, there are so many places where one's wants can be supplied, that the success or failure of a business can depend on the ability to please customers or clients. Courtesy—another name for politeness—costs nothing, but can gain much both for an individual and for an organization.

B. C. Forbes

The chief business of the American people is business.

Calvin Coolidge

CHAPTER

1

Understanding the Corporate Culture

Every corporation has its own culture, a culture that is very real and very powerful. There is no getting around it; you have to recognize and deal with it. According to a leading management consulting firm, even the CEO of a Fortune 500 company, whose average tenure is five to ten years, has little ability to change the corporate culture while he's in office. And, any influence he does have on the culture tends to be more noticeable after his departure.

The only way to survive in a corporation is to learn to function within its structure according to its rules. Just as etiquette is the manifestation of good behavior in a culture, the corporate culture determines acceptable business etiquette within that organization or industry.

American corporate cultures are pyramidal. They operate from the top down with a broad base that increases as the level of power decreases. This leads to a natural antagonism between the layers in the structure. It's somewhat like trying to get onto the subway at rush hour. The people behind are trying to push the ones in front out of their way, the ones in the middle are pushing the people in front while snapping at the ones behind them, and the people in the vanguard are trying to keep their position without being trampled from the rear.

That pyramid structure is your first clue to the acceptable behavior within an organization. **Business etiquette is based on hierarchy and power rather than chivalry.** Going back to the subway, if the person at the front is a 250-pound wall of muscle who gets annoyed by your pushy behavior and decides to block the door and not let you on the train, you're going to be left back on that platform, waiting.

By learning to work effectively within the corporate system your ascent through the corporate hierarchy won't be blocked. You may even find yourself pulled up the ladder because skilled professionals are a boon to any organization.

Corporate culture is a two-tiered set of values shared by management and employees and composed of both philosophical principles and daily principles, according to Stanley M. Davis in his book *Managing Corporate Cultures*. Philosophical principles guide how to conduct business, how to compete and how to manage. Daily principles determine how the philosophical principles are implemented within the organization.

ing to decide the priorities of everyone's assignments. Check the secretary's workload. If your project really is urgent and your associate's work has to be put on hold to accommodate you, confer with your peer to work out a list of priorities for the secretary. Don't cajole, threaten or try to impose your will upon the secretary directly; you'll alienate both the secretary and your peer.

Be especially sensitive when someone else's secretary is helping to cover your secretary's absence. It is best to establish the rules of the exchange beforehand. Executives tend to feel very proprietary about their secretaries and where the secretary's loyalty should lie. **Never ask someone else's secretary to do work for you without first clearing it with the secretary's boss.**

Never, ever insult someone in front of his or her secretary. Not only is it embarrassing to both parties, but you undermine the boss-employee relationship that should be based on mutual respect.

Peers

The secret to moving up in any organization is to gain the confidence of both your superiors and your peers. Your peers can be your greatest source of strength in business. That may sound like a contradiction because they are also your competitors for increasingly infrequent promotions as you rise on the corporate ladder, yet you will also be judged on your relationship with your peers. How well-liked are you? How much respect do you command with your co-workers? How much of a power base are you able to establish among your peers? People are seldom promoted because they are disliked, disrespected lone wolves.

Treating anyone badly will make you look like you're not a team player, and team players are prized in most American corporations as effective contributors toward the corporate good. Corporate etiquette helps relieve stress among peers by creating a warm, friendly environment that is conducive to productivity. When productivity and creativity flourish, the entire organization benefits.

By being supportive of your team members in meetings and by complimenting them for the way they've handled an assignment, you will both look good. **Always compliment the work, though, not the person's physical appearance, regardless of the gender of your co-worker.** Don't divert the focus from the professional to the personal.

Never refer to anyone in your office as "sweetie," "honey," or "dear." Nor should anyone ever be referred to as a

"hunk" or a "dish." Don't call anyone a boy or a girl after the age of puberty. All of these terms are highly insulting and derogatory, and they do not elevate your position by comparison. Treat your peers with respect. Greet your associates the first time you encounter them each day. Then nod and smile when you meet throughout the day.

Listening attentively to your peers will make them feel as though you care about them and their work. By cooperating with one another, you build a source of mutual support and loyalty. However, it is bad manners to ask a co-worker to cover for you.

Peers are natural allies, but if you alienate them, you'll never need any other corporate enemies to sabotage your career. When confrontations occur, curb your anger and exercise diplomacy in your communications. **Diffuse the hostility with a tactful suggestion to discuss the dispute in private and you will look in control and powerful.** As someone once said, you get along by getting along.

When you move from one office to another, don't try to revamp the existing structure. Watch and listen at first, and you may even learn that their way is better without having created any undue antagonism. No one wants to hear how you did it back in New York or at your former employer any more than you want to hear that you should go back where you came from.

Being a team player requires a special set of skills because it requires getting along with your rivals and still looking after your own interests. Good etiquette does not entail becoming a doormat for anyone. Corporate manners demand you take responsibility for your own deeds without being anyone's fall guy. The best way to protect your turf is to deal from a position of strength. The best way to move up and increase your turf is to do your job so well, so smoothly and so effectively that you'll be given a bigger, better job.

Superiors

The tone of a working relationship is always set by the person in upper management. Because like attracts like, take your cue from the boss's behavior and dress. Indications of what is acceptable in the corporate culture come from your superiors. Bucking the trend set by their example will not endear you or make you look like a team player. **If your managers address you formally, make sure you do likewise.** However, if they call you by first name, it is still better to wait before responding in kind until you've been invited to do so. Don't call your superior "Sir" or "Ma'am"; address the person as Mr. or Ms. followed by the surname until you are invited to use a first name.

Addressing your boss by first name, having lunch together, or being invited to play squash, tennis or golf at his or her club does not mean that you've established an intimate friendship. Nor is it likely that a good boss will try to seek that type of relationship. Remember that corporate America is based on hierarchy and power, and power expects to be acknowledged.

A powerful person is unlikely to want to be surrounded by yes-men because a powerful person does not need that kind of ego stroking. A good boss knows that you will make him or her look good by making valuable contributions, not by giving rubber-stamp approval.

Promising more than you are capable of delivering will not gain your boss's esteem. Not only is it bad company manners, it is bad corporate politics. Your boss is responsible for the smooth operation of his or her turf and its relation to the organizational structure. Performing below your promise will upset the organizational applecart and make the boss look bad. You have to be honest about your work and any problems you may be encountering or your boss will not be able to go to bat for you.

If you do encounter problems, or if your performance review is less than glowing, accept the criticism graciously. Your superior is trying to help you, so retain your composure. It is ill-mannered to get hostile or defensive. And, don't deflect the criticism by joking or being flip. You'll only look immature and unsuited to the responsibility you've been given.

WHEN SOMEONE CALLS ON YOU

When a client, a vendor or a co-worker visits your office, you are, in effect, the host or hostess. As such, you control the visit. First and foremost, greet the visitor. Either you or your secretary should go out to the reception area, make the introductions and extend a hand in welcome, then escort the visitor back to your office. **If the secretary has gone to fetch the visitor, be sure to get up and out from behind your desk.** Preferably, be at the door to welcome the visitor. Unless you are planning to fire someone, never stay behind your desk; it acts as a protective barrier that conveys a confrontational message and distances you from your caller.

As host, it is your function to guide visitors to the place you would like them to sit. Many offices have a conversational seating area, more conducive to a friendly exchange than speaking across a desk. If you have a choice of furniture for your office, opt for chairs that are not too deep to get out of easily and gracefully rather than a sofa. Chairs offer more flexibility in the seating structure. If you have only one chair for visitors in your office, move it to the side of your desk. Offering coffee or tea often acts as an ice breaker and puts the visitor at ease.

Should someone enter while you are on the telephone, try to terminate the call as quickly as possible, especially if that person has an appointment with you. The person with an appointment has priority on your time unless you're dealing with a crisis. In that case, apologize and try to indicate how long you'll be. Keeping someone waiting at any time for no good reason is a feeble power play that makes you look weak.

TIME MANAGEMENT

Visitors often can cause serious disruptions to our concentration and productivity. As long as you receive a paycheck, your responsibility is to the corporate good, and you have to deal with visitors accordingly. For instance, when you are interviewing someone or when you are listening to someone else's sales presentation, you are very much in control of the time you allot the person. To draw a meeting to a close, indicate that you have only a few minutes left so they have an opportunity to summarize. Thank them for coming, let them know when they can expect to hear from you and escort them to the door.

While subordinates can be dealt with politely, but firmly, with instructions to get to work, talkative colleagues may require a bit more tact. Guard your time without creating unnecessary friction. Explain that you wish you could chat with them, but you have work that must be attended to immediately; you might suggest continuing the discussion over lunch. If that doesn't work, try walking over and gently ushering the person toward the door as you continue to speak. If that doesn't work, you may have to firmly ask the person to leave.

Senior executives seldom achieve their level of success by hanging out around the water cooler or in other people's offices;

they appreciate the value of time. But, if you have been blessed with a talkative boss, grin and bear it and work late if necessary. If it is a serious problem for you, politely explain that you are having difficulty finding the quiet time necessary to complete the workload and ask for the boss's help. If that doesn't work, consider a job switch.

Everyone's work is important to the smooth operation of an organization. **Don't be the person who disrupts others. State your case and get back to your own work.** Treat others fairly and extend the same respect for their time that you expect of them and you will create a win-win situation that makes everyone look good.

Visiting Someone Else's Office

When visiting someone else's office, whether in your own company or at a client's office, your role is equivalent to that of a guest. The person you're visiting should act as host. It is up to the host to guide the visitor through the appointment rather than having the visitor make him or herself at home.

Arrive punctually to ensure the success of any business appointment. Americans treat time as a tangible object, something that can be spent, saved or wasted. Wasting someone's time is a serious personal infringement because time is an irreplaceable commodity. You should arrive a few minutes early. Present your card to the receptionist and state your business. If you have a coat, ask where to hang it before you go in to your appointment.

Wait to be shown to a chair; never take the seat of power. If your host sits without offering you a seat, don't remain standing because it can look like an attempt at intimidation. If there are several chairs, ask where the host would like you to sit.

Don't put a briefcase or a handbag on someone's desk or chair; keep it on the floor. Don't touch anything on the person's desk and don't spread papers all around. If you do have files that you are working from, keep them on your lap unless the host suggests you use the desk. No one appreciates an intrusion into his or her space.

State your case succinctly and take your leave. A good rule of thumb is to stay no longer than fifteen minutes. If your host is really interested he or she may ask you to stay or to schedule another appointment.

Always follow up an appointment with a thank you note within twenty-four hours of the meeting. Refer back to a shared moment, an interesting point that was brought up or information that was requested of you. Avoid the formula note that begins, "Thank you for taking the time out of your busy schedule to see me. I know how busy you must be." While that was effective a number of years ago, it has become overworked and has taken on the tone of a trite form letter.

When follow-up has been requested of you, make sure you do it. There is nothing more refreshing and nothing that will get you noticed faster than keeping your word. While keeping your word is basic to good manners, doing what you say you're going to do has become all too rare in the business arena.

DOORS

There is a great deal of confusion about who goes through a door first. **In the business arena, whoever reaches a door first, regardless of gender, should open it, go through and hold it to ensure it doesn't hit the person behind.** If the door pulls toward you, it is courteous to hold the door for the others, especially if they hold a more senior position.

There is an unspoken etiquette based on pecking order that the most senior executives, male or female, go through the door first.

Men no longer hold doors open for women because it implies that the woman is incapable of doing it for herself. And, if a woman is incapable of opening a door, she must be incapable of handling more serious matters. As in all rules, of course, there are exceptions. If you would hold the door open for another man, then it would probably also be appropriate to hold the door for a woman. For example, it is only courteous to hold the door for anyone who is laden down with stacks of files, regardless of position in the corporate pecking order.

When hosting others, your role as host preempts pecking order or gender. An executive acting as host should always open the door for visitors and motion them to walk ahead. If, however, the door is a revolving door or if it is particularly heavy, the host should push through the door and wait for the others on the other side. Be sure to stand aside so that you allow them sufficient room to get out of the doorway.

When someone holds a door open for you, always remember to thank that person.

ELEVATORS

When getting on a crowded elevator, the person nearest the door enters first. In a self-service elevator, hold the door open until everyone has entered. If you're near the panel in a crowded elevator, ask the other passengers what floor they want and press the buttons for them.

If you are nearest the door, step aside or step out to allow those in the rear to exit. The person nearest the panel should press the door open button until everyone who is not exiting at that floor has had a chance to reenter. If you are one of the first to enter an elevator and you are getting off at a low floor, step immediately to the side of the elevator rather than to the back; it is usually much easier to exit when you don't have to make your way from the rear.

Men should not remove their hats in a crowded elevator. While holding your hat in front of you may give you a bit more personal space, it is extremely inconsiderate because it adds to the crowding.

Even when you're alone in an elevator, don't do anything you would not do in the presence of others. Elevators in office buildings often have security monitors that capture your every move on screen.

ESCALATORS

Whoever gets to the escalator first gets on first. **Step to the right and hold on to the handrail so that you don't block anyone who is in a hurry and wants to pass on the left.** Do not stop as soon as you get off the escalator. Not only is it bad manners to those behind you, it is positively dangerous. If you don't know where you're going, step away before you stop to get your bearings.

SMOKING

Smoking is not only hazardous to your health, it can be hazardous to your career. In recent years a strong anti-smoking movement has gripped the working world. Smokers have become *persona non grata* because studies show that smoking is responsible for absenteeism and higher medical, disability and life insurance premiums, a major problem for American business.

Smoking is now considered a sign of weakness rather than a sign of sophistication. Inability to conquer a nicotine habit labels you as someone lacking in self-control, an undesirable failing in top management. Many states have even enacted legislation against smoking in the workplace, because breathing secondhand smoke is at least as dangerous, if not more so, than inhaling directly. The federal government has also banned smoking in all of its buildings.

Even when a person is not allergic to cigarette smoke, smoking is still annoying to others because it invades their olfactory space. One winter, a client from out of town drove in to see me. Because it was cold, he must have kept the car windows closed while chain-smoking for the entire trip. I could smell his stale tobacco odor from across the reception area. That odor hung in my office for almost an hour after he left. Smokers are seldom aware of that stale tobacco odor on themselves or others. I had stopped smoking only a few months earlier, and it came as a shock to realize the offense I must have given others all the years I smoked.

If you are a smoker, don't smoke if you don't see an ashtray. **Lack of an ashtray is a clear signal that smoking would be considered offensive. Nor should you ask, "May I smoke?"** While few people will refuse permission, they may fume silently while you smoke. Even if you see an ashtray in another person's office, don't light up unless they do.

While it is acceptable to smoke in your office, as long as it is not against company regulations, you should always ask visitors if they mind you smoking. A courteous host is attentive to his visitors' wishes. When you do smoke, keep an eye on the direction of your cigarette smoke and move the ashtray or your cigarette if it is drifting into someone's face. Even other smokers are offended by someone else's smoke blowing into their eyes. Be neat; make sure you don't litter cigarette ashes and butts everywhere.

When you invite a client to lunch, always ask beforehand

if he or she smokes and sit in that section whether you're a smoker or a nonsmoker, provided you are not allergic. Never smoke at a table when others are still eating. Wait until coffee is served at the end of a meal, rather than lighting up between courses.

Never smoke a cigar in a restaurant or in someone's home or office unless the host offers a cigar. Because cigar and pipe smoke is even more offensive to many than cigarette smoke, the courteous host invites those who choose to smoke cigars to join him in another area, preferably one that is well-ventilated.

While nonsmokers have every right to politely request others to smoke elsewhere or extinguish the cigarette if they are being bothered by the smoke, nonsmokers do not have the right to rebuke smokers about their perceived vice. It is as rude to force your personal opinions on other people as it is for them to blow smoke in your face.

THE FAST TRACK

1. Learn the corporate culture because that determines the acceptable business etiquette within that company.

2. Beware of sensitivities caused by regional or cultural differences and make the necessary adjustments.

3. While all employees may not merit equal attention, it is still a first class faux pas to treat anyone second class.

4. Always deal with problems in private. Never embarrass or chastise someone in front of others.

5. Greet superiors, peers and support staff when you first meet them each day.

6. Don't forget to say "please" and "thank you" to your staff.

7. Let your secretary know how you would like to be addressed.

8. Don't delegate personal chores to your secretary.

9. Take your assistant out to lunch occasionally, but don't monopolize personal time.

10. When sharing a secretary, arrange the priorities of the workload with your peer.

11. Never ask another person's secretary to do work for you without first clearing it.

12. Compliment work, not physical appearance.

13. Don't use derogatory terms like "honey," "sweetie," "dear" or "hunk." Avoid "sir" or "ma'am."

14. Diffuse hostility with kind remarks instead of returned hostility.

15. When someone calls on you, it is your responsibility to act as host or hostess to the visitor.

16. If you can't greet the visitor in the reception area, have your secretary go out to get the visitor.

17. Don't greet a visitor from behind your desk.

18. Be punctual.

19. Don't disrupt others from their work by loitering. Don't allow others to monopolize your time.

20. Keep your briefcase, handbag or coat off others' desks.

21. Never touch anything on someone else's desk.

22. Keep appointments brief and to the point.

23. Always follow up an appointment with a thank you note and complete any promised follow-up.

24. Whoever gets to a door first opens it unless that person is laden down.

25. Junior executives hold doors for senior executives.

26. The person closest to an elevator door enters or exits first.

27. Step aside to allow people in the rear of an elevator to exit.

28. Stay to the right on an escalator and clear the top quickly when getting off.

29. Don't smoke if there are no ashtrays. Never ask if you may smoke.

PERSONAL PRESENCE

Our image is a silent introduction of ourselves to others. It speaks volumes.

Carolyn Gustafson

The most important thing in communications is to hear what isn't being said.

Peter F. Drucker

If you've ever read the speeches of some of the world's great orators, you may well have shrugged and wondered how they acquired such a reputation. It's simple; the words have very little to do with it. According to the research of Albert Mehrabian, which was substantiated by the similar findings of Dr. Ray Birdwhistle, **words account for only 7 percent of the impact of our message. Vocal quality accounts for 35 percent and nonverbal image, the way we look and** act, accounts for a whopping 58 percent in our culture and even more in some others.

Our personal presence is the sense of ease and composure we project by the way we use space and send signals with our body language, our appearance, our dress and our personal grooming. It determines the perceptions others have of us, our attitudes, our motives and our opinions of them. **This nonverbal response, whether it's called intuition, a sixth sense or a gut reaction, is that first impression formed within ninety seconds of meeting someone.** And you never get a second chance to make that first impression, which seldom changes for the better.

Unfortunately, we are all too often unaware of the signals we send and the offense that we may be giving. Paying attention to these seemingly inconsequential matters will help pave the way for a smooth interchange of communication that can lead to a successful relationship.

PERSONAL SPACE

While space implies the sense of touch, or rather a lack of it, we actually perceive space with all our senses. You can invade someone's personal bubble of space by the way you smell and the volume at which you speak as much as by the proximity at which you stand. Your use of space has a direct bearing on your ability to relate well to other people.

As you travel around the country, remember that space varies with location and, because Americans are very space conscious, you will have to adjust your personal bubble to communicate effectively. In crowded New York, people tend to be perceived as very private. Midwesterners appear much more open, and southerners more approachable still.

There are no hard and fast rules about the amount of space to give someone, but the average acceptable personal space in the United States ranges from about eighteen inches to four feet. As the intimacy decreases, the space increases. At the outer limit of four feet, you are keeping the other person just out of reach, whereas normal conversation tends to be conducted at arm's length. In a more convivial atmosphere, like a cocktail party, space tends to decrease slightly.

Be aware of the spatial clues someone is sending you. If the person steps away or leans back, you may be too close and creating discomfort. If, however, the person keeps edging closer and you keep backing away, you may be coming across as aloof and cold. Either way you'll hamper an open flow of communication.

The volume at which you're speaking may be the culprit. If the person is backing away and the distance is making you uncomfortable enough to affect your ability to communicate, try lowering your voice to bring him or her closer to you. If, however, you are forever being asked to repeat what you're saying because your voice is so soft or you mumble, you may have to raise your voice to keep others from getting too close.

Space is an indication of status. Status is displayed not just by the large corner office on a high floor, but by the deference we show a superior by keeping a respectful distance, or by the intimidation caused by a boss who leans over an employee's desk and invades that person's territory and personal space. By moving into someone's personal space, you signal "You are a non-person. You do not matter." This message can also be signalled by ignoring someone who enters your space, even to someone such as your secretary who may be in and out of your office regularly. While you are not expected to chat, you might occasionally look up or nod to indicate that you are aware of them.

OFFICE SPACE

Offices are an extension of personal space. They are an individual's staked-out personal territory. Where you seat someone who comes to your office conveys volumes about the formality or informality of the meeting. Having someone sit across the desk from you creates a great deal of distance and formality that can be difficult to bridge. Simply by moving the visitor's chair to the side of the desk, you narrow the distance and imply that, while you're there to do business, you're working in close harmony and you are approachable. Showing someone to a seating area in your office indicates a much more informal, conversational meeting.

As the visitor to someone's office, you should always be aware that you are invading another's territory, with or without an invitation. All your actions, even if you are the person's boss, should indicate a degree of respect for that person's space unless you want to appear hostile, aggressive, threatening or rude.

BODY LANGUAGE

Every movement of our body, every posture we adopt communicates a message. Whether we stand, sit, shuffle our feet, drum our fingers, tap a pencil, fidget with a strand of hair, tense our facial muscles, cross or uncross our legs, our actions reveal our unspoken thoughts. Pay attention to all those telltale signals and learn to control them because they distract others from paying attention to your words and may even be contradicting your verbal message.

Several excellent books on body language can be found in your library or neighborhood bookstore. You may learn a great deal by reading them, but be wary of interpreting someone else's motives by a single movement. Look at the overall picture, at what the entire body is expressing. A man sitting with his arms crossed is sending very different signals if he is leaning in toward you, or sitting very erect with legs also crossed or leaning back with his head cocked to one side.

The less you rely on gestures, the more powerfully you'll be perceived. Studies show that the higher a person is on the socioeconomic scale, the less that person gestures. The vocabulary range of someone higher on the scale tends to be far greater, so that person relies less on nonverbal communication.

When you walk into a room, move with vigor and vitality and stride toward a destination, even if that destination is only three feet into the room. Keep your head erect and your shoulders back. By entering with confidence and energy, you set the stage for what you're going to say and do. Others not only expect but also accept you taking charge when you exhibit poise.

Standing and sitting with good posture helps you project authority. Keep both your feet planted firmly about hip distance apart for solid support when you converse with others. By leaning or swaying, you lose much of your presence. Sit with your feet firmly on the floor or possibly crossed at the ankle. Crossing and uncrossing your legs not only reveals tension, it also creates problems because it cuts off circulation. By keeping both your feet flat on the floor, you prevent fatigue and perform in a much more alert manner for a longer time.

Never slouch. Not only does it make you look listless, lazy and bored, it is a drain on the other person who has to do twice the work to sustain the energy of the conversation. Sit erect with the back of the chair supporting your back. To indicate the intensity of your interest in the other person and what is being said, lean forward slightly.

Eye Contact

I ne'er could any lustre see
In eyes that would not look on me.

Richard Brinsley Sheridan

The eyes are more exact witnesses than the ears.

Heraclitus

Your eyes convey an entire scope of both positive and negative emotional responses. Through your eyes, you send messages of enthusiasm, excitement, approval, sincerity, admiration, empathy, interest and concern. Through your eye contact, you signal to the other person that you are listening.

The amount of eye contact that is made between two people varies greatly from culture to culture, and even within cultures. **In the United States, polite eye contact normally ranges from 40 percent to 60 percent of the time.** Less than 40 percent, and you appear shifty, devious and untrustworthy. By making eye contact more than 60 percent of the time, you appear imperious, authoritarian and intimidating.

When you are speaking to people, you may want to pay close attention to their eyes to see if you are holding their attention. If not, you may want to adjust your style of communication and possibly ask a question to get them to speak and to refocus their attention.

Dressing Appropriately

Dress gives one the outward sign from which people can judge the inward state of mind. One they can see...the other they cannot.

The Queen of England to the Prince of Wales

> If a woman is poorly dressed, you notice her dress, and if she
> is impeccably dressed, you notice the woman.
>
> **Coco Chanel**

Americans dress with a great deal more self-expression and with a much greater emphasis on ease and comfort than people in other cultures. The absence of dress codes in schools in the last twenty-five years has made it even more difficult for younger executives to understand the importance of appearance.

Your appearance is an indication not only of your self-respect, but also of the respect you have for the person with whom you are dealing. If you can't make the effort to appear at your best, you imply that the person you're dealing with is not worth the effort. The extended assumption will be that the quality of work or service to be expected from you will probably be no greater than the quality of your appearance. The way you dress is the outer expression of the inner person, and you will be judged accordingly. The way you dress leaves an indelible impression.

Radical dressers do not last in many organizations. Success breeds success because people like the security of dealing with someone who is a proven commodity. **If your company has a dress code, observe it; dress to suit the authority figures who ultimately control your destiny.** If you have no idea of what is acceptable in your organization, emulate the senior management.

If that doesn't give you a clear idea, look at the pictures in the business publications. The people you see there may not be the illustrations of sartorial splendor that you find in the fashion publications. However, these are the success stories you not only want to emulate, but whose approval you will probably want to garner to further your career. Unless you are in the fashion industry, avoid the extremes of fashion. The fashion industry exists to make money, not to guide you up the ladder of success, and it will sell you whatever you are foolish enough to buy.

You cannot judge an outfit by itself. You must consider regional variations based on climate and geography; what is appropriate in Maine will look out of place in Miami. A conservatively dressed Philadelphia banker will look stiff and unapproachable in Los Angeles. Colors that look fine in the bright Houston sun will look garish in New York, whereas New York's basic black will appear funereal in southern California.

Consider the business environment, the type of company and the work you do. If a great deal of your work is on site a silk suit on a man or a narrow skirt and high heels on a woman will signal you are not there to do business or that you are inexperienced.

Consider the function. Wearing accessories appropriate to an elegant business dinner at a breakfast meeting may well give the impression you haven't changed from the night before.

Finally, consider the statement you want to make with your appearance and the audience you are addressing. The outfit that reeks of power won't be appropriate if you are in sales, trying to convey a message of friendly service. A lawyer once complained to me that he had tried to get a deposition from a reluctant witness and it was a fiasco. In speaking with him, I learned he had worn his best power suit and tie to impress upon the witness, an older woman, the seriousness of his intent. His presence agitated the woman so that he was unable to get any information from her and the deposition had to be rescheduled. By changing to a "user-friendly" outfit for the second attempt, the witness gradually calmed down despite initial apprehensions and gave him the information he needed. Success is not looking powerful; it is achieving the desired goals.

If you don't feel confident in your ability to make the proper selections, consider hiring an image consultant or a personal shopper. However, I caution you that it is really a case of buyer beware. Before hiring image consultants, take a good look at the way they present themselves. Do they have a business background and understand the needs of the business arena, or are they trying to make you feel good and look stylish? Would their appearance be out of place in your organization? Do they ask you about the company you work for, your position and the impression you're trying to make? Can they tell you about the psychological impact colors, styles and fabrics will have on others? If in doubt about their suggestions, check with someone whose taste and judgment you trust before you go out like the emperor in his new clothes.

There is no such thing as neutral clothing. Everything you put on communicates something. Your image is either working for you or against you. Own a full-length mirror and use it so that you can see the total image you're creating for others.

Consider the fit of the clothes. Jackets should never be skimpy; skirts or trousers should not be so tight that they convey a message of sexiness. Exposed cleavage and miniskirts are not appropriate business attire for women. Never wear 100 percent polyester.

It looks cheap, it doesn't wear well, it does not breathe so you perspire a great deal more and it retains odors. It is not appropriate for someone even moderately successful in business.

Double-breasted jackets on both men and women are meant to be buttoned, not left hanging open and flapping around. If you take a suit jacket off in your office, always put it back on before receiving a visitor or going to see a superior. Short-sleeved shirts on men and sleeveless blouses or dresses are inappropriate business attire. Keep them covered with a jacket.

Jewelry should not be obtrusive, nor should it move or jangle. Keep all jewelry simple and inconspicuous. Don't wear rings on the right hand and you'll feel much more relaxed about shaking hands when the rings don't dig into your fingers. Wear a watch even if your internal clock functions well. Business in the United States runs according to schedules and deadlines, and promptness counts.

Never brag about designer labels or the price of your clothes. It is not how much you spent but how you look that is important. Also, you should be wearing the clothes, not the other way around. Never ask people about the price of their clothing or where they got it.

Unless you're living in the Arctic, fur coats are not appropriate in the business arena. They imply ostentation rather than success. Many people are also opposed to the killing of animals for fur. If you wear a fur coat in the evening, keep it with you unless the maître d'hotel offers to take it. Don't impose the worry about possible theft on others.

Shoes must always be polished and in good repair. Keep fabric softener sheets in your briefcase for a great instant shine.

Dress well when shopping and you will get much better service from the sales staff. Buy quality not quantity. Quality shows, and it will enhance your image. You will also get much greater clothing mileage for your dollar; it's called investment dressing.

At social functions, it is acceptable to compliment people on their appearance if the compliment is sincere. Within the office, restrict compliments to the work. Don't give a compliment as a *quid pro quo* for a compliment received. **When you are given a compliment, a simple "thank you" is sufficient response.**

On a Business Appointment
Always take your coat off when you call on someone's office. If the receptionist offers to take your coat, give it. Otherwise,

ask where you may hang your coat before you go in to your appointment, especially in bad weather when you may also have an umbrella or galoshes. If there is no place to hang the coat, take it with you, but put it neatly on the back of your chair unless you are told to put it some other place.

Keep your suit jacket on when you are in someone else's office unless the host suggests you remove it. Even then, it is not mandatory to do so. Taking your jacket off without permission is equivalent to making yourself at home in a stranger's house. Never get so informal that you roll up your shirt sleeves in someone else's office, even if others do. Maintain your sense of decorum.

Keep your briefcase and/or handbag on your lap or on the floor; never put it on someone else's desk. Keep files on your lap, too. Never touch or move anything on someone else's desk.

At a Special Function

An invitation will often specify the appropriate dress for an occasion in the lower right-hand corner. Guests are expected to adhere to the requested dress. If in doubt about what to wear, call the host or hostess. The thoughtful host and hostess will tell you what they are wearing so that you will embarrass neither them nor yourself by appearing in something totally inappropriate.

Couples should discuss what they are planning to wear and coordinate the styles to avoid appearing as odd as a pair of mismatched socks.

Casual attire can be the order for parties at any time of day or evening. The type of activity will determine the clothing because what you would wear to a barbecue would not necessarily be appropriate for a casual cocktail party.

Informal, or semi-formal as it is called in some parts of the country, is a cut under black tie. Men would wear a dark business suit, a white shirt (preferably with French cuffs) and a dark silk tie, possibly with a tiny dot pattern. Women would wear a dressy suit in an evening fabric, a short cocktail dress or a long skirt and blouse.

Black tie formal can vary greatly according to geographic and climatic conditions, so it is always advisable to do your homework. **Basically, though, it refers to a tuxedo or, in summer, a white dinner jacket for men.** Women would wear either a short or a floor-length evening dress.

White tie formal is full evening dress. Men would wear a black tail coat with white tie, possibly a white dinner jacket if it's summertime, or the equivalent military uniform. Women would wear a floor-length formal evening dress. Gloves, once compulsory as part of a woman's formal evening attire, are now optional.

At any function, formal or informal, that includes a dinner, a woman should bring some sort of wrap, stole, jacket or evening cardigan if her dress is strapless or has thin spaghetti straps. Otherwise, the woman has the appearance of being topless at the table. After dinner the wrap would be removed.

GROOMING

It is important to wear the right clothes, but it is more important to be clean and well-groomed. A lack of personal grooming habits is an offensive intrusion into someone else's olfactory space.

Your skin is the largest organ in your body, and it is important for your health and for the impression you make on others to keep it in good shape. Bathe or shower daily to fight odor and wash off the buildup of bacteria. Because you perspire as much or more at night as you do during the day, it is a good idea to bathe twice daily. Better two brief showers a day than one long one. Then, use deodorant or antiperspirant and foot deodorant.

Clean your teeth after eating. To prevent bacteria and a smile filled with food particles, carry a toothbrush and dental floss. Be sure to clean up after yourself in a public washroom. No one wants to confront a dirty sink coated with toothpaste foam. Use a mouthwash daily and visit a dentist regularly to keep your teeth in good shape.

Fingernails should always be clean and manicured. Dirty, bitten nails are repulsive to look at. Nails that are too long do not look professional. A woman's nails should never be painted a blatant or extreme shade, and the polish should not be chipped. Our hands are constantly on view in business. When they are not looked after, when the nails are dirty or bitten, the cuticles ragged or the polish chipped the impression is one of slovenliness.

Hair should be kept clean, and the style should be appropriate to business. While shoulder-length locks or ponytails on men and cascades of curls halfway down the back on women might be acceptable in a few avant-garde industries, they are not acceptable in most offices. They suggest you are there for reasons other than business. Don't play with your hair either. If you do so as a nervous habit, make a concerted effort to stop, even if you have to sit on your hands till you get it under control. Don't comb your hair in public, especially in a restaurant. Go into the washroom to attend to any repairs to your hair and to lipstick. Never, ever spray hairspray in front of other people.

Facial hair, whether a moustache, a beard or excessive sideburns, seems to appeal to young men as a way to distinguish themselves. Unfortunately, the image it projects is not altogether positive. While facial hair is tolerated to a mid-management level, it is not popular among upper management, as you can quickly surmise from the faces in the photographs of business publications. When looking at a man with a moustache or a beard, the eye is drawn to the facial hair and away from the eyes. The moustache or beard acts as a barrier, something for the person to hide behind. A clean-shaven face, whose characteristics are clearly visible, gives the impression of openness and directness. If you insist on maintaining facial hair, make sure it is clean and trimmed. Stop by the men's room after eating to make sure no food is lodged in your beard or moustache. Always keep ears and nostrils free of excess hair.

Clothes should be clean and pressed at all times. Check after each wearing for stains, loose buttons and split seams. Brush clothes with a lint brush before putting them away.

If you wear sneakers to work, change both the shoes and the socks or hose when you get to work. Sneakers do not belong with business attire. Feet tend to perspire more in running shoes, and the socks absorb the odors. Keep shoes polished and heeled. Briefcases should also be kept clean and polished. Never cram a briefcase too full, nor carry one that is excessively large. Replace the case when it gets worn. Also replace worn watchbands, and clean metal bands regularly so they don't leave black marks on your wrists.

Use a handkerchief rather than tissues. If you have a cold or you're ill, stay home. Sharing germs is neither polite nor generous.

While it is important to wear the right clothes and more important to be clean and well-groomed, it is most important to have a positive attitude about yourself, your work and others. Your personal style is judged by the respect you have for yourself and that you show others, by your ability to keep your word, and by the way you make others feel welcome with the nonverbal signals you give.

THE FAST TRACK

1. You have ninety seconds to make a good first impression.

2. Components of a first impression: words, 7 percent; vocal quality, 35 percent; nonverbal communication including body language and appearance, 58 percent.

3. Stand about eighteen inches to four feet away from someone. Never invade someone's personal space by being too close, too loud or too smelly.

4. Avoid telltale body language like fidgeting, tapping, finger drumming, foot shuffling or hair twirling.

5. The less you gesticulate, the more powerful you'll appear.

6. Enter a room with energy and walk to a destination.

7. Stand and sit with good posture with feet firmly planted.

8. Make eye contact 40 percent to 60 percent of the time.

9. Dress appropriately to indicate self-respect and respect for others.

10. Take your cues of acceptable behavior and dress from upper management.

11. Dress according to the environment, the function and the message you want to convey.

12. "Thank you" is sufficient response to a compliment. Never deprecate a compliment.

13. Hang your coat up before you go in to an appointment. Keep your suit jacket on.

14. Adhere to the dictums of dress on an invitation.

15. Maintain the highest standards of good grooming.

16. Have a positive attitude.

MEETINGS AND GREETINGS

In nothing do we lay ourselves so open as in our manner of meeting and salutations.

Lavater

Consider yourselves introduced because I can only remember one of your names and that wouldn't be fair to the other.

Sir Herbert Beerbohm Tree

Remember that a man's name is, to him, the sweetest and most important sound in any language.

Dale Carnegie

Every day we encounter people in a variety of business and social situations. The way we meet and greet them creates lasting impressions and paves the way for a productive encounter.

CHAPTER

3

Mastering introductions puts people at ease and conveys the respect we have for them and the way we view their status. The rules for introductions really aren't that complicated.

The most important point about introductions is to make them; failing to do so causes embarrassment and discomfort. **Most people would rather have you make the introduction incorrectly or forget their names than to stand there and be disregarded.**

In any introduction, the names of the people being introduced are mentioned last and the persons they are being introduced to are mentioned first. The rules for who is introduced to whom depend on whether it is a business or a social introduction.

As you make the introduction, include a brief but important piece of information about each of the people to explain their uniqueness or importance. "Sally is the PR consultant who helped me get all that coverage in the national press. Bob is the photographer whose work you admired in my office, Sally." Best is to introduce two people through their mutual interest. "I wanted you to meet because you're both such jazz lovers." Never qualify a description by saying "my best client" or "my dearest friend" because the automatic implication is that the other person holds a lower position in your personal hierarchy. When in doubt, be less personal rather than more personal.

As you say each of the individuals' names, look at them. In this way, you focus attention on them and make them feel important while appearing as if you are in control. Once the people have started a conversation and seem to feel at ease with one another, you may excuse yourself.

BUSINESS INTRODUCTIONS

As in all business etiquette, the rules for business introductions are based on power and hierarchy. Gender plays no role in business etiquette, and it does not affect the order of introductions. **Persons of lesser authority are introduced to persons of greater authority regardless of gender.** You would say, "Mr./Ms. Greater Authority, I would like to introduce Mr./Ms. Lesser Authority." While that might seem fairly simple in the hierarchical structure of most companies, in some egalitarian organizations, the hierarchy is more difficult to define. Yet even when the hierarchy is clear-cut, the CEO may not be Mr./Ms. Greater Authority. A client always takes precedence over anyone in your organization, as does an elected official. Here are examples of pecking order:

1. Introduce a non-official person to an elected official.
Example: Senator Watson, I'd like to introduce Mr. Dan Jennings of the *San Francisco Examiner.*
Note: Whenever introducing anyone from the media, include affiliations in your introduction to let the people, especially public officials, know that they may be on record.

2. Introduce someone from your firm to a client or customer.
Example: Mr. Dawson, I would like to introduce Ms. Saunders, our chief financial officer. Mr. Dawson is our client from Atlanta.

3. Introduce a junior executive to a senior executive.
Example: Mr. Senior Executive, this is Mr. Junior Executive.

4. Introduce a junior military officer to a senior officer.
Example: General Schwarzkopf, may I introduce Lieutenant Jones.

SOCIAL INTRODUCTIONS

According to rules of international diplomatic protocol, people are presented to royalty, chiefs of state, ministers in charge of legations, ambassadors and dignitaries of the church regardless of age or gender, similar to the pecking order or precedence in business etiquette. In these situations, the woman's or the man's name would be mentioned last and the more distinguished person mentioned first. For example, "Cardinal O'Connor, may I present Mrs. Doyle." But these are the exceptions to the rule.

Social etiquette is based on chivalry, so both formal and informal introductions are made according to age, then gender, and then social status. The man would be introduced to the woman in a social situation unless the man is obviously a great deal older, in which case one would defer to age over gender. For example, if both persons are of the same generation, you would say, "Mrs. Jameson, I'd like to introduce Mr. Horton." But, if the woman is considerably younger, you would say, "Mr. Horton, this is my daughter Hilary."

When introducing relatives to other people, always clarify their relationship to you; it avoids any possible faux pas that could result from inadvertent comments.

Never refer to your own spouse as Mr. or Mrs. in a social introduction. "Matt, my husband," or "Kitty, my wife" is sufficient. **However, if the woman has kept her maiden name, she should include the husband's surname with some emphasis on it.** This avoids the awkwardness caused when a husband is referred to by the wife's professional name.

When a couple is living together but not married, introduce both by their first and last names, but do not comment on their living arrangements. It is the couple's option, not yours, to divulge that information should it be necessary.

When introducing peers to one another, mention both the first and last names. It does not matter who is introduced to whom. Include a tidbit of information that might start the conversational ball rolling. For example, "Mary McMillan, I'd like you to meet Gary White, my mixed doubles partner. Mary was the junior varsity tennis champion at college."

Even if everyone in a group is on a first name basis, introduce the two people by both first and last names. But, if you only know one person by first name, be consistent in your introductions and use both their surnames, "Ms. White, Mr. Clark."

INTRODUCTIONS AT SOCIAL/BUSINESS FUNCTIONS

At a social event, it is not necessary to introduce a newcomer to everyone in the room. Introduce the person to the closest group of people by saying the newcomer's name first and then giving the names of the others in the group. Ask the members of the group to introduce themselves if you can't remember everyone's name. Make sure from time to time, though, that the person is circulating.

At any function, the host should meet all the guests to make them feel as if their presence matters. At many business functions, the guests may not know the host, so he or she should appoint several representatives of the corporation to stand by the door and act as greeters. When the guests arrive, the greeters introduce themselves and escort the guests to the host, make the introductions and then escort the guests to the bar or introduce them to others so the host remains free.

If there are more than fifty guests, it is preferable to have a receiving line within the party area to insure that everyone meets the host. The receiving line remains in formation until all guests have arrived. To relieve the pressure on one host at a large social function, list several corporate officers as hosts on the invitation so that they can relieve one another. To keep the receiving line short, all the hosts need not stand in line at once. When the receiving line is shorter, it moves more quickly and easily, and the guests are not bogged down in a long, tedious line.

While spouses are expected to stand in a receiving line at social and political affairs, they should not stand in the receiving line of a business related event. If the guest of honor has been accompanied by a spouse, though, the host's spouse should also stand in the receiving line with the guests of honor and the host.

Members of a receiving line should not drink while in line. Nor should a guest drink while going through the receiving line. However, if the line is very long, it is acceptable for the guest to get a drink and return to the line, as long as the drink is disposed of before the guest reaches the host.

INTRODUCING YOURSELF

If no one introduces you, step in and introduce yourself. The person may be too embarrassed to admit forgetting a name or may be distracted by other matters. Feeling slighted because you were not introduced only puts you at a disadvantage. Introduce yourself by extending your hand, smiling and saying something like, "I'm Matt Jones, David's partner." Avoid making any comment such as "Helen works for me" that might be misconstrued as arrogance or superiority. Instead, say, "Helen and I work in the same office."

As a guest, it is your duty to circulate and introduce yourself at any function, large or small, especially if the host or hostess is busy. The fact that you are both there is sufficient justification to introduce yourself to anyone at the gathering. By only sticking to those people you already know you'll never expand your horizons or make new acquaintances.

Always use both names when introducing yourself to convey the message that you take yourself seriously as an adult and expect the same treatment from others. And, until you know how comfortable the other person feels with formality or lack of it, give the other person the chance to set the tone that is most comfortable.

Be clear and concise in your introduction; the fastest way to turn a new acquaintance off is to ramble on about your life history, or worse, your problems or illnesses. Leave your problems on the doorstep and make sure your tone is engaging. Then, construct an introduction that is interesting and catchy, yet still professional. I like to think of it as a one sound bite commercial. A sound bite, the length of time available in television to engage viewers' attention before they tune out, is now only seven seconds because we are so overexposed to visual stimuli.

Try to gauge the information that will be of interest to the other people. At a business function, it would be appropriate to mention where you work. However, just saying "I'm in public relations at IBM" is not likely to stir a great deal of interest or conversation, whereas "I try to lure investment in IBM by working on the company's annual reports," will. Don't focus too much attention on yourself with grandiose pronouncements.

Don't expect someone else to be forthcoming with their job information at functions that are not strictly business because many people feel that they are not defined by employment. At an organized event, such as an environmental fund raiser, you can mention your connection to the organization. If you know that you both have a mutual interest, you may want to mention that, as long as you phrase it in such a way that the focus is on the other person. For example, "Gina tells me that you are a member of the Global Business Association. Since I'm also involved in international trade, I'd be very interested in learning how the association has been of benefit to you."

At any business meal, always introduce yourself to the people sitting next to you to open the way for conversation. Not introducing yourself when you sit at a table can cost you a potentially valuable business lead because few people want to deal with someone who comes across as aloof or unsavvy.

RESPONDING TO INTRODUCTIONS

The way you respond to someone else's introduction is just as important as making the introduction. **In response to an informal introduction, a simple "hello" is sufficient.** Add a phrase like, "I've heard so much about you, Barry," only if it is true and if it is complimentary. Beware of phrases like, "Pleased to meet you" because that may not be true after only a few minutes of conversation.

"How do you do?" followed by the person's name is the customary response to a formal introduction. Refrain from the use of first names until the person to whom you've been introduced has indicated that the familiarity is preferred.

RISING TO THE OCCASION

Always stand for introductions. Today everyone should rise to greet newcomers at both business and social functions. The old rule that a woman remains seated when new people enter a room and are introduced is obsolete. At a very large function, only those nearest the newcomer would rise and say hello. If you are wedged into a tight position in a restaurant, there may not always be sufficient room to stand properly, but at least make the attempt so that your remaining seated will not be misconstrued as aloofness.

In an office, the executive should always rise and come around the desk to greet a visitor unless it is a co-worker from down the hall or a secretary who is in and out of the office all day long. While a junior executive would customarily stand when a senior executive enters the office, this would not be necessary if the senior executive is constantly in and out. However, it is a sign of courtesy and respect for the junior executive to stop working on the project at hand and look up in acknowledgment.

SHAKING HANDS

To shake or not to shake should never be the question. Handshakes have become the universal physical greeting that accompanies our words, although Americans shake hands much less than any other culture with the exception of Asian countries like Japan. Initial impressions are formed by all our senses including touch. **A handshake is the acceptable physical contact for both men and women.** It is a universal indicator that conveys how we feel about ourselves, what our motivations may be and how we respond to others, regardless of any language barriers.

One business associate recently brought his younger son into the family business. The younger son was overshadowed for some time by his older brother's success. The first time I met the young man, I received one of the limpest handshakes I had ever encountered. Several months later, I learned of a major accomplishment by this young man. Sure enough, the following week he gave me a firm, confident handshake that spoke volumes about his improved self-esteem.

A handshake signals in the most personal yet professional manner what you and your business are all about. You are judged by your handshake. In fact, many people feel they can "take the measure" of another person by the person's handshake. And, whether you are aware of it or not, you judge others by their handshake, too! A good handshake creates a favorable impression of self confidence and interest in the other person.

A proper handshake:
- is firm, but not bone-crushing
- lasts about three seconds
- may be "pumped" once or twice from the elbow
- is released after the shake, even if the introduction continues
- includes good eye contact with the other person

A good handshake consists of keeping the fingers together with the thumb up and open, then sliding your hand into the other person's so that each person's web of skin between thumb and forefinger touches the other's, and squeezing firmly. When making the handshake, lean in slightly, smile and make eye contact.

Extend a hand when:
- meeting someone for the first time
- meeting someone you haven't seen for a while
- greeting your host(ess)
- greeting guests
- saying good-bye to people at a gathering
- someone else extends a hand. It is rude not to accept someone's hand.

Handshaking Tips:

- If your hands tend to be clammy, spray them with antiperspirant at least once a day. But remember, it takes at least twenty-four hours before antiperspirant starts to work.

- Avoid giving a cold, wet handshake at any function by keeping your drink in the left hand.

HUGS AND KISSES

Hugs and kisses entered the workplace with women and, while women should stay, the hugs and kisses must go. **It is strictly taboo to hug and kiss in any business atmosphere, with the possible exception of the fashion and entertainment fields.** It is impolite to touch colleagues of the opposite sex, regardless of how close you may feel, even if it is to put an arm around them or to place a hand on the shoulder. And, since business etiquette is not gender based, you would not treat someone of the same sex differently than someone of the opposite sex. The only acceptable kiss in a social/business function is if you are greeting your spouse when the two of you meet at a business function. Even then, keep it simple and friendly; save the passion for private moments.

DEALING WITH NAMES

Pronounce difficult names correctly. If in doubt about the correct pronunciation, ask. If you don't catch it the first time, apologize and ask again. Never crack a joke or make a disparaging comment about someone else's name. A name is representative of a person's identity and you would be insulting the person. I swear my aversion to science is the fault of my ninth grade physics teacher who purposely mispronounced and made fun of my name so often that I dreaded the embarrassment of science class. You don't want any business associate to develop that kind of aversion to you or your company.

If you have a difficult name, as I do, assist the person in trying to pronounce it. Word associations and rhymes help.

In place of my first name, I am often called Hilda, Helga and Elke. Depending on the mispronunciation, I might say "Remember the actress Ilka Chase? Well, it's like that with an *h* in front," or "Just change the *d* in Hilda to a *k* and you've got it!" or "it rhymes with milk, then add an *a*." And with Klinkenberg, I usually smile and say "It's a mouthful, isn't it?"; then pronounce it for them. Never make too much of an anecdote about your name lest you put too much focus on the other person's error and cause more embarrassment. Keep a smile on your face and in your voice when gently correcting the pronunciation of your name.

REMEMBERING NAMES

If you forget someone's name when making an introduction, try putting the other people at ease rather than concentrating on your own embarrassment. Remain calm; if you fall apart, the person whose name you forgot may feel obliged to put you at ease, compounding your faux pas. Be straightforward yet tactful in admitting your memory lapse. By saying, "I've forgotten your name," you imply the person wasn't worth remembering. "I've just drawn a blank," or "my memory seems to be malfunctioning" connotes a more temporary condition that doesn't have the same insulting implications. Or, if you can't remember someone's name, but you remember an interesting point about them, cite it. You might say, "I clearly remember the conversation we had about exporting to Canada at the Jones' party, but your name seems to have temporarily slipped my mind. Please help me out."

Then, whatever happens, get off the subject of the memory lapse and on to something more interesting to everyone. Profuse apologies only make everyone uncomfortable. The sooner you forget about it, the sooner everyone else will...and the happier everyone will be.

When you're introduced to someone, say the person's name, then repeat it several times during the conversation. Not only do you project a genuine interest in someone by repeating a name, but the repetition is more likely to imprint the name on your memory. **When someone seems to have forgotten your name, just jump in, hand outstretched, a smile on your face, and offer your name.**

INTRODUCING A GUEST SPEAKER

Prior to the event, have the guest speaker supply background information and ask how he or she prefers to be introduced. Keep the introduction short but enthusiastic, giving the speaker's name, credibility on the subject and the title of the presentation. Then ask the audience to join you in welcoming the speaker and begin the applause.

Don't alienate the audience by informing them that they'll learn something. And don't undermine the speaker by talking so much about the topic yourself that you give part of the presentation.

THE FAST TRACK

1. Always make introductions, even if you can't remember the name.

2. If you forget a name, apologize for the mental slip and ask for help.

3. Mention the name of the person being introduced last, the person the introduction is made to first.

4. Include a brief but meaningful remark about the person being introduced.

5. As you say the person's name, look at him or her.

6. Business introductions are based on pecking order. The rule is: "Mr./Ms. Greater Power, Mr./Ms. Lesser Power."

7. Social introductions are made according to chivalry, which means that they are made according to age, then gender, then social status.

8. Exceptions to social introductions are royalty, chiefs of state, ministers in charge of legations, ambassadors and dignitaries of the church. Both women and men are introduced to them and the woman's or man's name would be mentioned last, the dignitary first.

9. Always clarify the relationship when introducing a relative.

10. Never use "Mr." or "Mrs." when referring to your own spouse.

11. Be sure to include the husband's surname if the wife has retained her maiden name.

12. When an unmarried couple is living together, give the full names of both people, but do not comment on their living arrangements.

13. With peers, it doesn't matter who is introduced to whom, although make sure to introduce them equally with full names or surnames only.

14. It is not always necessary to introduce a newcomer to everyone at a party.

15. At large affairs, a receiving line may be preferable.

16. As a guest, it is your duty to circulate and introduce yourself.

17. "Hello" is sufficient response to an informal introduction, "How do you do?" to a formal introduction.

18. Both women and men should always stand for introductions.

19. Shake hands. It's the acceptable physical contact for men and women.

20. Hugs and kisses are taboo in the business arena.

21. Make the effort to pronounce someone's name correctly.

Now that you have a better understanding of meeting and greeting people, heed Lord Beaverbrook's admonition, "Be fearless and each day you must meet someone new."

FORMS OF ADDRESS

The true test of moral courage is to ignore an insult.

Unknown

I have known a German Prince with more titles than subjects, and a Spanish nobleman with more names than shirts.

Oliver Goldsmith

Addressing someone incorrectly, whether verbally or in writing, is improper etiquette. It indicates a sloppy, uncaring attitude toward the person that is totally devoid of respect. And people do care. They are sensitive to those nuances of respect shown when they are addressed properly. **It behooves every company to make sure that any correspondence that leaves its premises is properly addressed.** This enhances the corporation's image and furthers good business relationships founded on mutual respect.

CHAPTER

4

As executives move up the corporate ladder, their exposure to officialdom as representatives of their company will increase. **Knowing the basics of verbal forms of address is only smart.** Addressing someone incorrectly is one of those minor gaffes that have major consequences. While you should always do your homework before any function to find out who will be present, you can never be completely certain who you might encounter.

For further information on official American protocol, I would recommend *Protocol* by Mary Jane McCaffree and Pauline Innes, the revised edition published by Devon Publishing Company, Inc., in 1985. In addition, you might want to check the *Diplomatic List* (a Department of State publication), or *Burke's Peerage.*

HONORIFICS

Never, ever omit the honorifics Mr., Ms., Mrs., or Miss from any envelope whether it is business or personal correspondence. To do so implies that you just don't care. Computer generated mail seems to be one of the worst culprits, and it is precisely that uncaring mass approach which indicates a lack of respect for the individual. It takes virtually no time to insert Mr. or Ms., and the added courtesy adds immeasurably to the positive impression made by your correspondence. Do not use an honorific with your own name, though.

Ms. is the appropriate address for a woman in business regardless of what she chooses to call herself in her private life. Unlike Ms., Mrs. and Miss imply social, marital and sexual distinctions that have no place in the business arena although there are still some women, usually of an older generation, who prefer to be addressed by those titles. If that is the case, it is always better to comply than to offend. **However, when using Mrs. in a business context, use the woman's first name rather than her husband's,** i.e., Mrs. Susan Smith rather than Mrs. Samuel Smith. As accepted as Ms. is in the business arena, Ms. is not used in diplomatic or official correspondence.

TITLES IN BUSINESS

Because the hierarchical structure of corporate America is based on military structure, rank and status are very important. Just witness the explosion of vice presidents, assistant vice presidents, senior vice presidents and executive vice presidents, to say nothing of chief financial officer, chief operating officer, chief executive officer, president and chairman of the board.

Whether you privately address your chief by the first or the last name depends to a great degree on the formality, or lack of it, within your corporate culture. **In the company of others, especially from outside your firm, show your boss respect by addressing him or her formally as Mr. or Ms. Smith.** You do not address someone verbally by a corporate title. Save "Mr. President" for the president of the United States.

In writing to a business associate, it is not necessary to include the corporate title, but people do like to see the position they have earned spelled out.

With inclusion of the title, the envelope would read:

Mr. Frank Forbes
President, The Tool and Die Company
12600 Industrial Way
Akron, Ohio 00000-0000

Without the title, it would read:

Mr. Frank Forbes
The Tool and Die Company
12600 Industrial Way
Akron, Ohio 00000-0000

PROFESSIONAL ACCREDITATION

When a person has a professional title, like Dr. or Professor, you drop the Mr., Ms., Mrs. or Miss when you use the title before the name or the initials of the profession after it. **Do not use both the title and the initials of the entitling degrees at the same time.** Dr., by the way, is the only title to appear before a name that is abbreviated, with the exception of Mr., Ms. or Mrs.

A doctor would be addressed as:

Envelope— *Official:*	David Dannis, M.D. (or D.D.S. or D.V.M.) or Dr. David Dannis
Social:	Dr. (and Mrs.) David Dannis
Introduction:	Dr. David Dannis
Salutation:	Dear Dr. Dannis
Conversation:	Dr. Dannis or Doctor
Place Card:	Dr. Dannis

A professor would be addressed as:

Envelope— *Official:*	Dr. John Jones (with doctoral degree) or Professor John Jones (without doctoral degree)
Social:	Dr. (or Professor) John Jones
Introduction:	Dr. (or Professor) Jones or Dr. (or Professor) Jones of (name of university or college) (The academic position is preferable)
Salutation:	Dear Dr. Jones Dear Professor Jones

Conversation: Dr. Jones
                                               Professor Jones

Place Card: Dr. Jones
                                               Professor Jones

Note: The title Dr. pertains to a professor only if he has earned a doctoral degree. Otherwise he is referred to as Mr. If a person has the doctoral credentials, but not the academic position, he would only be referred to as Dr., not professor.

When initials of professional organization memberships like A.I.A. (American Institute of Architects) are used after the name, the name is not preceded by Mr., Mrs., Ms. or Miss on an envelope, for example: Hal Roach, A.I.A. In all other situations, the person would simply be referred to as Mr. or Mrs.

THE "HONORABLE" COURTESY TITLE

"The Honorable" is a title of respect in America that is held for life by a high-ranking official in either federal, state or city governments, including some presidential appointees and federal and state elected officials. It is also accorded to foreign diplomats, chargés d'affaires of ministerial level and heads of international organizations unless those individuals are otherwise entitled to use "His Excellency."

"The Honorable" is a title of distinction that is conferred by others on the person, not by the person upon himself. In other words, you would never refer to yourself as "the Honorable." Nor would you have it printed on your stationery or invitations. If, however, you were to work for a law firm or a magazine, the company could refer to you by that title on their masthead.

When writing to an individual who holds the title, "The Honorable" is written out in full on the line above the person's name. It is not used in the salutation of the letter, though. Nor would you address someone as "the Honorable" in conversation. If you are writing about someone who holds the title, you would only capitalize *h* in "Honorable"; "the" remains in lower case. For example "...will be represented by the Honorable James John Doe."

ADDRESSING THE SPOUSE OF A TITLE HOLDER

The spouses of high-ranking officials do not share their mates' titles. Out of respect for her husband's office, the wife of the president of the United States is always referred to only by her surname, never with a first name or initials, whether it is in written communication or verbal address or introductions. Everyone else, even the spouse of the vice president of the United States, is referred to by the name and title they would hold in private life. If either the husband or the wife holds the title, correspondence to the couple would be addressed as:

> The Honorable
> The Secretary of the Treasury
> and Dr. (or Mr. or Mrs.) Doe
> (depending on the title the spouse
> holds in private)

When the wife of an official uses her own name, you would introduce them and send correspondence to:

> The Secretary of Labor
> Mr. Joe Doe
> and Dr. Mary Smith

When both husband and wife hold rank, both names are listed individually with rank. The person with the higher rank is listed first, as in:

> The Honorable
> Elisabeth Doe
> and
> The Honorable
> John Doe

Addressing Officialdom:

Title	Introductions & Envelopes	Salutation	In Conversation	Place Card
The President	The President The White House Washington, D.C. 20500 *social:* The President and Mrs. Bush	Dear Mr. President	Mr. President	The President
The Vice President	The Vice President United States Senate Washington, D.C. 20510 *social:* The Vice President and Mrs. Johnson	Dear Mr. Vice President	Mr. Vice President	The Vice President
Speaker of the House	The Honorable John Doe Speaker of the House *social:* The Speaker of the House and Mrs. Doe	Dear Mr. Speaker	Mr. Speaker or Sir	The Speaker of the House of Representatives
Secretary of State	The Honorable John Doe Secretary of State Washington, D.C. 20520 *social:* The Honorable The Secretary of State and Mrs. Doe	Dear Mr. Secretary	Mr. Secretary or Mr. Doe	The Secretary of State

Title	Introductions & Envelopes	Salutation	In Conversation	Place Card
Cabinet Member	The Honorable Mary Doe Secretary of the Treasury Washington, D.C. 20530 *social:* The Honorable The Secretary of the Treasury and Mr. Doe	Dear Madam Secretary	Madam Secretary or Mrs. Doe	The Secretary of the Treasury
U.S. Senator	The Honorable James Doe United States Senate Washington, D.C. 20510 *social:* The Honorable....	Dear Senator Doe	Senator Doe Senator Mr. Doe	Senator Doe Mr. Doe
U.S. Representative	The Honorable Joe Doe House of Representatives Washington, D.C. 20515	Dear Mr. Doe	Mr. Doe	Mr. Doe
Governor of a State	The Honorable John Jay Doe Governor of Virginia *social:* The Governor of Virginia and Mrs. Doe	Dear Governor Doe	Governor Doe Governor Sir	The Governor of Virginia

Title	Introductions & Envelopes	Salutation	In Conversation	Place Card
State Senator	The Honorable Jerry Doe California Senate *social:* The Honorable Jerry Doe and Mrs. Doe	Dear Mr. Doe	Mr. Doe	Mr. Doe
Mayor	The Honorable Jean Doe Mayor of Dallas *social:* The Honorable The Mayor of Dallas and Mr. Doe or Mr. and Mrs. John Doe if a man: The Honorable Jack Doe and Mrs. Doe	Dear Mayor Doe	Mayor Doe or Madam Mayor (if a man, Mr. Mayor)	Mayor Doe

THE JUDICIARY

Because American society is very litigious, the legal profession has become a daily part of doing business in America. You won't create any unnecessary offense that may make the judge more impatient with your case if you address the bench correctly.

The term Esquire, abbreviated to Esq., is optional after the surname of a lawyer, whether that person is male or female. The initials J.D. (for Doctor of Jurisprudence) are also optional if the lawyer has that degree. Both terms would only be used in a professional context. With either Esq. or J.D., the honorifics Mr. or Ms. would not be used. **When writing to a lawyer, you would only include "Attorney at Law" on the line under the lawyer's name if he or she had passed the bar.**

Title	Introductions & Envelopes	Salutation	In Conversation	Place Card
Chief Justice of a United States Lower Court	The Honorable James Doe Chief Judge United States Court of... *social:* The Honorable James Doe and Mrs. Doe	Dear Mr. Justice Doe	Mr. Justice or Sir	Mr. Justice Doe
Judge of a Lower Court	The Honorable John Doe United States Court of... *social:* The Honorable John Doe and Mrs. Doe	Dear Sir or Dear Judge Doe	Judge Doe or Judge or Sir	Judge Doe
Clerk of a Lower Court	Mr. Jack Doe Clerk of (Court Name) *social:* Mr. and Mrs. Jack Doe	Dear Mr. Doe or Dear Sir	Mr. Doe	Mr. Doe

INTERNATIONAL PROTOCOL

The global village is upon us. Increasingly, companies look to expanded international markets, production facilities or sources of supply. Invariably, business dealings with other countries involve a much greater degree of government participation, both here and in the other country.

Studies have shown that the United States is the most egalitarian society in the world. This means that almost every other country places a much greater emphasis on rank and status than Americans do. Honorifics abound in some countries, and titles are as common as vice presidencies are here. Every country has its own established domestic protocols. Before you get on a plane, do your homework. The best place to start is by placing calls to the desk officers for the target country at both the Department of State and the Department of Commerce.

HIS/HER EXCELLENCY

While Americans use the term "the Honorable" to connote the importance of someone's present or former position, in former Commonwealth countries like Great Britain, Canada, Australia and New Zealand, the correct title would be "The Right Honorable."

Heads of state and ambassadors of other countries would be addressed as His (or Her) Excellency before the first and last names on envelopes, in correspondence and when making introductions. **However, while ambassadors might be called "Your Excellency" in conversations abroad, they are addressed as Mr. (or Madam) Ambassador when they are in the United States.**

Title	Introductions & Envelopes	Salutation	In Conversation	Place Card
American Ambassador	The Honorable James Jay Doe American Ambassador	Sir (or Madam) or Dear Mr. (or Madam) Ambassador	Mr. (or Madam) Ambassador or Mr. (or Mrs.) Doe	The American Ambassador
	social: The Honorable The American Ambassador and Mrs. (or Mr.) Doe			
Former American Ambassador	The Honorable James Jay Doe	Dear Mr. Doe or Dear Mr. Ambassador	Ambassador Doe or Mr. Doe	Ambassador Doe
U.S. High Commissioner	The Honorable Jerry Doe United States High Commissioner for	Dear Mr. Doe or Sir	Mr. Doe	Mr. Doe
American Consul General	Jay Doe, Esquire American Consul General	Dear Mr. Doe or Sir	Mr. Doe	Mr. Doe

Title	Introductions & Envelopes	Salutation	In Conversation	Place Card
Foreign Ambassador	His Excellency José Doe Ambassador of (& full name of country)	formal: Excellency	Your Excellency or Mr. Ambassador	The Ambassador of (country)
	social: His Excellency The Ambassador of (country) and Mrs. Doe	informal: Dear Mr. Ambassador		
Foreign Ambassador with Personal Title	His Excellency Count José Doe Ambassador of . . .	Dear Mr. Ambassador	Excellency or Mr. Ambassador	The Ambassador of (country)
	social: His Excellency The Ambassador of (country) and Countess (Surname)			
British Ambassador with Personal Title	His Excellency The Right Honorable The Earl of York British Ambassador	Excellency Dear Mr. Ambassador	Your Excellency or Mr. Ambassador	The British Ambassador

Note: When the American Ambassador is away from his/her post, add "to (full name of the country)" after "Ambassador."

"The Right Honorable" signifies personal rank in the British Commonwealth and should be used in addition to the complimentary diplomatic title of "His Excellency."

United Nations Diplomats:

Title	Introductions & Envelopes	Salutation	In Conversation	Place Card
Secretary General of the United Nations	His Excellency Jorge Doe Secretary General of the United Nations New York, NY 10017	Excellency or Dear Mr. Secretary General or Dear Mr. Doe	Excellency or Mr. Secretary General or Mr. Doe	The Secretary General of the United Nations or H.E. Jorge Doe
Foreign Representative to the United Nations	His Excellency (Dr.) Jorge Doe Representative of (country) to the United Nations New York, NY 10017	Excellency or Dear Mr. Ambassador	Mr. Ambassador	H.E. Jorge Doe or The Representative of (country) to the United Nations or Ambassador Doe

Title	Introductions & Envelopes	Salutation	In Conversation	Place Card
U.S. Representative to the United Nations with the rank of Ambassador Extraordinary and Plenipotentiary	The Honorable Jay George Doe United States Representative to the United Nations	Excellency or Dear Mr. Ambassador	Mr. Ambassador	Mr. Doe or Ambassasor Doe

Rank and precedence at the United Nations change on a rotating basis with no regard for the importance of the country or for length of service. To determine the current rank, call the United Nations Protocol Office at (212) 963-7171.

THE FAST TRACK

1. Make sure all correspondence is properly addressed.

2. Never omit Mr., Ms., Mrs. or Miss from any envelope.

3. Know the basic verbal forms of address and do your homework before a function to make sure you'll know how to address any official who will be there.

4. Ms. is the appropriate title for a woman in business, regardless of what she calls herself in private life.

5. When obliged to use Mrs. in a business context, use the woman's first name rather than the husband's.

6. Never underestimate the importance of rank and status.

7. How you address your chief in private depends on the chief's wishes and the corporate culture.

8. In front of others, especially outside the company, address your boss formally.

9. It is not necessary to include the corporate title when writing a business associate.

10. With medical or Ph.D. doctors, do not use both Dr. and the entitling degrees at the same time.

11. With professional accreditation initials, don't use Mr. or Ms.

12. "The Honorable" is a title of respect held by high-ranking officials for life. The title is conferred by others and you would never use it in reference to yourself.

13. The spouses of high-ranking government officials do not share their mates' titles.

14. The wife of the president of the United States is referred to only by Mrs. and her surname. The first name is not used.

15. When both husband and wife hold rank, both names are listed individually with rank, highest first.

16. The term esquire (Esq.) is optional after the name of a lawyer.

17. A lawyer should only be addressed as "Attorney at Law" in correspondence, on the line below the name, if the lawyer has passed the bar.

18. High-ranking officials in countries that were formerly part of the British Commonwealth are referred to as "The Right Honorable."

19. Heads of state of other countries would be addressed as His/Her Excellency.

20. Ambassadors from other countries are referred to as Mr./Madam Ambassador when in the United States.

21. Rank and precedence at the United Nations change frequently on a rotating basis. Always call the U.N. Protocol Office first.

CONSUMMATE CONVERSATIONAL SKILLS

God gave us two ears but only one mouth. Some people say that's because he wanted us to spend twice as much time listening as talking. Others claim it's because he knew listening was twice as hard.

Unknown

Conversation...is the art of never appearing a bore, of knowing how to say everything interestingly, to entertain with no matter what, to be charming with nothing at all.

Guy de Maupassant

I'll pay more for a man's ability to express himself than for any other quality he might possess.

Charles Schwab

CHAPTER

5

The best way to keep your word is not to give it.

Napoleon Bonaparte

Corporations prize interpersonal communication skills, including good manners and the ability to get along with others, above all other skills. Of next importance are writing and speaking skills. Good manners are essential to effective communication skills.

Use language your listener is comfortable with. Don't sound pretentious by using fancy words, but don't talk down to the person either. Say what you mean in such a way that the other person can understand the intent of your message. A good acronym to remember for successful communications is KISS—"Keep it simple, smartie."

Everyone responds more positively to warm, open and friendly communication. **A smile says more than a mouthful of words.** It invites and encourages conversation whereas harsh words and anger effectively curtail communication.

Arguments are an ineffectual way to conduct business. As someone once said, **an argument is something that even if you win you lose.** Yelling shows a lack of control that will cost you the edge in a dispute. If the disagreement has become too heated and adversarial, it is better to tactfully suggest you reconvene later.

TWO EARS, ONE MOUTH

George Bernard Shaw said, "No one ever listens himself out of a job." Good listening skills are essential to success in the business arena, and we all think our skills are just fine, only because we are unaware of what we missed.

Men and women have different listening styles, so you may feel that some of the following points may not apply to you. However, by following the guidelines, you'll adopt a gender neutral style of behavior that will flatter everyone with your undivided attention.

A conversation is an exchange of ideas and information, not a monologue. **Don't monopolize the discussion; give another person the chance to speak, too.** The ability to listen, without constantly interrupting to regain the spotlight, gives the impression that you care about the person and what he or she has to say.

To listen effectively, listen actively. Active listening means you don't shuffle papers, rattle keys, doodle or make other distracting gestures that signal boredom or inattention. **Use positive body language such as leaning slightly toward the speaker.** By leaning away or turning your head to the side, you signal that you are not paying attention, even if you actually are.

Active listening encourages people to talk. **Indicate that you are listening by giving some type of acknowledgment while the person is speaking, even if it is only a nod of the head.** Writer and lecturer Carole Hyatt once interviewed Walter Cronkite, who complimented her by saying that he had never been interviewed so well. Ms. Hyatt swears she only said "mmm," "interesting" and "tell me more" throughout the conversation after the initial question. A good listener gains a great deal of insight into another person and makes that person feel valued.

If you spend too much time listening to yourself or thinking about what you're going to say when the other person finally stops talking, the conversation resembles two ships passing in the night, with little connection between the two sides of the conversation. **Too often people are so caught up in the message they want to deliver that they miss the nuances of the other person's message.**

Effective listening is the primary factor in eliciting the response you want from the other person. If you are not getting the results you want, change your style of listening to become sensitive to those nuances. Then you'll build those solid relationships that develop into invaluable business alliances.

By being a good listener and controlling what you say, you are much less likely to be indiscreet. **Curb the urge to speak impulsively or to "tell it like it is."** A loose tongue only makes you appear immature and consigns you to lower management forever. A good rule of thumb is **"Don't complain, don't blame and don't explain."** No one wants to hear negative remarks. Powerful communications are positive.

At times it is necessary to interrupt a speaker or to interject a comment. If you've been listening well, you'll have picked up the rhythm of the person's speech and you'll know when it's appropriate to break in to his or her speaking pattern.

Don't interrupt in mid-sentence; let the speaker finish before interrupting or changing topics. Try to be polite, perhaps by saying, "Excuse me, I have some relevant information to add." **Don't apologize for interrupting.** If you feel the need to apologize, you should question your reasons for the interruption. A comment like, "I'm sorry to interrupt but..." usually has the speaker wondering why you are interrupting instead of paying attention to what you have to add.

VOICE

In face to face contact, our words count for 7 percent of the initial impression we make and our vocal quality counts for 35 percent. It doesn't take a great mathematician to realize the importance of your voice. **Your tone should always be appropriate to the situation you're in, and it should reflect the topic of conversation.**

Learn to control the volume of your speech. Speaking too loudly alienates listeners because they turn off. The strain of trying to understand someone with too soft a voice or someone who mumbles irritates listeners.

Control the pace at which you speak. Speaking at a breakneck speed, like those Federal Express commercials several years ago, makes it very difficult for others to follow your words. A snail's pace has listeners chomping at the bit to complete your sentences—or checking their watches.

Sloppy diction displays an uncaring attitude toward your listener. A monotone or a high whiny voice distance the listener. Both make effective communication difficult.

Get a tape recorder, listen to yourself and practice so your tone of voice won't be misconstrued as hostile, arrogant, patronizing, sarcastic or condescending. People are swayed by the positive or negative use of your voice.

While a mild accent is charming, thick accents hamper communications. Both the speaker and the listener must be aware of this. **If you have a heavy accent, whether it is European, Asian or regional American, retain your sense of humor if listeners have difficulty comprehending you. Suggest they interrupt you when they don't understand.** Speak slowly, especially on the telephone. A temporary receptionist on the verge of tears once buzzed me to say a man was calling the president of the company and wouldn't give his name but kept shouting "wrong" when she asked. It was a major client, a Mr. Wong, but because of his accent and because he had not used "Mr." or his first name, there had been a breakdown in communication that created a lot of frustration on both sides.

Make that extra effort to listen to Americans to learn the rhythm and phrasing of their speech. If you realize that your accent is impeding the smooth flow of communication, you may want to work with a speech therapist to take the edge off the accent.

BREAKING THE ICE

According to *The Book of Lists,* speaking in front of a group outranks the fear of death two to one. Walking into a room full of strangers brings out a similar terror. Don't stand alone like a wallflower. Mastering a few simple techniques will make meeting people more pleasurable and will build your network of business contacts.

The easiest way to enter a conversation that is already in progress is to approach the group and position yourself so you can be seen. Stand there, make eye contact with one of the people in the group and listen to what is being said. If you are listening actively, you'll be reacting instinctively to the others. Be patient and eventually you'll be invited to join in because everyone enjoys a good listener. Or, you may find the conversation unappealing, in which case you are free to move on.

The easiest way to start a conversation is to ask questions. We are all our own favorite topics of conversation. People are usually so glad of the opportunity to talk about themselves that they are not concerned if your question was less than brilliant. Just be sure that those opening questions aren't meddlesome or prying and that they are acceptable topics for discussion. You could ask, "Do you attend these functions often?"

Follow that initial question with one or two other questions based on what the person has revealed. For instance, you may ask, "What have you found to be the main benefits of membership in this organization?" or if this is a first appearance, "This is my first time, too. What do you hope to gain from this organization?" Include a few comments of sincere praise or appreciation and you have a successful conversation.

Be friendly and smile. **Often a statement with a rise in vocal inflection at the end sounds much gentler than a direct question.**

If you have trouble taking the initiative, think of yourself as the host whose job it is to make people feel good. Think about what you would have to do to look after them. At a gathering you could put a selection of hors d'oeuvres on a plate and offer the other person some. "These are delicious. Would you like to try some?" is a gracious opening gesture.

SMALL TALK

Small talk is important because it helps strengthen the bonds of business by building trust and loyalty. Small talk allows us to connect without the threat of intimacy and to test each other by observing gestures, body language, tone of voice and eloquence. Being able to converse easily makes you appear relaxed, approachable and confident rather than uptight or hostile.

Many businessmen profess to have great difficulty with small talk, yet they make it all the time without realizing it. Discussing Sunday's football game or last week's golf score all fall into the realm of small talk. The problem lies with topics of conversation rather than the actual act of making small talk. **Almost any topic is up for grabs as long as it is not malicious, derogatory, inflammatory or indiscreet.** Take a look around the room and you'll see any number of things you can comment on. Avoid put downs or sarcasm, though; they only make you look insecure. Read a daily newspaper and a weekly news magazine. Keep abreast of books, movies, television shows, if only to ask, "What do you think of the latest...?"

Eleanor Roosevelt ran through the alphabet to come up with topics of conversation that might spark the interest of the people with whom she was speaking. She might start with apple pies, then move to baseball, until she found a topic that clicked. After returning from a social event one evening, she told the president that talking to one man had been a chore because she had reached *W* before finding a topic that interested him. Obviously that man had a great deal to learn about his responsibilities in company.

Small talk is an acquired social skill that is facilitated by a sincere interest in other people. **Flatter people by focusing on their interests and feelings rather than your own.** The whole world is not watching you, so relax. You don't have to be profound or brilliant. Social situations don't demand long, serious conversations, just an exchange of niceties.

Make eye contact, regardless of the brevity of the conversation. A warm, friendly expression makes the other person feel valued for that brief encounter and you make a lasting positive impression. Successful politicians and diplomats are masters at this intense eye contact. Contrast that to the person who is always look-ing around and over your shoulder to see if anyone more important than you is there. Invariably that type of person rushes off without so much as a fare-thee-well.

Always make a concerted effort to close a conversation (no matter how brief) by shaking the person's hand and saying, "I enjoyed talking to you," or "It was nice meeting you," rather than dashing off without bringing the encounter to a proper close.

Buzzwords

To give the impression of seriousness, sophistication and credibility, use jargon and buzzwords sparingly. Every industry has particular jargon known to insiders. It acts as a form of shorthand when used within the industry, but it alienates those who do not know what the words or acronyms mean. Just think back to the last time someone spoke to you in legalese, computerese or technicalese without bene-fit of an interpreter.

Corporations, too, have code words that act as motivat-ing phrases. To be perceived as a team player, learn these words as quickly as possible. The fastest way to learn them is to ask the presi-dent's secretary. The secretary is in a position to observe the power core first hand and share it with you without feeling threatened or competitive.

Buzzwords can give the impression that you're at the fore-front of the latest trends. However, using buzzwords that have be-come hackneyed affects your credibility as quickly as wearing last year's fashion fads. Overuse of buzzwords, jargon and slang, no matter how *au courant,* will give the impression that you are imma-ture and overeager to impress.

Some buzzwords should always be part of your corporate vocabulary. "We" signals you're a team player; "they" is the compe-tition or a former employer; "No problem" demonstrates a positive attitude.

Straightforward English, spoken in a well-modulated voice, is always well received as an indication of class, whereas trendy language can make you look trite.

TABOOS

Abrasive words and phrases like "You're wrong," "You don't understand" or "How stupid can you get?" trigger a defensive response that is not conducive to effective communication. Avoid them and rephrase your message in a more tactful manner.

Don't use demeaning terms like girl, gal, guy or boy. The appropriate term in the business arena is man or woman, not lady. Never address anyone as sweetie, honey or dear. **Reference to spouses like, "My husband said..." or "According to my wife..." do not belong in business-related conversations.**

Avoid extraneous expressions such as "right," "you know" and "like," which contribute nothing to your message. Well, right like you know man what's wrong with speaking like that? Nothing, if you want to stand in the unemployment lines.

Street slang, localisms like "y'all" and careless speech like "dontcha," "hafta," "wanna," "gonna" are all going to ensure you remain in the lower echelons of your firm, along with unprofessional expressions like "uh," "uh-huh," "uh-uh," "yah," "nah," "hi" and "bye."

The four-letter words that became so popular as an expression of rebellion in the late sixties and remained as a sign of aggressive, macho power behavior into the eighties are definitely taboo. Cursing, swearing and blue language only indicate someone who is hotheaded and inarticulate.

The following topics are also taboo:

- off-color and discriminatory jokes
- personal relationships and sexual proclivities
- health
- personal tragedies
- diets
- cost of anything personal
- income
- controversial topics, e.g., politics and religion
- free professional advice of doctors, lawyers, accountants or other professionals

Constantly talking about yourself is another taboo. "I" trouble essentially ignores and usually bores others. I'm reminded of that Yellow Pages commercial for "Vanity Cases" that has the woman saying, "Enough about me. What do you think about my dress?"

If you must toot your own horn, whether it be to the press or to upper management, make sure you have a strategy. **Talk in terms of goals, strategies and results rather than what you did, and the "I" will be there loud and clear without you ever suffering "I" troubles.**

GOSSIP AND RUMOR

Light, harmless gossip that deals with who-is-doing-what-where-when-how is a staple of small talk as long as it is not malicious and backbiting. Malicious gossip causes anger, tension, stress and embarrassment that demoralizes those involved. Everyone's productivity suffers. **If you can't tell the difference between the harmless and the malicious varieties, ask yourself, "Would I want what I am about to say of someone else written boldly across the office walls about me?"** If not, keep your mouth closed.

The best way to avoid the taint of vicious gossip is not to indulge in it. Being a gossip is unprofessional, and it will have people wondering what you say about them behind their backs. There is no faster way to create distrust among your peers.

When someone has spread gossip about you, confront that person directly as quickly as possible and ask them to explain the source of the information they are spreading. Invariably the gossip will deny having said anything, leaving you the opening to reply, "Good, then I won't be hearing any more about this." Everyone should get the message.

Often people inadvertently feed information to the gossip by answering questions that are really an invasion of privacy. **If you are asked about your age, income, personal relationships, the cost of your possessions or religious and political beliefs, you don't have to answer.** It is perfectly proper to politely decline to comment. You can even be flip. For instance, if someone asks your age you can reply, "On a beautiful spring day like this, I feel like a kid," or "After working all weekend to complete that proposal, I feel about a hundred years old."

TACT AND DIPLOMACY

Webster's defines tact as "intuitive perception, especially a quick and fine perception of the proper thing to say or do to avoid giving offense; sensitive skill in dealing with people." Someone else once defined diplomacy as the art of saying and doing nothing nicely.

Diplomatic handling of the many situations that crop up in a business day means that a great deal gets done nicely because conflicts are avoided, people are not backed against a wall and relationships continue to flourish.

The tactful way to deal with information is to keep your boss informed, to include your peers and to instruct your subordinates. Resist the urge to tell all to the people who work for you unless the news is good. You should shoulder your own concerns and not create undue stress for others.

Tact helps you to sidestep business gossip and rumors that could be detrimental to you or your company. It allows you to say, "I don't pay attention to rumors," or "It is my policy never to give statements," or "I'm not the person to ask," if someone, possibly even the press, makes a comment like, "I hear your company's stock is going to take a nose dive when the market opens in the morning."

Tact requires that you think as much about the effect of your words on another person as about the message you want to impart. Framing your statements diplomatically gives you the edge because you stay in control of the situation. Choosing your words tactfully will get you the results you want much more effectively than blunt honesty.

Honesty is not always the best policy. **The little white lie is an essential business tool that helps smooth potentially sticky situations or protect someone's feelings.** When a business associate calls to invite you to lunch, for example, you could say, "I'm sorry, but I already have a previous commitment," rather than "I wouldn't be caught dead in public with an ill-mannered slob like you."

Tact also means that you don't call a boor a boor. You'll gain nothing but enmity. If the seventy-five-year-old founding father of a company chooses to call a forty-year-old executive "my boy" or "young lady" and treat you accordingly in front of a major client, smile sweetly and continue with your business. Nothing you say or do will change the person, and you will probably be the one who ends up looking bad.

"No" and "never" are the two most dangerous words spoken in the business arena. They create hostility and divisiveness. The person on the receiving end loses face. Phrase your refusal tactfully: "Let me think about that and get back to you," or "What an ingenious idea! Let me see if there is room in the budget." **"Yes" and "always" are almost as bad as "no" because they are absolutes that allow you no room to maneuver.** "That is an excellent possibility. Why don't we give it a try," is a great deal more flexible.

There is nothing wrong with admitting that you don't know the answer to a problem or that you need help. However, saying "I don't know" too often will begin to erode your credibility. A comment like "Let me check" or "I'll look into that" suggests the possibility of positive action without making you look like you are in over your head.

CRITICISM AND COMPLIMENTS

Delivering criticism requires a great deal of tact. Always think through what you are going to say so that you can phrase it positively. Harsh, negative criticism creates inordinate hostility and is counterproductive. Rather than saying, "Saunders, you idiot. You made a mess of this report. You totally forgot to include the figures from the branch office," you might try, "Saunders, I see you've put a great deal of effort into the preparation of this report. However, I don't see the figures from the branch office. Is there some reason you chose not to include them?" Then Saunders can explain the rationale or oversight without confronting you from a defensive posture.

Calling people idiots or telling them they were wrong is a personal attack that is not constructive. **Concentrate on criticizing behavior rather than personality if you want to elicit a positive response.** The purpose of criticism is to improve corporate behavior, not to destroy self-esteem. Instead of a character attack like, "You're lazy and incompetent," which leaves the person totally unreceptive to what you have to say, you could try, "Because you're spending so much time at the water cooler, John has to shoulder a far greater workload. I want you to handle..."

Be specific with your criticism and deal with only one item at a time. A shopping list of complaints is overwhelming. Vague criticism undermines people's confidence without giving them anything to build on; it will only strain relationships. Don't criticize at all if there is nothing a person can do about a problem, like height.

Never, ever reprimand someone in the presence of others. Censure them in the privacy of your office.

In response to criticism, keep your hackles down. Listen to the criticism without interruption, because you risk irritating the critic and you may miss what is really being said. If you're so busy reacting emotionally to the criticism, you won't benefit from it; you may even incite harsher words. **It is far better to listen quietly and then request some time to think over what has been said. Accept the criticism as an attempt to help you and thank the person.** You may even want to consider writing a note.

Schedule a follow-up appointment at a later date to discuss the matter when you can deal with it calmly. Avoid sentences beginning with "but" or "however" because you set up a confrontation; use "and." Responding to your boss's complaint about an overdue report with "And I've been working on it around the clock without the temp that was promised me," is much more positive and effective than, "But I've been working on that around the clock. However, the temp I was promised never materialized." Humor in mild doses helps, too. Never discuss the criticism with others because it will only undermine your credibility.

In response to a compliment you need only say "thank you."

ENDING A CONVERSATION

While you should never just walk away without bringing a conversation to a satisfactory conclusion, it is sometimes difficult to do so.

In social situations, it is acceptable to excuse yourself. You might say, "Please excuse me, but I see someone across the room I must talk to. I have enjoyed meeting you and hearing about your new consulting venture."

When the conversation is tedious or repetitive, it is not impolite to offer to help the person move to a conclusion by saying, "Allow me to summarize to see where we are." Or, ask for a solution, "You've explained the situation in such detail that I believe I understand it clearly. Now, how would you propose to resolve it?" If all else fails, ask the person to get you out of the conversation. "We seem to be covering the same ground over and over. I need your help to move us to a conclusion."

When the conversation becomes heated, critical or unpleasant, table it till it can be dealt with calmly. "I don't believe this is the most expedient time to pursue this topic. Let's continue the discussion at a more opportune time."

THE FAST TRACK

1. Use language your listener is comfortable with.

2. Smile.

3. Stay calm.

4. Don't monopolize a conversation; give others a chance to speak.

5. Listen actively and use positive body language.

6. Don't make distracting noises or gestures while someone else is speaking.

7. Indicate you're listening by giving acknowledgment.

8. Listen; don't get caught up in what you plan to say next.

9. Resist the urge to speak impulsively or "honestly."

10. Don't complain, don't blame and don't explain.

11. Don't interrupt in midsentence.

12. Don't apologize for interrupting.

13. Adjust your vocal quality to the situation and the topic.

14. Speak clearly in a well-modulated voice.

15. Heavy accents require extra patience and effort on the part of both the listener and the speaker.

16. The easiest way to start a conversation is to ask a question, followed by another question and a few comments of sincere praise or appreciation.

17. When attending social events, think of yourself as the host trying to make others feel good.

18. Make small talk about any topic that is not inflammatory, derogatory, indiscreet or malicious.

19. Focus on the interests and feelings of others rather than on your own anxieties.

20. Make eye contact when speaking.

21. Always close a conversation with an appropriate remark.

22. Speak in plain English. Use jargon, acronyms and buzzwords sparingly and only if they are current.

23. Tactfully rephrase abrasive words and phrases like "You're wrong."

24. Keep your spouse out of business conversations.

25. Avoid extraneous expressions like "you know" or "right."

26. Hi, bye, uh, uh-uh, uh-huh, yah and nah are unprofessional.

27. Don't curse, swear or use foul language of any kind.

28. Avoid taboo topics like health, diet, salary, price and off-color or discriminatory jokes.

29. Talk in terms of goals, strategies and results. Don't start every sentence with "I."

30. Don't spread malicious gossip.

31. If someone asks prying questions, politely decline comment.

32. Be tactful. Consider how you say something as much as what you say.

33. Resort to the little white lie when it is kinder than blunt honesty.

34. Don't call a boor a boor.

35. Avoid absolutes like "no," "never," "yes" and "always."

36. Admit you "don't know" but don't make a habit of it.

37. Inform your boss, include your peers, instruct your subordinates.

38. Criticize behavior rather than personality.

39. Deliver only one criticism at a time.

40. Never reprimand in front of others.

41. Accept criticism as an attempt to help you. Ask for time to consider it before you respond.

42. Don't discuss criticism with others.

43. Respond to a compliment with "thank you."

TELEPHONES AND OTHER MODERN CONTRAPTIONS

The telephone call starts with the sound of your voice.

Unknown

The first telephones had cranks on them. Some still do.

Unknown

Remember that as a teenager you are in the last stage of your life when you will be happy to hear that the phone is for you.

Fran Lebowitz

How you and your staff handle your phone system can be crucial to the success of your business because business can no longer function without telephones. Telephones give us instant access to almost anyone almost anywhere in the world; telephone lines also connect our FAX machines and our computer modems.

CHAPTER

6

Every ring of the telephone means business. Too many rings, and the business may go elsewhere. Often the only contact a caller has with your company is via the telephone, and that becomes the dominant impression of the firm. Rude or indifferent voices answering the phones can escalate a minor complaint into a major problem. Research shows for every client you alienate you lose many more potential customers. Discontented clients do spread the news of their dissatisfaction. However, when callers feel that you and your staff are treating them with courtesy and respect and giving them personal consideration, they will have confidence in your company and its products or services.

You represent your company when you place calls as well as when you receive them, and the results can be just as devastating. Most appointments are scheduled over the telephone. Offend someone when placing the call and that may be as far as you'll ever get. Handle the call well, and you've already made a positive first impression.

VOICE, DICTION AND MANNER

When you meet someone in person, vocal quality counts for only 35 percent and words spoken a mere 7 percent of the initial impression you make. **Those statistics jump to a whopping 70 percent for vocal quality and 30 percent for words spoken when the impression is made over the telephone.** The impression you make will be a lasting one, so make sure your voice and manner always show you at your alert and professional best.

The Golden Rule for the telephone is: "Speak unto others as they would like to be spoken to." Callers base their opinion of you on what you say, how you say it and the tone of your voice. Making a customer strain to understand you is impolite. It is your responsibility to be understood, not the caller's responsibility to decipher your words. **Speak clearly and distinctly. Avoid colloquialisms and slang but don't resort to pomposity in your speech.** If you have a strong regional accent or dialect, take speech lessons or have someone else answer the phone for you.

Be friendly; an unpleasant manner can cost you precious business. **Smile when you speak on the telephone because that smile can be heard.** Keep a mirror by the telephone so you can see yourself as others hear you. Make sure your eyes and face are conveying the same message as your words.

Don't eat, drink or chew into the mouthpiece. **Sounds are greatly magnified over the telephone.** It trumpets to the person on the other end of the line that you are not paying close attention. **Background noises from radios, televisions and computers are also magnified and make it difficult to be heard.** Either turn them off or get a telephone with a mute button.

Be alert and helpful. If, for instance, you cannot connect a caller, don't just hang up. Ask if someone else could help or if you could take a message. It indicates a regard for positive customer relations.

ANSWERING YOUR PHONE

Never leave the phones unattended. It signals to callers that you couldn't care less about their business. If you have to be away from your desk, have someone else answer your phone for you. In fact, leaving a desk without informing anyone is one of the most frequent complaints about executives by support staff.

Show efficiency by answering your phone promptly, before the second ring if possible. Identify yourself with both your name and your department; don't leave the caller guessing. Identifying yourself often encourages callers to do the same. Add a warm and friendly greeting that will encourage the caller to talk. Always say "hello" rather than "hi," which sounds unprofessional and trivial.

When you have to interrupt a long-winded caller, do it as politely as possible. You may say, "Janet, my two o'clock appointment has just arrived, so I'll have to cut this call short." **Someone with a scheduled appointment has priority over a person you're talking to on the phone, unless it is a crisis.**

The way your telephone is answered is your responsibility. Make sure your staff knows what you expect. It is a good idea to call your office occasionally yourself to see if your staff does respond with a pleasing telephone manner. If not, be sure to take steps immediately to correct the image conveyed of your company.

SCREENING CALLS

Screening telephone calls irritates most callers. Yet there are times calls do have to be intercepted if you want to get any work done. Whether a caller feels insulted or feels courteously treated depends on the way you have your receptionist or secretary handle the situation. **Abrupt phrases like, "Who's calling?" "Can I have your name?" or "What are you calling about?" sound crude and confrontational.** A caller will rightly assume you're screening calls and be offended. Normally you would have your assistant ask, "May I tell Mr. Doe who's calling?" and respect the person's right to say "No." If you definitely do not want to be disturbed and only want to talk to specific people, have your assistant say, "I'm very sorry, but Ms. Doe is unavailable at the moment. May I ask the nature of this call so someone else might be able to help you or would you prefer to leave a message?" Or, your secretary might inform the caller, "Yes, Mr. Smith is in. He's stepped away from his desk for the moment. May I take a message and have him call you?" Sometimes a little white lie is the better part of good manners; just don't make a habit of it. **Always have the secretary announce that you are unavailable before asking for the caller's name or message so the caller will not feel screened.**

ANSWERING ANOTHER'S PHONE

When you answer someone else's phone, give that person's name, then yours. For instance, "Ms. Adams' office. Gary Graham speaking." If the other person is unavailable, say so and offer to help the caller or take a message. If you ask for the caller's name, then say "Ms. Adams is not in," the implication is that the call is being screened and the caller didn't make the cut.

Comments like, "He hasn't come in yet," or "She just stepped out for coffee" are not professional responses. They can easily convey the wrong impression. Instead, a comment like, "Mr. Green has stepped away from his desk. May I ask him to call you?" would cover all situations without giving the impression that the person is a slackard.

If the person being called is on another line, say so and let the caller decide whether or not to be put on hold. If so, keep returning and reassuring the caller that the person is still on the other call, but will be there shortly. Never leave the caller dangling on a silent phone. **Never leave callers on hold for more than twenty seconds without checking back to see if they would like to continue holding.** While twenty seconds may not seem long to you, it can seem an eternity to someone listening to silence or muzak. Callers will feel that they are not getting the personal attention they deserve.

 When you take a message, be sure to get all the information and get it right. Listen carefully. When full attention is given to the caller, the caller shouldn't have to repeat anything except to verify a telephone number or the spelling of a name. If the caller has a difficult name, explain that it is important to you to get the name right but, because it is not familiar to you, you need to have it repeated. It is better to get the message correct than to create confusion and embarrassment to others with your personal interpretation. Note the date and time of the call and take the caller's name, phone number and message. **Ask the caller the best time to have the call returned.**

PLACING CALLS

Place your own calls to clients and other managers despite your busy schedule. Calls placed through a secretary create the unfavorable impression that you consider yourself more important and your time more valuable than the person you're calling. Before you've even said a word, you've set up a confrontational tone. Placing and answering your own calls is much more personal and more efficient.

 No one should ever have to ask you, "Who's calling?" when you place a call. **Begin telephone calls by introducing yourself and identifying your company before asking for the party you are calling.** Not only is it polite to do so, but you usually have far greater success in reaching the person you want to speak to because you have presented yourself as a powerful individual who has a right to be calling.

 Place your calls when you think it may be convenient for the person you're trying to reach. Interfering with someone's job will not endear you. If in doubt, ask the person when it would be convenient for you to call. Avoid calling businesses just before closing if you want friendly, first class service. It is rude to expect someone to stay late to accommodate your needs.

The call you place has priority over an incoming call. Tell the caller you'll call back and return to the call you placed. Leaving a person you called listening to a dead receiver may mean you get the cold shoulder.

A telephone call is an intrusion into a busy person's life, so make sure you have a good reason for placing the call. When you interrupt someone, be brief and get to the point of the call quickly. A lot of chitchat will make the person you called think your job is not very important and you have nothing better to do than make idle calls.

If you are disconnected on a call you placed, it is your responsibility to call back immediately, even if the call is long-distance, and even if responsibility for the disconnection lies with the other party.

CLOSING A CALL

The manner in which you end a telephone call leaves a lasting impression. **Take the time to end the call on a positive note.** Thank the person at the end of the call. Guard against trivial, unprofessional phrases like "bye" or "see ya"; the professional close to a conversation is "good-bye." Let the caller hang up first, then replace the receiver carefully and quietly.

Follow through on all calls; it is courteous and it will be favorably noticed. If you've promised information, try to call back promptly or have someone else call for you if you can't return the call right away. In his "Ten Commandments of Street Smarts," Mark McCormack says, "If an executive promised (a) to consider one of our proposals, which conceivably represents enormous fee income for us, and (b) to call me at 3:00 p.m. next Monday with his final decision, I would be pleased when he told me the good news but even more impressed if he did so at 3:00 p.m. next Monday." In business you are only as good as your word.

TELEPHONE TAG

Telephone tag is the business game of the nineties! You've all played it at one time or another, and you know it is not amusing. The scenario is this: You place a call, but the other person is on long-distance and will be a while. He phones you back just after you've gone to a meeting. You call back, but he's just left for lunch. He calls back and you're in a meeting with your most important client. And on it goes, if your call wasn't screened in the first place by a zealous secretary.

Telephone tag is one of the major sources of frustration an executive can experience. Studies show that an executive places an average of twenty-five calls per day and that the likelihood of reaching the person on the first try is only 20 percent. As bad as those odds may be, they can improve greatly with the second call.

It's possible to win and make the person you're calling feel good too. If you can create a win-win situation, you're always ahead of the game. First, plan before you ever place the call. Do you know why you are calling? Don't waste anyone's time. **Give some thought to the message that you plan to leave before you call; consider it the commercial for your call.** Be specific, but make it enticing enough that the person will want to take the time to call you back. With a clear idea of the reason for your call, you're in a much better position to have your call returned.

Often the individual you're trying to reach is right there the entire time, being protected by a well-meaning employee. Face it, part of a secretary's job is to give the boss a chance to get some work done. That secretary can become a real ally for you, though, if treated with consideration and respect. If you don't know the secretary's name, ask the receptionist when you first place a call. "This is Hilka Klinkenberg from Etiquette International. May I please speak to Mr. Smith? Oh, before you connect me, what was his secretary's name? It's slipped my mind." Then, when you reach the secretary instead of Mr. Smith, you'll be able to address her by name. "Hello, Mrs. Watson. It's Hilka Klinkenberg from Etiquette International. Is Mr. Smith available?" Using the secretary's name and introducing yourself displays courtesy and confidence and implies that you have an established relationship with Mr. Smith. She'll be much more likely to respond favorably to you. **The secretary who is well treated by a caller will often be an invaluable source of information.**

When you're leaving a message, give a time period that is best to reach you. It is bad form not to return calls, but many executives try to get around it by calling when they think you're likely to be at lunch. That way, they look golden for having done the right thing, and they've still managed to elude you. If you've left a time to return your call, it becomes harder for them to outmaneuver you. A choice of times to return your call is even better.

Most courteous is to take the burden of returning your call off the other person and to place the return call yourself. Ask the secretary, "When is the best time to reach Mr. Smith?" Then, let her know that you will be calling Mr. Smith back at the specified time to spend five minutes discussing whatever you've already decided as your message. If you've given a good enough commercial for your return call, so the person you're trying to reach knows that it might be beneficial to take your call, you are very likely going to have a high rate of success on your second call. The secretary might even schedule an appointment for your return call.

While you are trying to obtain information about your target, you may have to be put on hold because other calls are coming in. Just remember, the secretary is doing you a favor, so be considerate about the interruptions. It's a smart idea to send a thank you note for any special help the secretary may have given you. Because so few people show their appreciation, you'll be remembered and treated even better the next time you call.

VOICE MAIL

As companies try to streamline operations and cut costs, they resort increasingly to technology. Unfortunately, it can cause a great deal more client irritation than the company has bargained for.

Computer-related companies seem to be in the vanguard of this technological movement. Recently I had problems with some software from a company in Massachusetts. To obtain assistance, I spent four minutes and thirty-six seconds on a long-distance call dealing with their voice mail system, listening to one set of options after another and pressing the appropriate buttons, only to get an automated voice telling me that all lines to that department were busy. I did leave a message, but felt less than pleasantly disposed to this organization.

Later that day, a friend told me that she had an even worse experience with a major software company in California. She spent more than five minutes on a long-distance call maneuvering her way through voice mail, only to be told the lines were busy and she would have to call back later. The company in Massachusetts might have done the same, because no one returned my call.

Voice mail is excellent for relaying information within an organization. But when dealing with clients, especially if they have problems or complaints, it is only a small step better than rude and hostile employees.

Voice mail is here to stay, and there are ways to make it work. **Give the option of leaving a message on voice mail, dialing someone else's extension or being switched back to the receptionist.** Never have the caller switched through an endless trail of menus and options without reaching a human voice.

When recording an outgoing message, always do it in your own voice, clearly identifying yourself and your department. A recorded message makes even more demands on your vocal quality than the telephone. Make sure you practice, practice and practice some more until your voice sounds natural. Nobody likes to hear a stilted, artificial message. Avoid those generic messages like, "I'm unable to come to the phone right now." That was obvious when we got a recorded message. Instead, leave a specific message like, "This is Bob Smith. I'm in a client conference at the moment. Please leave a message or call back after 4:00 p.m. You can reach my secretary by dialing extension 672 or a live operator by dialing zero." Not only does this make the caller feel that the call is important to you, but that you check your messages frequently. The caller should always be given the option to go back to a real person.

ANSWERING MACHINES

Like it or not, answering machines, just like computers, are here to stay. They are part of the total communications package, and they are a useful tool. Answering machines are the butlers of the twentieth century, receiving calls in your absence and screening them when you don't want to be disturbed. While many people complain about them, answering machines really are preferable to a phone that rings insistently without being answered. Some callers are annoyed by a recorded voice and will hang up. But, since you've already placed the call, it would be far more efficient to leave a brief message stating the best time for the person to return your call.

Too often people stutter or sound as if they were reading a funeral announcement. **Before recording your message, practice what you are going to say from a written script. Recording in a nor-**

mal speaking manner may still sound very bland, so put some energy into your voice. Sound upbeat.

Then, leave a clear, concise message without any theatrics or avant-garde sound effects. Be concise. Don't waste the other person's time. Eliminate the obvious; we know you're unable to answer the phone at the moment. Short, simple messages are best. "Caren Cross speaking. At the sound of the tone, please leave your name, your telephone number and the best time to reach you. I'll return your call as soon as possible." Keep listening to playbacks and keep recording your message until it has a pleasant and professional sound. Remember that cute, clever or amusing messages are not professional.

If you reach someone's answering machine, leave a message. Not all machines are voice activated. Not only is it annoying to listen to thirty seconds of silence, punctuated by a series of beeps, but it is frustrating to wonder about the missed call. You wouldn't hang up on someone's secretary or receptionist, and you shouldn't do it with an answering machine.

As a caller leaving a message on either an answering machine or voice mail, be sure to identify yourself. It is presumption beyond belief to assume that someone will recognize your voice, especially when the sound can be distorted in a recording.

Be succinct. Leave the same message that you would have with a secretary. **In other words, briefly explain who you are, why you are calling and the best time you can be reached or the time you will try to call back. Don't forget to leave your telephone number** because the person may be away from the office and the Rolodex when checking in. Also remember the area code. A client once left me a message and telephone number, and I tried to return the call. And I tried, and I tried. After several hours, someone answered and informed me I had the wrong number. When my irate client called back the next day, I learned he was several blocks from my office in New York; I had been trying to reach him in San Francisco where he is headquartered.

ANSWERING SERVICES

Answering services cannot act as your replacement; they can only answer your phone. Don't expect them to give out detailed information or take detailed messages. Be sure your instructions to the service are clear and simple. Answering services get very busy at "peak" hours, so callers can be put on hold too long and messages can be taken incorrectly. Keep in mind that the person taking your calls is a human being working under a great deal of pressure at times, and human errors can be made. Losing your temper will not undo a mistake. However, when you treat the staff with dignity, they will respond in kind. Let them know occasionally how much you value their professional help with a box of candy or a basket of fruit that everyone can share.

FAX Machines

Although FAX machines have been around for many years, only recently has the technology become sufficiently cost-effective to make the equipment affordable to a broader spectrum of companies. The ability to transmit documents instantly makes this an ideal piece of machinery for today's business environment. Faster than the technological developments is the proliferation of abuses.

The paper the transmissions are printed on and the cartridges used to do the printing all cost money. The irritation to the support staff who have to get up and go to the machine only to get junk transmissions hurts your cause and costs the employer time.

Rule number one, then, is unless the transmission has been requested, **it had better be important and to someone you already know.** Don't send anyone your resume; it won't impress and may even cost you the job.

Rule number two is to always include a cover that states who the FAX is from, who it's to, the date and the number of pages. Recently while I was on the phone to a business associate, I asked her if I needed a cover on the urgent FAX I was about to send her. Late that afternoon, she called and told me she had waited all day for the FAX but it had never arrived and now she had to leave. What happened? The FAX had been received before we had finished our call, but because I hadn't included a cover letter, when she asked her support staff for her FAX, she was told nothing had arrived for her. Fortunately she found it, dealt with it at home that evening and caught a critical error before I sent the document off the next morning. I was lucky, but I'll never send a FAX without a cover again.

E-Mail

E-mail, or electronic mail, is an addictively easy mode of communication if your computer is connected to a network or to an external e-mail system via modems. It enables you at any time to send a message that the recipient can recall at his or her convenience, thereby keeping you out of those telephone tag loops with your colleagues.

Unlike formal correspondence, don't compose a carefully constructed letter that you then retype onto the computer. **Exploit the speed and convenience of e-mail by typing brief, spontaneous, informal messages directly onto the screen.**

Because message headers provide the date, time and name of sender, it is not necessary to repeat that information. However, I feel that a direct use of the person's name, without "Dear," and your name at the end, without a "Yours truly," personalizes the communication and avoids some of the coldness of technology. "Bob, I received the artwork with time to spare. Thanks, Tom" sounds a great deal better than, "Artwork arrived" and only takes a second more to type, even by the "hunt and peck" method I employ.

Be careful of excessive informality or flippancy that crosses traditional lines of respect. A good rule of thumb is that if you wouldn't say it to a person's face or put it on paper with your signature, don't put it on e-mail.

Linda Ellerbee, the newscaster, once wrote an unflattering description of her boss and printed it out to send to a friend, without realizing it had been saved on e-mail. When the back-up of information was released the next morning to all the Associated Press offices in four states, Ms. Ellerbee's letter went with it, and so did her job.

Skip jokes, teasing, wisecracking or any other attempts at humor that may offend people or be misconstrued. Adding comments like "haha!" or "smile" doesn't alter the insult and only makes you appear juvenile.

The Fast Track

1. Speak unto others as they would like to be spoken to.

2. The impression made over the phone is 70 percent vocal quality and 30 percent the actual words spoken.

3. Smile when you speak on the phone.

4. Speak clearly and distinctly. Avoid colloquialisms and slang.

5. Don't eat, drink or chew into the mouthpiece.

6. Turn off background noises like radios, TVs and computers or get a phone with a mute button.

7. Never leave phones unattended.

8. Answer phones promptly, before the second ring if possible.

9. Identify yourself and your department.

10. If you cannot connect a call, ask if someone else can help.

11. Say "hello" instead of "hi," "good-bye" instead of "bye."

12. Give someone with a scheduled appointment priority over a phone call.

13. Avoid abrupt phrases like, "Who's calling?" Say, "May I ask . . ."

14. Always let the caller know the person being called is unavailable before you ask for the caller's name or message.

15. When answering someone else's phone, give that person's name, then yours.

16. Let the caller decide whether or not to be put on hold.

17. Never leave someone on hold longer than twenty seconds at a time.

18. When taking a message, get all the information: date, time, name, number, message and best time to return call.

19. Place your own calls.

20. Begin calls by introducing yourself and your company before asking for the party you want to speak to.

21. Give the call you place priority over an incoming call.

22. If you are disconnected on a call you placed, it is always your responsibility to call back immediately.

23. End a call on a positive note.

24. With voice mail, always give the caller the option to switch back to a live person.

25. Before recording your message for your voice mail or answering machine, practice from a written script and make sure your voice has some energy. Rerecord until you get it right.

26. Cute, clever messages are not amusing or professional. Make sure your answering message is clear and concise.

27. When leaving a message for someone, always identify yourself and leave your telephone number with area code.

28. Always include a cover with a FAX transmission stating who it's to, who it's from, the date and the number of pages.

29. Don't send unsolicited FAXes unless they're important.

30. E-mail should be brief, spontaneous and informal, but avoid flippancy that crosses traditional lines of respect.

31. With e-mail, avoid teasing, wisecracking or attempts at humor that can be misconstrued.

PEN TO PAPER

People judge you by what you say and write. I don't know a successful man in business who is not a good letter writer.

L. A. McQueen

A pen is certainly an excellent instrument to fix a man's attention and to flame his ambition.

John Adams

THE BUSINESS STATIONERY WARDROBE

From entrepreneurial start-ups to Fortune 500 firms, the stationery, graphics and logo of a company reflect upon it as much as the image presented by the firm's employees. However, whereas an employee's poor appearance can be tempered by in-depth product

CHAPTER

7

knowledge and a concern for and understanding of the client's needs, the letter stands alone.

The impression created by your corporate correspondence involves what you write, when you write and send it and what you write and send it on. The quality of the paper, the graphic design and color, the process used for printing, the wording, the neatness and style of typing, and the signature all contribute to the impressions we create and the impressions we form of others.

Image and Design

Whether a company is in a conservative, contemporary or avant-garde business determines the paper, color and design to be used. Then, the particular market segment the company plans to appeal to, whether it is mass market or very upscale, has to be considered. So a bank, a conservative business, might want to appeal to either a very elite market, as does J.P. Morgan and Co., Inc., which has very impressive and powerful ecru stationery with black lettering, or to a mass market, like Citibank which incorporates a bold graphic with contemporary type in a bright medium blue.

An established corporate trademark or logo is like a shorthand representation of the company and should be immediately recognizable by its public. To that end, its message must be clear and relate to the organization it represents. While a flower as part of the design may be suitable to a fragrance house, a bull or a bear is more suitable to a financial institution. **Logos are unnecessary for small firms with a narrow market appeal. For very traditional firms, such as law offices, they may be inappropriate.**

The typeface you select is also reflective of the nature of the organization. Two basic categories are serif faces, like Times Roman, that have little lines along the bottoms of the letters, and sans serif faces, like Helvetica, that do not have lines. Within those two categories is a wide range of traditional, contemporary and avant-garde type styles to choose from.

Color

People respond more strongly to color than they do to design, yet color is one of the most misused elements in graphic design. **While black and white (or ecru) are the most powerful and conservative combinations, color also has potent physiological and psychological effects that can be a major determinant in reaching your audience.** Don't select color because it is pretty or your favorite. Make sure your designer can tell you what effect the color in your logo or type will have on the people you're trying to reach, not just that it's the "in" shade.

A management consulting firm I know of had its stationery and business cards redesigned by a graphic designer. The final package was a very attractive failure. The predominant feature was a strong geometric shape in pastel turquoise that had no relevance to the company, with deeper turquoise lettering for the company's name. Turquoise, especially in frilly pastel, appeals to women but is not well received by men, according to studies by color researchers at the Carleton Wagner Institute in Chicago. The remaining type was in grey, a good business color, only it was so light a shade that it was difficult to read the company's address and telephone number. In addition to audience appeal, stationery and business cards must also be legible.

If in doubt about the effects of color, go to the library and look up the works of Faber Birren or Carleton Wagner among others.

Lettering Process

Printing is the most common process. If your organization uses a laser printer, it is most likely the only process that the printer will accept. For a new business, printed stationery is all that is required.

Engraving, which can be felt on both sides of the paper, is a sign of status and success that is usually reserved for the executives of an organization because it is a luxurious and expensive process requiring a special steel die. While engraving is a sign of prestige to many, it conveys excess and fiduciary irresponsibility to others; consider your type of business and your target audience. If the letterhead is engraved, the envelope should also be engraved.

Thermography, a heat process that causes the ink to rise slightly so it feels like engraving on the top side of the paper, is the poor man's engraving. The ink can melt in a laser printer, so be sure to use a typewriter. To me, thermography is an imitation, and I don't like imitations because they speak volumes about the people who use them.

Embossing raises the design considerably and enhances the effect of a logo or monogram. Some companies emboss their logos on everything, including business cards and stationery, that may have all the other information printed. Embossed stationery may also cause a problem in some laser printers and may require the use of a typewriter. Embossing a design without color is referred to as blind embossing.

Paper Selection

If words are worth putting on paper, the paper should be worthy of the words and of the organization.

Always use a good quality paper that has a substantial weight. The rag content indicates the quantity of cotton fiber as opposed to wood pulp in the paper. Twenty-five percent rag means it has 25 percent cotton; 100 percent rag is 100 percent cotton. The greater the quantity of cotton, the more luxurious the look and feel of the paper.

For a conservative presentation, the paper should have no surface texture. Contemporary and avant-garde stationery can have a texture interest.

Office letterheads measure $8^1/_2$-by-11 inches. The company name, logo (if applicable), address (including zip code), telephone (including area code), FAX and telex numbers should all appear on it. Legal and accounting firms often list the partners. Without an individual's name and title, the sheets may be used by anyone corresponding on behalf of the firm. Partners or executives may use the letterhead with their name printed below the corporate identity on the upper left.

The size of the corresponding envelopes is Com10. The company name and address is shown on either the face or on the back flap of the envelope. However, the post office threatens to stop returning letters that do not have the return address on the envelope face.

Monarch sheets measuring $7^1/_2$-by-$10^1/_2$ inches, with the company identity at the top, are used by the executive to send a personal message on behalf of the firm or to write to an associate with whom the executive is on a first name basis. Professionals such as doctors, lawyers and consultants often use Monarch sheet as letterhead. Matching envelopes have the name and address imprinted on the back.

Memo pads can be of any size. They may have the company name with or without the address, and they can be personalized with the name of the sender. Memo pads are usually used for brief informal internal or external communications.

Message cards can be used for short interdepartmental messages or to forward items of interest when a business card with a slash through the name (see page 103) is inadequate. Message cards, which usually measure $3^7/_{16}$-by-$4^7/_8$ inches or $3^{11}/_{16}$-by-$5^1/_8$ inches and have only a name and possibly the title of the person printed on them, also can be mailed as a note in their corresponding envelopes.

PERSONAL STATIONERY WARDROBE

Corporate letterhead should never be used for your personal business correspondence like thank you or condolence notes, letters of congratulations, fund-raising, personal lawsuits or job searches. Always keep a supply of personal stationery on hand for business use.

Correspondence cards with only the executive's name at the top are ideal for short notes, written invitations and acceptances or written thank you's. In fact, correspondence cards can be used for almost all personal correspondence by the savvy executive. They are flat, heavy cards, usually $4^1/_2$-by-$6^1/_2$ inches or 5-by-7 inches. The executive's name and the company address, without the company name, appear on the back flap of the envelope.

Other personal stationery you may want to consider are fold-over notes, often with an embossed or printed monogram, called informals. Informals are usually about $4^3/_4$-by-$3^1/_2$ inches with matching envelopes. If the monogram is in a color rather than blind embossed, be sure your ink matches.

Small letterhead, $6^1/_2$-by-8 inches, with matching envelopes, can also be ideal for much of your personal correspondence. Remember that the company name should not appear on this letterhead, even if the address is that of the company.

Confusion can arise when a woman who is married retains her own name in business and entertains jointly with her husband. **To avoid having the husband addressed by the wife's name and embarrassing both business associates and the husband, invitations, acceptances and thank you's should be sent on joint personal stationery.**

STRUCTURING A LETTER

Address and Salutation

A quick telephone call to the company you are writing will provide you with the name and correct title of the person you should address, the correct spelling of the name and whether the person is a Mr., Ms., Mrs. or Miss. Even a cross-country call is less expensive than having your letter thrown out, as I tend to do to anything addressed to Mr. Hilka Klinkenberg. **No letter or envelope should ever be without an honorific or title.**

Although the temptation is to develop an instant rapport by switching to the person's first name in the salutation, don't. **Wait until you have established a relationship with the business associate and use first names in person before you jump to that type of familiarity in a letter.**

Body

Several points can make a major difference in the impact of your letter. **First, write in a style reminiscent of your everyday style of speech, eliminating any slang or expletives.** Read the letter aloud so you can hear how it may read to the recipient. Be careful of those pat introductory sentences like "It was a pleasure to meet you. Thank you for the time you gave me..." that sound as if you found them in a beginners' book of letter writing and that can signal you are going to waste the reader's time. Instead, relate to a need, a challenge or a humorous shared moment that engages your reader.

Always remember the guideline questions who, what, where, when and how, and make sure your first paragraph addresses at least one, if not all, of them. **Be concise.** Respect the recipient's time. Give some thought beforehand to what you want to convey, keep it to one page and edit the first draft to make sure you have no redundant or extraneous material in the letter. If the tone or content is inflammatory, put the letter aside and review it the following day before deciding to send it.

In closing, eliminate phrases like "Please don't hesitate ..." that sound very presumptuous; instead revert to more traditional and direct phrases like "I'd be happy to answer any questions you have," or "Please let me know if there is anything I can do for you."

Before a single word is ever read, the recipient has a visual impression of your correspondence. **No letter should contain any**

spelling errors, typos or corrections. If your spelling is atrocious and you don't have a crackerjack secretary, get a word processing program for your computer that has a spell check and possibly also a thesaurus and grammar check. It is even possible now to get Strunk and White's classic little guide to the proper use of the English language, *Elements of Style,* on software.

If you use a computer to write your correspondence, always make sure that you format the page to left justification only. This means that only the left side has an even margin; the right side has a slightly jagged look. Full justification, with even columns on both sides, is harder to read because of the irregular spacing that results from making the words fit within the margins. It also makes your letter look like a form letter, with little personal attention or consideration for the recipient.

If you don't know the difference between a block and extreme block set up for your letter, any basic book on typing or secretarial skills will explain the positioning of the various parts of the letter and how to set up margins.

Closings and Signatures

Closings like "Very truly yours" or "Very sincerely" have an excessively formal and old-fashioned air for most contemporary business communication. **Closings like "Sincerely," "Cordially" or "Regards" are sufficient for most business letters.** If writing to the president of the United States or to a high church official, "Respectfully yours" is appropriate.

Always make sure your closing matches your salutation. Since Americans quickly adopt a familiar tone by switching to first names early in the relationship, letters are often addressed "Dear Tom," yet signed with the full name of the person sending the letter. That may be appropriate when writing to children or servants, but it is extremely disrespectful to do so in business. If you are concerned that the recipient of the letter may not know which Bob at Fortune 500 Company is sending the letter, you either do not know the person sufficiently to use first names or your letter lacks specificity.

The reverse, addressing a superior by Mr. or Ms. and the surname and signing with your first name is acceptable but not advisable unless you want to appear subservient.

In a properly structured letter, the full name and title of the sender should be typed under the signature whether you sign your first name or your full name.

PENMANSHIP

Your signature and your handwriting can reveal a great deal more about you than spelling skills. You might want to consult with a good graphologist to see what secrets you're giving away.

THE WRITING INSTRUMENT

The fountain pen is the writing instrument of choice among savvy executives today. **Whether you use fountain pen or ballpoint, the color of the ink should match the stationery.** If your company letterhead is printed in black, that's the color ink you use. If it is blue, use blue ink. If your stationery is a bold color statement, stick to black ink to correspond to the type in the body of the letter. While purple ink might be interesting for a New Age related business or green ink to tie in with the environmental movement, they have no place on most business letters. Save them for your personal informal correspondence.

TIMING

Write all your notes and answer all your correspondence promptly. The nuances of sending a note or letter are completely lost by too much elapsed time. Writing promptly also means you won't have to apologize for not having written. However, if you did delay, don't apologize so profusely that it appears as if writing was the penultimate of many burdens you're shouldering. No one likes to be made to feel guilty for your compliance with the most basic dictates of good manners.

HANDWRITTEN CORRESPONDENCE

Handwritten correspondence is more personal and less time-consuming than a telephone call. Writing a note takes only a moment and you don't have to worry about interrupting people because they can deal with it at their leisure. Handwritten notes are also a way of networking and keeping in touch with people you don't see often. Lyndon Johnson wrote to everybody he met so that, no matter what you thought of him, you felt good getting a personal note from the president of the United States. Powerful people get that way by paying attention to details like writing notes.

At times a handwritten note is preferable to a typewritten letter, regardless of your penmanship; at times a handwritten note is mandatory.

Write a note when:

- you write an informal invitation.
- you reply to a written invitation.
- you receive a gift.
- you have been a weekend guest in someone's home. Flowers accompanying the note are even better.
- writing a condolence note if you were a friend of the deceased or of the survivor.
- you want to be thoughtful and gracious after a lunch, a dinner or cocktail party.
- a colleague receives a promotion, an honor or an award.
- when a business associate or a member of the family is married, has a child, graduates or achieves some other milestone.
- someone has taken time to see you for an appointment.
- you've been interviewed for a job.
- you owe an apology.

THANK YOU NOTES

It is simply a smart business move to send thank you notes because everyone in our culture appreciates praise and recognition. Thank you notes demonstrate your flair and personal style while bringing business to a more personal level that improves client relationships. At times, the omission of a thank you note may be considered rude.

So that the nuances are not lost, thank you notes should be sent immediately. It is not necessary to write glowing praise; keep it simple and sincere.

CONDOLENCE NOTES

Condolence notes seem to be the most difficult for most people to write, possibly because they make us confront our own mortality and that of the people we love. **Condolence notes need only be a sincere expression of sympathy, especially if the deceased is not personally known to you, rather than an elegy.**

For example: "Dear Larry, I was saddened to hear of the death of your father. Please accept my sympathy for you and your family. If there is anything I can do, please don't hesitate to call. Sincerely, Ted."

HOLIDAY GREETING CARDS

Many of the world's religions have some form of holiday during the winter solstice. Because business is conducted on a much broader scope than in the past, your business associates may not all appreciate receiving a Christmas card, Hanukkah card or even New Year's card. **A more generic greeting will not give the offense that a card sent without thought and with a religious message different from the recipient's beliefs can.** This is not to deny anyone's freedom of religious expression; it simply shows consideration for another person's potential sensitivities. After all, the greeting extended is about the recipient, not the sender.

While it is correct to have your full name printed or engraved on the cards, a personalized message signed with your first name should be added. When cards are signed on behalf of a couple, the name of the person signing is last. **If the imprinted names include the first names of both husband and wife, the wife's name comes first, as in "Carol and Don Jones."** Corporate cards are printed with the name of the firm, not with the name(s) of the owner or president. **If the card is being sent to a person's office, the card should only be addressed to that individual. If the card is being sent to a person's home, address the card jointly, "Mr. and Mrs. Sam Smith," even if you only know one of the pair.** Don't add "and Family," but include a message for the family on the inside. **When a couple retains separate names or is not married, use two lines for the names of the two individuals.**

Holiday greetings are a wonderful way to let clients know you care about them and appreciate the business you receive from them throughout the year, while subtly reminding them of your services. Taking the extra time to select a card that won't offend, to personalize the message and to address it properly ensures your message will be received in the spirit it was intended.

BUSINESS CARDS

Business cards are one of the most frequently used forms of printed corporate communications because they give potential clients and business associates a means of contact. If someone looks upon your card with disfavor because it looks cheap or soiled, or if they lose respect for you because the card is too cute, you will lose business and do yourself more harm than if you had never given the card out at all. While professionals in avant-garde industries like fashion or design can be more expressive in their choice of color and design, other professionals and executives should stick with the conservative white or ecru 3½-by-2 inch cards of good quality stock with black or grey ink.

Business cards should not contain a shopping list of services that belong in the company brochure, nor should they have your picture or your bio on them. In a neat and precise manner, free of all clutter, the card should include this pertinent information:

```
                        Name
                        Title
       Company name           Telephone number
       Business address         with area code
         including full       Telex and/or
          zip code              FAX numbers
```

If necessary, also include a home number if you do a great deal of work from home, or other office locations if you also work from those offices. However, do not include other businesses you may own on the same card; print separate cards for each business.

A professional title like doctor, professor, or general, or the degree initials following the name are included as part of the information on a business card. **Do not use Mr., Ms., Mrs. or Miss on**

your card. Often a name, like mine for example or others like Robin or Leslie, can be either masculine or feminine. While it is acceptable in those circumstances to use Mr. or Ms., I prefer to include the full middle name. Hilka Elisabeth Klinkenberg or Robin Jean Cohn sufficiently indicates that the person is female without the addition of the honorific that can sound pretentious.

Presentation of the Business Card

Never present a card that is out of date, soiled or dog-eared; keep cards current, protected and fresh.

Be selective about handing out your card. Handing your card out indiscriminately to everyone in sight will make you appear pushy and overly zealous, and may undermine your professional credibility.

While business cards are often exchanged in other countries when an introduction is made, in the United States you should never give your card out early in a conversation. Speak with the person long enough to determine that you really want to give your card.

Never force your card on anyone, especially a senior executive. If their's is a more senior position, always let them request your card. Don't ask for their's; surely your memory is good enough to remember name and company long enough to jot it down after the conversation is over. The telephone book will give you the company's address and telephone number if the person is truly a prospect. And, instead of trying to get the executive to take your card, focus on the conversation and making a good impression. Showing interest in them, their company and their interests should give you information that you can use to approach the company at a later date.

Never present your card during any meal, regardless of how informal or formal it may be.

Only ask for someone else's card if you sincerely want to remember the person and the company.

Be gracious about receiving someone else's card. Take the time to look at it because it is representative of the person. And don't write on the card in the person's presence. Wait until after the person has gone if you need to make notes to remember the conversation.

When calling on someone, present your business card to a receptionist to help her get your name right.

Present your card when calling on a new client. However, if you are in a meeting outside your office with a group of people you don't know, wait for someone else to begin the exchange of cards unless you are clearly the most senior person in the group.

Personalize your card by putting a slash through your name and writing a note on the back when enclosing it with a gift or flowers or when attaching it to someone's resume or other material that you are forwarding on.

Always carry your card when you attend social/business functions. But, if you are asked for your card, hand it out discreetly, in private.

Never ask for or hand out a business card at a social occasion like a dinner party in a private home; carry a social card.

Social Business Cards

Social occasions often present us with excellent business contacts. However, by exchanging business cards, you appear opportunistic and you insult the host or hostess. The canny executive can usually remember the name and company of the new contact without having to ask for a card. However, if you distrust your memory or the function is very large, you may feel more comfortable discreetly exchanging social cards at social/business events. Social cards, which are the same $3^1/_2$-by-2 inch size as a business card, are engraved or printed with only your name and telephone number. By making no reference to a company, the stigma of commerce is removed from the card.

Business Announcements

Informing clients and other interested parties of a change in the status of your business with a business announcement card is good etiquette. Announcing a new address, an appointment or a promotion, a new partner or introducing a product with the announcement card gets the recipient's attention in a way that a phone call or a passing reference in conversation doesn't. But, beware of trying to communicate too much in one announcement.

Use a good quality stock with the message either engraved or printed. For formal announcements the card should be engraved in a conservative color type on a white or ecru correspondence card.

In composing the text, remember that a company is a singular entity; the verb should be in the singular, too. When sending an announcement to someone you know well, it is perfectly acceptable to personalize the announcement with a handwritten note.

The envelopes should always be handwritten, typed or printed on a word processor. Never use labels.

It is not necessary to acknowledge a business announcement card. But, if the sender is a friend or a close business associate, sending a brief note of acknowledgment or congratulations will long be remembered.

MEMOS

Memos are sent to those people who are working directly on a project and those whose departments or jobs will be affected by it. **Sending copies to people only to impress or to gain prestige can backfire.** Most people can see through transparent self-aggrandizement and are only annoyed by having their time wasted perusing irrelevant paper.

In listing the names on a memo, follow the corporate hierarchy. If no hierarchy exists, listing names alphabetically is the most democratic and avoids indistinct nuances of rank. Never list people according to your perception of their degree of involvement in a project because not everyone may agree.

Unless you enjoy living life on the edge, don't try to outmaneuver peers by omitting them from the list. It is unprofessional, risky and guaranteed to trigger retaliation. **Nor is it a good idea to send a so-called blind copy of a memo to someone who is not listed on the memo because word invariably leaks out and damages your credibility.**

THE FAST TRACK

1. The type of business determines the quality of paper, the colors, the graphic design, the type and the printing method.

2. Logos are inappropriate for very traditional firms and unnecessary for many small firms.

3. Don't use corporate letterhead for personal correspondence.

4. When a married woman retains her name, correspondence from her and her husband should be written on joint stationery.

5. When writing someone, always make sure the person's name is spelled correctly and the title is correct.

6. Be sure to include Mr., Ms. or any other appropriate title on an envelope.

7. Write like you speak, eliminating any slang and expletives.

8. Be concise.

9. Eliminate pat phrases.

10. Make sure there are no spelling errors, typos or corrections.

11. Format letters on the computer to left justification only.

12. "Sincerely," "cordially" or "regards" are sufficient closings for business correspondence.

13. "Respectfully yours" is an appropriate close when writing the president of the United States.

14. The way you sign the letter must match the salutation.

15. The color ink you use should match the color of the type on your stationery.

16. Write all notes and answer all correspondence immediately.

17. Thank you and condolence notes, informal invitations and replies to invitations should all be written by hand.

18. Send generic holiday cards that don't offend other religions.

19. Include a personalized message on printed greeting cards.

20. The wife's name is printed first; the person signing for a couple writes his/her name last.

21. Cards sent to an office are addressed only to the individual; cards sent to the home are addressed to the couple.

22. When a couple has different last names, put the names on two lines.

23. Business cards should only contain the pertinent information, i.e. name, title, company name, business address and zip code, telephone number and area code, and FAX or telex numbers for one company.

24. Include a professional title on a card, but not Mr. or Ms.

25. Business cards must always be clean and current.

26. Never force your business card on anyone, especially a senior executive.

27. Never present your business card during a meal.

28. Never present or ask for a card at a social function.

29. Receive someone's card graciously.

30. Hand your card to a receptionist when calling on someone.

31. Personalize your card by putting a slash through your name and writing a note on the back when using it as an enclosure.

32. Envelopes should be handwritten, typed or printed on a word processor. Don't use labels.

33. Don't send memos only to impress or gain prestige.

34. Follow the corporate hierarchy or the alphabet when listing names on a memo.

35. Don't purposely eliminate peers from the list on a memo.

36. Don't blind copy someone with a memo.

Invitations and Replies

First impressions always count because lasting impressions are formed within seconds. As the first official communication of your event, invitations are the drawing card to whet your guests' appetites and to entice them to attend.

In receiving an invitation all invitees want to know WIFM ..."what's in it for me?" Therefore, you must first know your audience and the impression you want to make. Determine what makes this corporation or event special and how you are going to convey that message. Does the invitation carry out the theme of the event? Does the design attract the eye? Do the words stimulate the imagination? Even the feel of the paper is important because we form those initial impressions with all our senses. A well-thought-out and well-designed invitation is the best way to create a first impression and get a positive response.

It's amazing how often invitations leave out pertinent details like date, time or location. The basic composition of every properly worded invitation, formal or informal, includes:

CHAPTER

8

Official or Corporate Symbol (if applicable)

the Host Line   = WHO
the Request Line
the Event Line   = WHAT
the Date Line   = WHEN
the Time Line
the Location Line   = WHERE
the City & State Line

the Special Instruction
Line (e.g. "Black Tie"
the Reply Request Line   or "Dancing")

"To meet..." or "To honor..." a guest could appear either at the top of the invitation or in the body.

FORMAL INVITATIONS

If the event is a formal or diplomatic function, this format is iron-clad. The invitation should be engraved on ecru or white letter sheets, or on plain white cards $5^3/_4$-by-$4^1/_2$ inches for official functions. **The wording is always in the third person, i.e., "Mr. and Mrs. John Brackenbury request...."** While formal invitations usually "request the pleasure of your company," the most formal, the most personal and the most expensive "request the pleasure of the company of" followed by a blank line with the name of the guest inserted by hand, preferably in calligraphy in black ink.

If you want to get the right people to attend your event, let them know they are important to you by personalizing the invitation with their name inserted in calligraphy. A secretary will seldom bother to show a Fortune 500 CEO an invitation that is not personalized.

INFORMAL INVITATIONS

If the company's image or the nature of the event doesn't demand formality, intrigue your audience with an innovative design and eye-catching typeface that reflect the mood of the event. Either go classic or go fun. Just beware the overzealous designer who gives free rein to creative impulse. Too many invitations have become too cutesy with glitter and all sorts of things falling out of them. Don't outsmart yourself because there is nothing like a beautiful formal invitation. Some of the best invitations are in black and white; it is unnecessary to waste money on four-color designs.

Although the basics of an informal invitation are the same as a formal invitation, there is a great deal more flexibility. People should be given as much information as possible to help them feel comfortable when they come to an event. In addition to the information given on page 108 you may want to indicate:

- Type of food to be served
- Whether card is required for admittance
- Whether card admits one or two
- Any necessary travel data

RESPONDING TO AN INVITATION

R.S.V.P. is the French abbreviation for *répondez s'il vous plaît* which means "please reply." Nothing is more frustrating to an event planner or a host than the sloppy attitude people have about responding to an invitation. **Unless a guest is paying, by buying a ticket or by attending an auction for instance, everyone should always respond to an R.S.V.P., even if it is to express regrets.**

New Yorkers seems to be especially negligent about replying whereas, in Washington, it is not uncommon to respond favorably to every invitation, then wait until the evening of the event to decide which to grace with one's presence, much to the frustration of many a Washington hostess who has counted on the person to honor the acceptance.

An invitation from the White House or royalty takes precedence over all others and is only refused because of a death in the family, a wedding in the family, an illness or an unexpected trip abroad. These, as well as official duties and the demands made upon one's time by the arrival of one's superior in business are also the only acceptable excuses to cancel any previously accepted invitation. And I do mean cancel—and immediately upon discovering you cannot attend—rather than simply failing to show up.

ELICITING REPLIES

Unfortunately there is no secret formula to getting people to R.S.V.P. For major non-profit events, a great deal of effort should go into putting together the committee and chairpersons who are listed on the invitation because people sell events...and tickets. A paragraph about the organization on the back of the invitation never hurts because people have become very savvy and don't want to throw their money away.

You can pull in a great number of chits and raise the response rate tremendously by personalizing every invitation with a note from someone in your organization who knows the invitee. In fact, as soon as the date is set, begin a telephone campaign by having the people call the CEOs' secretaries to put the event on the executive's agenda. Then, two weeks prior, have them follow up with a phone call to the guests who haven't replied.

Many corporations now include fill-in reply cards to facilitate responses. Although it is an excessive accommodation to missed manners, prestamped envelopes also help. Reply cards should match the invitations, and they must be at least 3 1/2-by-5 inches to be accepted by the post office.

For a standard R.S.V.P., the company's address, zip code and telephone number should be included in the information. If you request only a telephone reply, it is a good idea to include the name of the person in the organization to whom the replies should be made. Stressing that it is "essential" to R.S.V.P. or that it must be made by a certain date also increases the reply rate by adding urgency.

"Regrets only" responses should be eliminated from invitation vocabulary. "Regrets only" sets a negative imprint on an invitation that is supposed to make a positive impression. Moreover, a person who is not planning to attend is probably the least likely to make the extra effort to call or write, making it more difficult for you to obtain an accurate count.

Formal and Informal Replies

Replies to formal invitations should be made within two days. They should be handwritten in the third person on white or ecru letter sheets with black ink. Acceptances repeat the event, date and time. Regrets repeat the event and date and give a brief reason for declining.

The wording of an informal reply is dictated by the invitation and the relationship to the host or hostess. Informal replies can be written on correspondence cards, monogrammed notes or calling cards. When declining, a reason must be given.

Regardless of how people reply, it's a good idea to get a telephone number because you never know what will happen at the last moment. When the guest of honor became seriously ill the day before an event, an event planner I know was able to inform all the guests because she had contact numbers.

Enclosure Cards

A savvy idea that assists the busy executive is an enclosure card for the secretary, with printed details on where and how to contact the executive in case of emergency during the function. This is particularly useful for daytime events.

Planning

In order to plan successfully, start with the time an invitation should arrive. Important conferences or seminars, especially those lasting several days and requiring travel, should be made six to eight months in advance. For an important dinner that requires out-of-town travel, allow four to six months. Luncheons require three to five weeks notice. Evening receptions in conjunction with another event require four weeks notice. Cocktails require two to four weeks notice, as do large breakfasts. Teas require two to three weeks.

Working in reverse from the date the invitation should arrive, allow sufficient:

- mailing or hand delivery time
- time to address, stuff and stamp envelopes, with plenty of extra time for calligraphy
- printing, proofreading and correction time
- design time

MAILING DO'S AND DONT'S

- Never use computer or pressure sensitive labels. Formal invitations must be addressed by hand in black ink. Informal invitations are more effective when addressed by hand, although individually typed envelopes are acceptable.
- Always use stamps rather than a postage meter.
- If using a mailing house, make sure that they have a sample of the invitation and any additional inserts, with specific instructions on how to stuff the envelope. The invitation should always be on top.

As everyone retrenches from the social whirlwind of the 1980s, it has become much more difficult to attract attendance at galas and benefits. Even corporate events have to serve a useful function for people to invest the time to participate. Not only does the event have to be presented as special, the invitees should feel special to elicit a favorable response. Little things do mean a lot. By paying attention to the details of your invitation, you have taken a major step toward insuring the success of your event.

VERBAL INVITATIONS

For many occasions, like a business lunch with an associate or an afternoon tea to get to know a new client better, you would extend only a verbal invitation. Unfortunately, as everyone's lives get increasingly hectic, the trend is to have the secretary issue an invitation by phone. In a word, don't.

It's tacky for someone other than the person calling to issue an invitation, and it makes many people feel uncomfortable. **Relationships should show respect, which is not evidenced by an invitation extended through a secretary.** This implies that your time is more valuable than the other person's, and even if you think that to be true, you should never insult someone by making so self-centered a thought obvious.

Secretaries should only be used to confirm a date, time or location of a get-together. **If at the last minute you absolutely cannot make an appointment and cannot get through yourself, have your secretary call to cancel. However, as soon as possible, get on**

the phone yourself to apologize personally. Ideally, you should send a handwritten note and, if the offense was serious, flowers.

You are likely to give even greater offense if you have your secretary, a businessperson, call to extend a social invitation. Secretaries should not be used for personal business because it makes unnecessary demands on their time and obliterates any sense of caring that should be part of any personal relationship. **Whether an event was business or personal, it is the height of bad manners to have a secretary call to extend your thanks for a lovely luncheon or dinner.** Having a secretary call implies that you know you should extend thanks but don't care enough to take even two minutes to write a thank you note. Someone would be justified in assuming that to be a greater insult than overlooking the note completely.

INVITING BUSINESS ASSOCIATES TO PERSONAL FUNCTIONS

Invitations to personal functions should be exactly that, personal. **Whether or not you invite someone from your office depends on whether or not you have a personal relationship.** Don't issue blanket invitations because they put people who are not close to you in the awkward position of either having to refuse or to attend when they really don't want to.

No invitation should ever be extended or discussed in front of people who were not invited. Whether the person wanted to attend or not, being so obviously left out could be misconstrued as a deliberate snub.

Senior executives are often invited to major functions such as the weddings of staff members. While some offices may be small enough that such invitations don't make excessive demands on the executive, in larger offices invitations from employees can become quite a problem. Accepting some invitations and declining others can create friction in an office. Consequently, many executives opt to decline all invitations from employees. **When an invitation to a wedding, shower or bar mitzvah is declined, it is not necessary to send a gift.** Nor should anyone in an office feel compelled to give a gift if not invited.

When everyone remembers that personal affairs are not business promotions, fewer feathers are ruffled or feelings hurt.

THE FAST TRACK

1. Basic invitations include who, what, when and where.

2. Formal invitations are always worded in the third person.

3. An invitation from the White House takes precedence over all others and is only refused because of a death or wedding in the family, an illness or an unexpected trip abroad.

4. Always reply to an R.S.V.P. It means *répondez s'il vous plaît* in French and translates into "Please reply."

5. Replies to formal invitations are handwritten in the third person and sent off within two days.

6. Address invitations by hand. Never use labels.

7. Use stamps rather than a postage meter.

8. Don't have a secretary issue an invitation by phone for you.

9. Only have a secretary call to cancel for you if you absolutely cannot make the call yourself. As soon as possible, call personally to apologize.

10. Never, ever have your secretary call to extend your thank you's.

11. Only invite business associates and colleagues who have become friends to personal functions.

12. Bosses need not attend the personal functions of their staff. Sending a note of felicitation is appropriate, but it is not necessary to send a gift.

Business Entertaining

They don't teach etiquette much anymore, but if you ever have to choose between Incredibly Advanced Accounting for Over-achievers and Remedial Knife and Fork, head for the silver-ware.

Harvey Mackay

Entertaining is an extension of the way you conduct yourself profes-sionally at the office. When done with style, with a concern for the guest and with attention to detail, business entertaining is an art. Like learning about line, color and composition in painting or prac-ticing scales in music, business entertaining demands a mastery of certain basic skills.

Table Manners

The world was my oyster, till I used the wrong fork.

Oscar Wilde

CHAPTER

9

Aside from the chivalry-based manners that mandate deferential treatment to women, for example holding the chair, table manners in the business arena do not differ from those in the social arena. Yet it is amazing to witness the absence of manners in restaurants, regardless of grade, across the country.

Regardless of your background, a lack of proper table manners will abort your climb up the corporate ladder. Companies do pay attention to these little details. The list is long, but none of it is advanced algebra. With a bit of practice, table manners can be mastered.

Demeanor

Let the host determine the seating arrangements. When you sit down and get up from the table, do so from the left side of the chair, unless some major obstruction prevents you from doing so. **Don't place a briefcase or a handbag on the table; keep them on the floor.** Sit a few inches from the table, and don't slouch. Don't lean back or tilt, either. **Sit up.**

Keep your elbows off the table until after the meal is over. It is acceptable to rest the forearms against the table while eating. Learn to keep both hands within view so that no one ever wonders what the other hand is doing.

Excuse yourself and leave quietly if you need to use the facilities. **Comb your hair, straighten your tie, apply lipstick and dislodge food with a toothpick while in the washroom.** None of these activities should ever take place at the table. Don't ask people where they are going if they excuse themselves, and don't volunteer directions.

Don't smoke before or during a meal. Assuming you are sitting in a smoking section and it is acceptable to the others at your table, light up only after dessert is finished.

If you must take medication, do so discreetly, preferably away from the table. Don't complain about the size of the tablets or the difficulty in swallowing. Nor should you explain why you are taking pills. Don't ask the reason if someone else takes medication. Business meals, in fact any meals in public, are not the time to lay out an array of vitamin supplements.

Accidents do happen, but don't make an issue of them. **If you spill or break something, quietly call it to the waiter's attention. Blot up whatever you can yourself, and let the victims of your mis-**

hap fend for themselves. Offer to pay for the cost of cleaning. Don't dip your napkin into the water glass to wipe off a stain.

Don't belch. Cover your mouth with your napkin and say "Excuse me" quietly to no one in particular if it happens.

Don't adopt artificial manners like crooking your little finger in an attempt to look sophisticated. It is a mockery of good manners, and will make you look even more out of place.

It is not necessary to thank the waitstaff or busperson repeatedly. If the waiter serves something while you're talking, don't stop. Let the service be unobtrusive. Let your tip reflect your thanks.

A guest is expected to "sing for his supper," figuratively not literally. **Be sure to keep up your end of the conversation. Control your intake of alcohol,** though, so you don't blurt out your life history or your company's trade secrets.

Seating Arrangements

While the host controls the seating arrangements, the guest gets the most important seat. When there are only two of you at a meal, don't sit across from one another at a square table; it is too confrontational. Sit next to each other.

When hosting two guests, don't place them on either side of you or you will be moving your head back and forth as if you were at a tennis match. Place the more senior person across from you and the more junior on your left if you are right-handed or on your right if you are left-handed.

When hosting multiple guests, sit at the head of the table with your cohost at the foot of the table. Then rank your guests in order of importance regardless of gender. The most important guest is on the host's right, the second most important guest is on the host's left. The number three guest is on the cohost's right, and so on back and forth along the table until everyone is seated.

When spouses are included at a business dinner, the host sits at one end of the table, the spouse at the other end. The spouse of a guest holds the same status as the guest. If the most important guest is male, his wife is the most important female; if a woman is the most important guest, her husband is the most important male. If, however, the spouse also holds rank, the spouse is seated according to that rank.

Assuming the host is male, the most important female would sit on the host's right. Continuing with that hierarchical

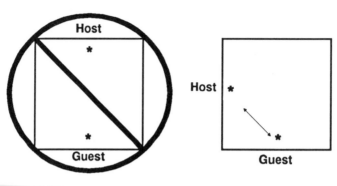

Hosting One Guest

Too Confrontational   **Congenial**

Hosting Two Guests

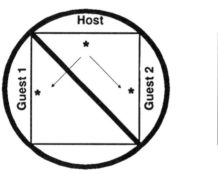

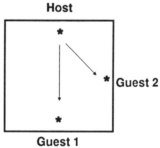

A Ping-Pong Game   **Better Sight Lines**

Hosting More Than Two Guests

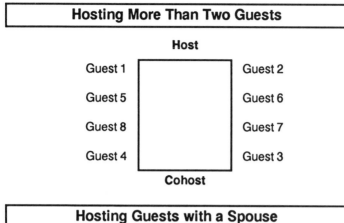

Hosting Guests with a Spouse

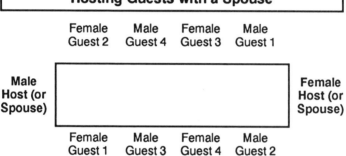

Hosting Multiples of Four with a Spouse

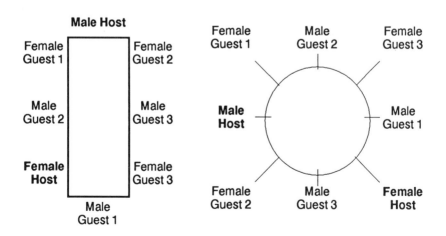

structure, place the second most important female on the host's left. The most important male, who is either the most important guest or the spouse of the most important guest, would sit on the hostess's right, the second most important male on the hostess's left. This male/female seating arrangement does not work in multiples of four, so the spouse would move one seat around, to the left of the end of the table.

As egalitarian as American society is, people do pay attention to these nuances of rank and status, so make sure you seat everyone accordingly.

Napkins and Flatware

In fine restaurants, the waiter will usually place the napkin on your lap. Otherwise, wait for the host to take the lead, usually immediately after being seated.

The most important thing to remember about a napkin is to use it—but not to wipe the flatware or glasses. If they are dirty or spotted, ask the waitstaff to bring you replacements. If you drop a piece of cutlery, leave it and ask for another.

The napkin goes on your lap, not on your chest. Using a napkin like a child's bib implies an insecurity in performing a basic physical skill you have had several decades to master. Less food on your fork or spoon helps prevent spills. A slimmer waistline can shorten the distance between plate and mouth, and reduce the possibility of mishaps.

A large dinner napkin is folded in half, with the fold closest to the body, while a luncheon napkin should be opened com-

Dinner Napkin on Lap

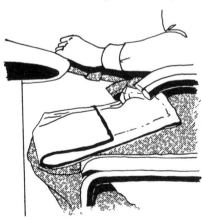

pletely. However, rules are made to be broken or re-invented. By unfolding the napkin, then folding a third back toward you, you can use the corner to blot your mouth without spilling any crumbs off the napkin and onto your clothes.

Never wipe your mouth with the napkin, blot it. Do not blot your lipstick on a cloth napkin; blot the lipstick onto a tissue before you start to eat. Don't use a napkin as a handkerchief.

Eat in either the American or the Continental style, but be consistent. Neither style permits you to wave your cutlery in the air to punctuate your conversation. Keep the hands down.

When you're finished, don't scrape and stack. Nor should you push your plate away. The proper placement of your flatware in the 'I am finished' position on your plate will signal to the waitstaff that you are done.

Place Settings

The amount of flatware on a table depends on the number of courses to be served. At a very formal dinner the waitstaff may replace the flatware prior to serving a course. The two illustrations show the place setting for a formal dinner and for a luncheon.

A Formal Place Setting

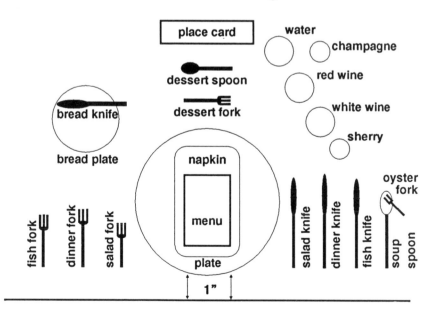

A Luncheon or Informal Place Setting

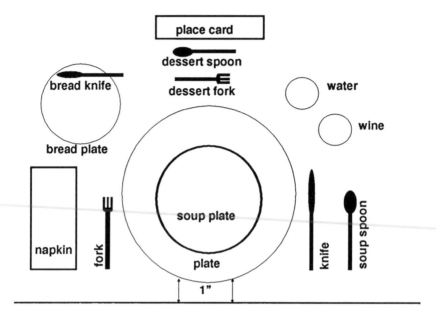

Spoons and knives are on the right, forks and the napkin are on the left. Liquids are on the right; solids, like a salad plate or a bread and butter plate are on the left. An astute diner can tell how many courses are to be served, and what those courses will be, by looking at the flatware.

Use the flatware from outside, in. Note that the salad fork and knife are nearest the plate because salad is the last course served before dessert. Salad is served to cleanse the palate after a main course. Those of you who have travelled to Italy know that waiters there regard you askance if you want your salad served as an appetizer. Follow the instructions described on pages 123–125 for placement of the flatware at the end of each course.

The dessert fork and spoon would not be on the table if finger bowls are being used. They would be brought out with the finger bowls.

American and Continental Dining Styles

Both American and Continental styles of dining are acceptable, as long as you don't switch back and forth between them.

The American Style of Eating

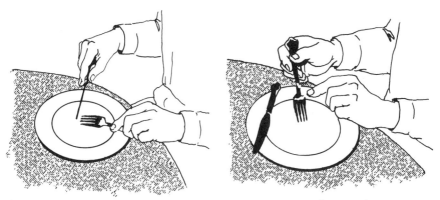

1. Cutting Meat   2. Switching Forks

3. Finished Position

As business becomes more global in scope, international travel is increasing and executives are finding that their perspectives are being broadened. More and more executives in the upper echelons are switching to the Continental style. The reason is simple. The Continental style is easier and looks more graceful.

As efficient as Americans are in most things, their style of dining is very inefficient. In the American style, the knife is used only for cutting. **Cut one piece of food at a time with the fork in the left hand and the knife in the right hand.** Then lay the knife down on the edge of the plate with the blade facing the center, and switch

The Continental Style of Eating

1. Cutting Meat

2. Bringing Food to Mouth

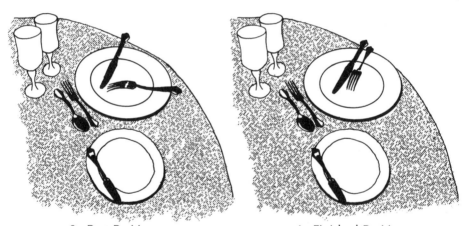

3. Rest Position

4. Finished Position

the fork to the right hand to eat with the fork tines up. The knife and fork are placed either at the right side or in the center of the plate with the knife over the fork to signal the "rest" and "finished" positions. Americans are the only people in the world who use this particular zigzag style of dining.

When eating in the Continental style, keep the fork in your left hand and the knife in your right hand throughout the meal. After the food is cut, it is pushed with the knife onto the fork, tines down, and conveyed to the mouth. Peas or creamed foods are pushed onto the fork, tines up.

To indicate to the waitstaff that you are only resting rather than finished eating, place your knife and fork (tines down) on your plate as if they were the hands of a clock at 3:40. The position to indicate that you are finished eating is at the 4:20 position on your plate.

Eating Habits

While it may be tempting to experiment and try new dishes when you dine out, business meals are not the time for new adventures. **Order foods that you know and that are not difficult or messy to eat.** Wait until your host starts to eat or indicates that you should begin.

Bring the food to your mouth; don't bend over and shovel it in. Eat neither too quickly nor too slowly, but try to pace yourself to the others at your table.

Don't chew with your mouth open, and never talk with food in your mouth. Chew your food thoroughly. Don't ever put so much into your mouth at one time that chewing or swallowing is difficult. Swallow all your food before taking another bite or a sip of your drink.

Scoop soup away from you so any drips fall into the bowl, not on your lap. Use a spoon to eat your soup. Sip the soup from the side of the spoon. Only a clear consommé, when served in a bowl with handles, may be drunk. **Crackers are never crumbled into the soup, but eaten as an accompaniment.** Don't blow on the soup, or any other food or drink for that matter, that is too hot. Wait till it cools down and eat from the sides first so you don't burn your tongue.

Put butter onto the bread plate or the edge of the dinner plate rather than directly onto your roll. Break, don't cut, then butter one bite-size piece at a time. Never butter a whole slice of bread at once or slice a roll in half and butter it.

Use a knife and fork to cut only one piece of food at a time. Although it is acceptable in the American style of dining to cut up to three pieces before laying down the knife and switching the fork into your other hand, it doesn't look very good. Don't clutch your fork in a fist. Never stab the food with your fork as if you're trying to prevent it from escaping. Don't saw your food, cut it.

Eating Soup

Ways NOT to Hold a Fork

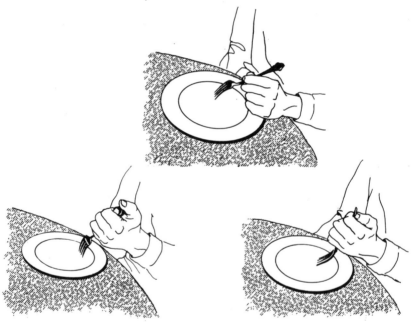

Never eat with your fingers unless you are grazing at a cocktail party or at a family barbecue. At a table, chicken is eaten with a knife and fork. Don't dunk, either. Not even doughnuts at breakfast.

It is acceptable to break one piece of bread at a time and pick it up with your fork to soak up sauce or gravy. Business dining is not about food, though, so it would look better to curb your gastronomic enthusiasm and leave the sauce on your plate.

Fishbones are removed with your thumb and index finger, then put on the edge of the plate. Use your fork, shielded by your other hand, to remove discreetly anything else, like pits, seeds or gristle, from your mouth. Camouflage whatever you may have removed under that ever-present ornamental piece of lettuce or lay it discreetly on the rim of your plate.

A glass of red wine is held by the bowl because the warmth of your hand helps release the bouquet. Brandy, too, is warmed by the heat of your hand. **Glasses of white wine and champagne, on the other hand, are held by the stem to keep the temperature cool.**

When packets of sweetener or sugar are served with tea or coffee, tuck the empty paper under the edge of the saucer or place it in the ashtray if no one is going to be smoking.

Pass It, Please

Waitstaff properly serve from the left and remove from the right. **When you pass any food around the table, do so counterclockwise to your right.** Pass the rolls, butter, condiments, cream and sugar even if you are not having any. Pass the salt and pepper shakers together. Pass the cream and sugar by placing them on the table within reach of the next person. **Gravy boats, pitchers and creamers should all be placed with the handle facing the next person.**

Don't reach! If you want something that is not within easy access, ask someone to pass it to you.

Don't sabotage your career. Eating with grace and good manners is an essential business skill. Table manners are not complicated. Social savvy and proper dining skills may pale in comparison to what is happening on your balance sheet, but they are bound to be important to your business contact. If you won't abide by the rules, confine your business dealings to the office.

RESPONSIBILITIES OF THE HOST

Many Americans are uncomfortable entertaining business associates over a meal, and it shows. No matter how much you spend, your guests will sense your unease and feel uncomfortable in your presence. To entertain successfully, it helps to enjoy the process and to have the confidence that comes of knowing what you're doing. Then you can concentrate on making your guests feel welcome and cherished. People prefer to do business with those who make them feel good, all other things being equal.

In exchange for the privilege of deciding with whom, where, when and what to eat, the host has the responsibility of handling every detail of the meal, from extending the invitation and making reservations to handling the tip and the coat check. Trust Murphy's Law; anything that can go wrong, will. Plan carefully.

The locale in which you entertain will be perceived as an extension of your business environment. Fancy establishments for the sake of fancy should be avoided. Familiarize yourself with several establishments with good food and polite, reliable service that reflect the image you wish to convey about yourself and your company. It is always impressive to your guests if you are greeted by name at an establishment, so start establishing a rapport with the maître d'.

Before extending an invitation, decide who should be invited. One-on-one meetings are the most productive. Invite others only if they are essential to your agenda. The more people at the meal, the less focused it will be. Never allow a guest to bring a friend or colleague who is not germane to your business. After all, you are paying the bill.

Know which meal—breakfast, lunch, tea or dinner—best suits your purposes in hosting. In business, every meal has a different reason for being. Allow an hour for breakfast or tea, two hours for lunch and the entire evening for dinner.

Always extend the invitation personally, and put some urgency behind it. To have a secretary extend the invitation on your behalf is impersonal and implies the person isn't worth that few extra minutes of your precious time. **Give the purpose of the get-together when extending the invitation so the guest can come prepared.** No one should ever be invited without an agenda.

Never ask your guests where they want to eat. Instead, offer them a choice of two restaurants according to their taste, personality and importance. "Janice, would you prefer to eat at Le Cirque or at Le Régence?" If you are unsure of their taste, offer a choice of two types of food, "Jim, would you prefer to eat Italian food or Mexican?" then offer a choice of two places. Take the location of your guest's office into consideration when deciding where to eat.

If several people are attending the luncheon or if time is of the essence, prearrange the menu. Doing so avoids the hassle of deciding what to order and the concern over the acceptable price range, eliminating a great deal of stress. Be sure to ask guests at the time of the invitation if there is anything they can't eat. Since most restaurants around the country now have separate sections for smokers and non-smokers, don't forget to ask your guests which they prefer and abide by it unless you are seriously allergic. In that case, say, "Because of my allergies, I have to sit in the nonsmoking section. Is that acceptable to you?"

Make reservations in your name and the name of your company as far in advance as possible. Specify where you would like to sit when booking the table. Choose a table for maximum privacy, avoiding tables near the kitchen, restrooms or mirrors. Decide beforehand where everyone will sit, remembering that the guest gets the best seat.

Avoid spreading out papers at a meal because it interferes with dining; it is better to meet in your office either before or after the meal. If you absolutely must review papers at the meal, be sure to request a large table.

Verify your arrangements with the restaurant the day before the meeting. Don't forget to call your guests the day before as well to confirm the date. If your guest is not available, leave a message with a secretary, repeating all the vital information.

Arrive early to be sure you're on hand to greet your guests. Make sure you won't be kept waiting. If you and your guest are going to be late for any reason, be sure to call the maître d' or you may find that he has given your table to someone else.

Use the time to recheck the table. If you have prearranged the menu, make sure it is in order. If you have not prearranged the meal, study the menu for possible suggestions. **Arrange with the captain the way you would like the check handled.** By confirming all the details, you leave no doubt in the minds of the maître d', the captain and the waitstaff that you are the host.

Wait for your guests in the lobby. If there is no lobby, go to the table, but watch for your guests. **Don't wait in the bar because that sends confusing messages about your agenda.** Don't order a drink or open your napkin when you sit down. You want to present your guests with a perfectly set table without implying that they have kept you waiting. If they apologize, reassure them that you just sat down yourself.

Handle chronic earlybirds or latecomers by adjusting the time you tell them to meet you. For example, if someone is always at least fifteen minutes early, tell that person the reservation is for 1:15 rather than for 1:00 p.m. Then you'll both be there at the agreed upon time. Allow your guests fifteen minutes grace before calling their office to find out why they are late. If they have not arrived half an hour after the scheduled time, feel free to order or to leave. If you decide not to stay, it is courteous to tip the waitstaff because you have taken up a table and reduced their source of income for that day.

If the maître d' seats you, he precedes the guests and you follow. When seating yourself, lead your guests to the table. Always offer your guest a drink, even if you don't want one. Let the guest decide whether or not to drink alcohol by asking, "Would you like some wine, mineral water or juice?" If the guest is having something, it is polite to order something too, although it doesn't have to be an alcoholic beverage.

Never table hop. It impresses your guests with your negligence and makes you look insecure. **Don't take calls at your table.** It announces to the entire restaurant that the person on the phone is more important than the person across the table from you. It is very rude to belittle someone so in front of others. You got out of the office to escape those calls and to focus on your guest.

Let guests order first if you don't have a prearranged menu. Since worry about the limits of your hospitality is one of the prime concerns of most guests, guide them to what is acceptable by suggesting an appetizer or a drink. You may want to take the lead by saying, "I'm having . . . What would you like." **Making a recommendation of one or two entrées indicates an acceptable price range for them.** Phrase your suggestion in such a way that your guests don't feel obliged to follow your suggestion. "John, everything on this menu is delicious. I especially enjoy the Dover sole and my partner insists the filet mignon here is the best in town." Keep the order simple.

Problems can occur in even the best run establishments. Never make a scene if you're displeased. Be firm, polite and businesslike about the service. If food is cold or not cooked properly, send it back. If reordering, never reorder the same dish. Never chastise a waitperson or a captain in front of others. **If something goes wrong during the meal, excuse yourself and have a quiet chat with the captain or maître d'.** Once at lunch in a very good New York restaurant, our food had not arrived after quite some time, and the waiter was nowhere to be seen. He had walked out ten minutes earlier because of a dispute with the sous chef, and the captain had not noticed it in the lunch hour rush. We could have waited a long time if nothing had been said. Let the captain or the maître d' handle the problem for you.

Even though this is a business meal and you've indicated your agenda to your guest when you proffered the invitation, don't jump right in to discussing the business at hand. Small talk allows you and your guest a chance to relax and to establish a rapport with one another, somewhat like allowing an engine to warm up before you drive off. Be sensitive to your guests and begin the discussion when they appear to be ready. **A good rule of thumb is to wait until after the orders have been placed and the appetizers have arrived.** Never wait until dessert and coffee to get down to business because it shows a lack of respect for the guest's time. As host, it is also your responsibility to adhere to the agenda and control the conversation, especially when several people are present.

Thank the maître d' with either a phone call or a note later that day. It will create a favorable impression for your return visit. Savvy hosts have even been known to send notes to their guests, thanking the people for joining them.

RESPONSIBILITIES OF THE GUEST

Once you accept an invitation, it is your obligation to follow through. Don't hedge your bets waiting for the best invitation, and don't cancel at the last minute because something better comes along. As was mentioned in chapter 8, only illness, the demands of one's superior, a trip abroad, an invitation from the White House or a marriage or death in the family are acceptable reasons to cancel an invitation. **If you do have to cancel a business meal, do it personally and as far in advance as possible.** Try to reschedule another meeting at the time of cancellation.

The realities of business life have a way of interfering with even the most organized executive's plans. **If a last minute crisis or deadline occurs and you cannot get away to call yourself, then have your secretary call.** It is imperative that you follow up with a personal call and a note of apology as soon as you are free. If you were unable to reach your host and you stood him or her up, send flowers with that note of apology.

Arrive punctually. **If you are going to be late, call your host at the office or at the restaurant.** It is just as rude to arrive very early as it is to arrive late. If you get to the restaurant with time to spare, take a walk around the block or window shop for a few minutes.

Show appreciation for the hospitality extended to you by participating in the conversation. Leave any other worries or problems back at the office and concentrate on your host's agenda. It is perfectly acceptable to have your own agenda, but don't bring it up before the host. If you find the host is not responsive to your agenda, drop it immediately. Don't let yourself be bought for the price of a meal, though. It is bad manners for a host to expect luncheon guests to impart knowledge or information for which they would usually charge.

Write a thank you note within twenty-four hours after the meal.

TOASTING

Toasting is an important exchange of esteem between host and guest, and both have a responsibility to handle a toast with style and grace.

When making a toast, don't roast the other person. Keep the toast simple, short and sweet.

The person being toasted remains seated and does not drink to himself or herself. **Afterward, always respond with a toast to the person who made the original toast to you.**

If you don't drink and someone is being toasted, raise your glass anyway.

HANDLING THE CHECK

Confusion abounds over how to handle the check at a business meal, especially when one of the people is a woman. The rule is very simple. The person who does the inviting pays unless the other person is the one who benefits from the association. **In other words, if you invite a client to lunch, you pay; if the client suggests lunch, you still pay because you are the one who benefits from the business relationship.**

Always make sure well in advance that the restaurant takes the credit card you are planning to use. Then check again when you reconfirm the reservation because things do change. If you find that you left your wallet at home, talk to the maître d' privately, and request the bill be sent to your office. Most restaurants will oblige, especially if they know you. If you frequent a particular restaurant, open a house account with your company's approval. Then the check need never be brought to your table.

If you are paying by credit card, give the maître d' an impression of your card upon arrival. This speeds the paying process and avoids any confusion over who is paying the bill. Handle the credit card slip in one of three ways: Arrange to sign it on your way out; request that it be held at the captain's station, excuse yourself as the meal is coming to a close and go there to sign the slip; or, sign the slip when the imprint is taken, instruct that your standard tip be added to the bill and request that it not be brought to your table. Have the receipt sent to your office.

If by some oversight the bill is brought to your table and not given to you, pick it up immediately without comment. While it is acceptable to silently add up the figures and calculate the tip, it is not acceptable to comment on the total. Put the check face down on the tray or in the folder with your card or money underneath.

Remember to handle all coat check charges and tips on your way out.

POWER BREAKFAST

Breakfast is a crisp and defined meal that is perfect for time conscious people. **Breakfast invitations imply a sense of urgency that is hard to decline.** Power breakfasts are a good meal for meeting with people who are always booked weeks in advance or who don't break for lunch. **Breakfasts are also a good time to strategize for events occurring later that day.**

Even if you are an early bird, avoid snafu's by preparing everything the night before. Read the paper, listen to the news or watch a television talk show so you'll know what is going on. Allow sufficient time to circumvent problems with rush hour traffic.

Think about what you order. Avoid potentially sloppy foods. Juice or a bowl of berries is preferable to grapefruit halves which can squirt everywhere. Scrambled eggs are less likely to leave their mark than soft boiled or poached eggs. Not everyone is stimulated by the smell of a hearty breakfast. Avoid sausages, bacon or other fried foods unless your guest orders them. Cereal is eaten like soup, scooping away from you so any drops of milk will fall into the bowl.

Because breakfast is a shorter meal, make some small talk, but get to the point of the meeting when the food is served. Respect your guest's need to get to the office.

POWER LUNCH

Power lunches are a staple of American business because the atmosphere in a restaurant is more intimate and friendly than an office. Unlike the urgency of a breakfast meeting, lunch is more relaxed. People tend to be more receptive to good ideas in such an environment.

While lunch is an ideal time to discuss your concepts, products or services, avoid giving someone indigestion with a hard sell. Entertaining should be pleasurable. If you use the time to develop a rapport with your guests and explore their needs in relation to your agenda, the business will follow.

Power lunches are primarily used to entertain clients or to establish business contacts. Lunches are also a great way to cement inter-office relationships and to show appreciation to staff and co-workers without serious infringements into their personal time.

Power lunches are the least compromising male/female dining situations. While being seen together early in the morning can cause talk, and while dinners can be difficult to terminate, lunch leaves no doubt you're there to do business.

Business is no longer conducted over three martinis. It is important to keep your head clear to manage the intricacies of successful entertaining. If you choose to have a drink, keep it to one and keep it light. Wine, beer or champagne are the alcoholic beverages of choice at lunch.

The fewer people you have at lunch, the easier it is to control the dynamics. Keep it to the two of you if possible. Be sure to specify that you will need a large, private table. It may require a bit of extra maneuvering in an establishment where tables for two are small, cramped affairs or side by side along a wall, often lined by a banquette, but most maître d's will oblige you if they know you.

Otherwise, take the time to find a restaurant that will accommodate your needs. Looking after the comfort of your guest takes precedence.

Never forget your duties as a host, whether the power lunch is held in a restaurant, a private club or your offices. Be early and make sure all arrangements have been attended to. Remember to check the menu so you can help your guest and place your own order quickly. Taking longer than five minutes to study a menu and make a decision calls into question your decision making abilities on larger issues. Avoid foods that are unfamiliar, difficult to eat, squirt, require slurping or demand all your attention. The focus of the lunch is business!

The most effective way to control a lunch and keep the focus on business is to have it in your office. Inviting your guests into your offices adds a personal touch that affords them an introduction both to you and your company. It's the next best thing to inviting them into your home.

Corporate dining rooms vary from small elegant rooms with one table to large rooms that resemble fine restaurants. If your company has a full time staff, confer with the chef or the person in charge to plan the menu and seating just as you would with the maître d' of a fine restaurant. Don't assume that because the dining room staff is employed by your company, you can relinquish your responsibilities as host. If anything, your performance will be even more visible to your senior officers. If the meal is being catered, give the person making the arrangements for you specific instructions about the menu and service. Check that everything has arrived and is in order before your guest arrives.

If you don't have an executive dining room, you can still use a conference room and a caterer. There is no need to have a formal sit-down dinner. A buffet of attractively displayed cold foods is always a welcome meal.

When hosting guests in your office, always go out to greet them in the reception area. Don't expect them to find you or the dining room.

POWER TEA

Power tea may sound like a contradiction in terms, but remember that power at its most effective is subtle. Tea is civilized, quieter and more relaxed than breakfast or lunch, and more conducive to conversation. **Tea is an ideal time to become better acquainted with someone with whom you want to establish a business relationship.**

Afternoon tea is normally served at 4:00 p.m., and should last no more than an hour to an hour and a half. Don't refer to tea as "High Tea" or you'll be considered low brow. High tea is a light supper for the children or the household staff served at 6:00 p.m. Alcoholic beverages are not served at tea, so it is ideal for clear-headed conversations and for those who do not like to drink.

MASTERING MINGLING

Walking into a room full of strange people has become the number one fear of Americans, even greater than getting up in front of an entire group to speak. Most people would rather have the earth open up and swallow them whole!

It's not so hard if you master a few simple skills. The secret is to plan ahead. **First, find out as much as possible about the event, the agenda and the other attendees by calling the organizer or person who invited you.** Every event has a hidden agenda, and by knowing about it and the other players, you're probably further ahead than everyone else.

Second, create your own agenda by deciding on your goal in attending the function. If it is to meet prospective clients, knowing who will be there will help you focus on who you want to seek out. No longer will you be walking aimlessly into a sea of strange faces who intimidate you.

Party styles change with the location, and what works in one city will not necessarily work in another. Attitudes to dress, punctuality and conversation change from city to city. For example, while it is appropriate to be half an hour late for cocktails in New York, and to arrive in business clothes carrying your briefcase, in Washington you dress for the occasion and arrive punctually or you may miss the guest of honor.

Basic business manners don't change, though. **It is the guests' responsibility to introduce themselves.** Never wait for someone to introduce you. Decide beforehand how you would like to present yourself, then make sure you meet several new people. It gets easier with practice.

Read that day's newspapers and think of a few appropriate topics for small talk. Join groups of people and listen to the conversation; join in when it is appropriate. Remember not to stand too close (a little more than arm's length with strangers) or talk too loud. Don't tell jokes that involve sensitive subjects like race or religion, and keep them clean.

Never park yourself at the bar or hang out at the hors d'oeuvres table. Get what you want, then circulate. Eating before you attend a cocktail party leaves you free to meet people rather than attend to a growling stomach. Invariably, you'll be introduced to someone of importance the moment you have a mouth full of food.

Keep the drink in your left hand so you'll be free to shake hands without a lot of preliminary fumbling and you won't offer a wet, ice cold hand. There's a simple trick to handling a drink, the hors d'oeuvres and the handshake simultaneously. Put the cocktail napkin between the baby and ring fingers of your left hand, the plate of hors d'oeuvres between the middle and index fingers and the glass on the plate, stabilized between the index finger and thumb. Then your right hand is free to shake, to graze, to take a

Mastering the Grazing while Mingling

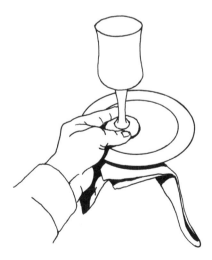

Hold Napkin, Plate and Glass in Left Hand

drink or to blot with the napkin. Just remember to put everything back between those fingers.

When you're ready to leave, don't turn your departure into an event. While it is a nice gesture to thank your host and say good-bye, it is not necessary if you can't find the person or if he or she is busy. It is necessary to send a thank you note the following morning.

BUSINESS DINNERS

Unless a guest is from out-of-town or a future client makes the suggestion, a business dinner should never be a first invitation. It is presumptuous to impose on someone's private time in the evening unless you have an established relationship and a very good reason for meeting.

Keep a professional attitude toward business dinners. As with any other business entertaining, have an agenda and let your guests know what it is beforehand. Include only those people who are working on the agenda under discussion. One-on-one business meals are almost always the most productive.

Whether or not the spouse should be included is an important consideration when extending a dinner invitation. If the guest is from out-of-town and the spouse has come along on the trip, definitely include the person. Otherwise, consider your agenda. The evening will take on a much more relaxed, social feel when you're entertaining a couple. **If the dinner is a special occasion intended to please your guest or if your spouse is accompanying you, include the guest's spouse.** It's more difficult to bring up business without ostracizing the spouse from the conversation if you're entertaining a couple unaccompanied.

Business dinners stretch over a longer period than other meals, and people have a tendency to drink more in the evening even though moderation is in vogue. The first drink is to relax your guest. Be sure to get to business before the second drink or you may find your guest too relaxed. You're the host, and it is your responsibility to guide the conversation to the point of the evening. Watch your own intake and remember that less is more effective!

Maintain your professionalism and dignity throughout the evening to retain your credibility. Dress appropriate to the occasion, but in a businesslike manner. That means no décolletage or strapless dresses for the women and no flashy jewelry or heavy scents for either men or women.

Never assume that your guest's dinner hour is your own. While dinners in large metropolitan areas are later in the evening, people from other parts of the country and parents of small children often eat earlier. Ask your guests when they prefer to dine. When your guests are ready to depart, don't try to cajole them into staying. Smile, shake hands and wish them a good evening. Gracious dinner guests also take into consideration their host's schedules and bid their farewells when the other guests leave.

THEATER ETIQUETTE

Dinner and the theater are an ideal combination for treating business associates to a special evening. To make the occasion as enjoyable as possible for everyone in the audience, there are certain rules of etiquette that everyone should adhere to.

First and foremost, be punctual. It is inconsiderate to the performers and others in the audience to expect to be seated after a performance has begun. Abide by the performance schedule, and stay until the end. Don't disrupt others by trying to get out before the rush.

Be quiet. Don't talk, rustle your program or candy wrappers or wear jangling jewelry. The audience did not pay to hear you.

Learn when to applaud. At the ballet, for instance, it is appropriate to clap when the curtain rises to an elaborate stage setting, when the prima ballerina or premier danseur appears on stage, when a dancer executes three leaps or four turns and when the music pauses at the end of a scene. If you feel compelled to shout "bravo," save it for the men. "Brava" is the correct term for a ballerina or an opera diva. **Don't sneak out before the applause.** The performers earned it; consider it part of the price of admission.

Don't get so carried away with a performance that you sing along or squeal with delight to the annoyance of your neighbors. Nor should you sigh with boredom. Stay awake, especially if you have a tendency to snore.

Unfortunately, theater etiquette is not printed on the back of every program in every theater. However, your admirable behavior can act as a role model for others and increase everyone's enjoyment of the theater arts in America.

SPORTING ETIQUETTE

Sports are an ideal compliment to business; perhaps that is why so much business is done over a game of golf, tennis or squash. Sporting events such as tennis matches or basketball games are great ways to cement business relationships in a more casual atmosphere. However, that does not mean you can let your hair down and behave in a juvenile manner.

Retain a semblance of professionalism and dignity at even the most exciting games. **Don't start calling names or yelling epithets at the referee or umpire.** Always cheer for the home team, especially if you are the guest. Loyalty is an important component of business relationships.

Dress appropriately. Attending a sporting event is not the time to trot out your old varsity letter. Nor should you dress like a participant. Only the players should be wearing tennis clothes at a tennis match. If in doubt, ask your host, "Are you going straight from the office, or are you going home to change first?" If the host is getting into something more comfortable, ask for clarification.

Every game has its own etiquette. The way you play the game says a great deal about the way you conduct yourself in business. Golf, for instance, has some very rigid rules of etiquette, like not talking when another player is making a shot, allowing the player farthest from the hole to play next and letting the group behind you play through when you've lost your ball. **Learn the etiquette of the game before you trip yourself up.**

ETIQUETTE AT PRIVATE CLUBS

Being invited to a club is an honor, whether it is for lunch or an afternoon of golf followed by drinks and dinner. **Never entertain a business associate in a club that permits discrimination whether on the basis of gender, race or religion.** Save it for your personal life if you must, but prepare to surrender your membership if you're planning to be in the public eye. **If you're hosting a major event and you want press coverage, don't entertain in a private club.** Most clubs frown on that public intrusion.

Deal with the staff at your club the way you would the staff at a good restaurant. For a large function, deal with the club manager like the banquet manager at a hotel. You are still the host and shoulder all the duties of a host.

While you need not worry about how to handle the check, remember to **handle the tip according to club policy.** If the club includes a service charge in the bill and the service has been excellent, leave an extra tip if it is allowed and let the club manager know with a note of appreciation.

As a guest at a private club, remember that your host is responsible for your behavior. **Respect the rules, and don't do anything that will cause the club to censure him. Obey the club's dress code.** Stay in the public areas of the club; don't wander around unescorted.

When you are invited to a private club, don't offer to pay, not even the tip. Return the hospitality in kind by inviting your host out. If you do not belong to a golf or tennis club, you could get tickets for a football game.

ENTERTAINING AT HOME

Entertaining business associates at home adds a personal touch to a business relationship and can be very impressive, but it can also be your undoing if not handled in a professional manner.

Unless there is household staff, it is a business investment, especially for a female executive, to hire a caterer. You cannot act as host, cook and server simultaneously. Nor should the spouse fulfill any role other than cohost. Leave the cooking to someone else. If gourmet cooking happens to be your hobby, at least have trained help to serve and clean up, and plan a menu that won't require your presence in the kitchen once the guests arrive.

Entertaining at home requires additional planning. **Make sure you have adequate seating and place settings for everyone. Book the caterer sufficiently in advance;** hiring a caterer is not like making a last minute restaurant reservation. **Confirm that the caterer will be handling the coat check, valet parking if necessary, cocktails and after-dinner drinks and all cleanup in addition to serving the dinner.** If not, make appropriate arrangements. Have the caterer provide any additional tables, chairs and place settings you may need. Make sure your home is immaculate. **Order flowers for the table.**

If you have pets or children, make sure they are out of the way and well cared for. No one feels comfortable having even the cutest children intrude on a business situation. Pets can be unpredictable regardless of the amount of training they have had. Even if you feel your pet has mastered petiquette, your guests may feel uncomfortable with animals around.

Give guests complete directions, preferably a map, so no one gets lost. If your party is large, have valet parking. If you live in a major city like New York or San Francisco where parking is inadequate at best, let anyone who is driving know where to find the nearest garage or most available street parking.

Plan your entertaining to allow everyone time to get home at a reasonable hour, especially on a week night. **Keep the cocktail hour short, half an hour to forty-five minutes, so no one consumes too much alcohol before dinner.** Serve hors d'oeuvres to help control the alcohol consumption.

If you are single and you are entertaining a large group, ask an executive of the same gender who is close to you in rank to act as cohost. It is inappropriate to have someone of the opposite gender or a secretary perform cohosting duties because there are too many personal implications.

If you are entertaining a large group of people, at a cocktail party for example, you may certainly invite your boss. Otherwise, let your boss extend the initial invitation or two. To extend an invitation to your boss first is pretentious. Don't discuss invitations to or from your boss with your colleagues unless you know for certain everyone is invited.

CORPORATE EVENTS

Large corporate events are best handled by professional party planners, whether they are in house or outside consultants. Every company should make certain, regardless of who plans the party, that a representative of the company sits at each table as a surrogate host to ensure everyone is introduced, conversation is lively and everyone is included in it and all problems are dealt with. When there is no receiving line, executives should greet guests at the door and take them to be introduced to the host.

As a guest at any corporate function hosted by your employer, you are there to work, not party. Socialize with the other guests and act in a manner befitting a host. Keep your alcohol intake down and keep your eyes open for any wallflowers who may need a bit of help socializing.

As a guest, your company manners should always be on display regardless of the size of the affair. Just because a party is large does not mean that you can arrive when you feel like it. Nor will your behavior be camouflaged by a crowd; it will be witnessed by more people who can pass judgement on you as a professional. Don't monopolize the host; it is your duty to circulate. Socializing in company can be a major boost to anyone's career.

Pass the Dictionary, I Can't Read the Menu

Many of the finest restaurants throughout the United States print their menus in French, Italian or Spanish, depending on the origin of the food the restaurant serves. While most have English translations in smaller letters underneath, those translations seem to be increasingly difficult to decipher as we mature; an acquaintance describes it as the "my arm's too short to read the menu" syndrome.

Whether you're the host or the guest, learn the terms for a few of your favorite foods to appear polished and professional at a business function.

The French Menu

Appetizers and Miscellaneous—Hors d'oeuvres et Divers

café complet—continental breakfast; rolls, coffee, butter, jam

céleri remoulade—celery root, cut in matchsticks, in cold zesty sauce

cornichon—type of pickle

crudités—raw vegetables

escargots—snails

foie gras—minced spread of goose or duck liver

frites—french fries

nouilles—noodles

oeufs—eggs

oeufs à la Russe—hard-boiled eggs with sauce made from chives, onion and a dash of Tabasco

pain—bread

sel—salt

sucre—sugar

Soups—Potages

bisque—a puree, more particularly of shellfish, served as a thick soup

blanquette de veau—veal stew in cream sauce

bouillabaisse—a soup or stew of varied fish and shellfish, usually garlic and saffron-scented, with tomatoes and parsley

cassoulet—a white bean stew, cooked with lamb, and/or goose, etc.

consommé—meat stock that has been enriched, concentrated, and clarified

madrilene—chilled clear chicken soup with tomato

petite marmite—a clear soup made from meat and vegetables, served with toast and sprinkled with grated cheese

soup à l'oignon—onion soup

Seafood and Fish—Fruits de mer et Poissons

anchois—anchovy

brochet—pike

coquillages—shellfish

coquilles St. Jacques—scallops, or scallops in a white wine sauce

crevettes—shrimp

hareng—herring

homard—lobster

maquereau—mackerel

saumon fumé—smoked salmon

tortue—turtle

truite—trout

Meat and Poultry—Viandes et Volaille

agneau—lamb

assiette anglaise—assortment of cold cuts

bifteck—steak; bien cuit—well done, saignant—rare

boeuf bourguignon—braised beef prepared with small glazed onions, mushrooms and red wine

boeuf rôti—roast beef

canard—duck

caneton—duckling

carbonnade à la flamande—beef cooked with beer

coq au vin—chicken braised in wine sauce with onions, ham or bacon and mushrooms

côte de veau—veal chop

entrecôte—rib steak

escalopes de veau cordon bleu—thin slices of boneless veal with ham and cheese

filet de boeuf—tenderloin

grenouilles—frog legs

jambon—ham

langue—tongue

lapin—rabbit

lard—bacon

pot-au-feu—boiled beef dinner

poulet chasseur—chicken with sautéed mushrooms, shallots, white wine and tomatoes

ragout—cut up meat, poultry or fish that has been browned, often with vegetables

ris de veau—sweetbreads

saucisson—sausage

suprême de volaille—choice fillet of poultry breast removed in one piece

tournedos—small fillet, filet mignon

Sauces and Styles of Preparation

amadine—made with almonds (often used with fish)

à l'anglaise—cooked in either water or stock

béarnaise sauce—buttery, egg-thickened sauce scented with shallots and tarragon

béchamel—sauce of milk thickened with butter and flour

beurre d'ail—garlic butter

beurre noir—brown butter served on eggs, fish, or vegetables

à la bonne femme—cooked with bacon, onions, potatoes and a thick brown gravy

brochette—anything cooked on a skewer

brouillé—scrambled

en croûte—in pastry

demiglace—thick brown sauce

à la duglère—a cream sauce made with wine and tomatoes, served with fish

hollandaise—thick, rich sauce of egg yolks, butter and lemon

à la jardinière—fresh vegetables, served with roast, stewed, or braised meat and poultry

lyonnaise—prepared with onions

maître d'hôtel sauce—butter, spiked with lemon and parsley

meunière—fish that is seasoned, dipped in flour and sautéed in butter

mornay—cream sauce with cheese

à la provençale—cooked with tomatoes, garlic, olives and eggplant

ravigote—white sauce highly seasoned with thyme and black pepper

rémoulade—a piquant mayonnaise-like sauce served with seafood or celery root

Salads, Vegetables and Fruit—Salades, Légumes et Fruits

ananas—pineapple

artichaut—artichoke

asperge—asparagus

aubergine—eggplant

avocat—avocado

cerise—cherry

champignon—mushroom

chou—cabbage

choucroute—sauerkraut

citron—lemon

courgette—zucchini

cresson—watercress

épinards—spinach

fraise—strawberry

framboise—raspberry

haricots—beans

haricots verts—green beans

macédoine—diced and mixed fruit or vegetables

pamplemousse—grapefruit

ratatouille—a vegetable stew, with eggplant, tomato, green pepper, onions and zucchini, served hot or cold

salade niçoise—a Mediterranean salad of greens and tuna, anchovy, boiled potato, string beans, olives, hard-boiled eggs, capers

salade verte—green salad

truffle—a rare and costly variety of fungi that grows underground in the roots of certain trees, used for flavor and texture

Desserts—Desserts

baba au rhum—rum-soaked cake

beignets—fritters

blini—thin, unsweetened pancake

bombe glacée—ice cream dessert

Brie—a creamy dessert cheese

café glace—ice cream with coffee flavoring

Camembert—a soft runny dessert cheese

choux à la crème—cream puffs

crème brulée—a rich dessert pudding made with vanilla and cream, which is lightly coated with sugar, placed under the broiler, and then cooled for two to three hours before serving

crème caramel—custard with a burnt sugar flavor

crème Chantilly—whipped cream

crêpes Suzette—pancakes in a sweet orange sauce spiked with Curaçao liqueur

petit-beurre—butter cookie

profiterole—puff pastry filled with custard, ice cream or whipped cream, usually covered in a chocolate sauce

tarte—pie

Beverages—Boissons

bière—beer

café au lait—coffee with milk

café noir—black coffee

demitasse—strong black coffee served in a small cup

jus de fruit—fruit juice

thé—tea

vin—wine

The Italian Menu

Appetizers and Miscellaneous—Antipasti e Agguintia

bruschetta—slices of toasted, crusty bread rubbed with garlic and seasoned with olive oil, salt, pepper and topped with chopped tomatoes

fontina—a rich, mellow cheese

frittata—omelet

grissino—breadsticks

mortadella—soft salami

pane—bread

panzerotti—potato croquettes or yeast dough stuffed with mozzarella

pecorino—sheep's milk cheese

prosciutto—smoked ham often served with figs or melon

provolone—a firm, mild cheese with a slightly salty flavor

ricotta—a mild white curd cheese

schiuma di mare—just spawned anchovies seasoned with oil, lemon and pepper

spiedino—fried cheese in a piquant anchovy sauce

Soups—Minestre e Zuppe

brodetto—fish stew

brodo—broth

minestrone—thick vegetable soup

stracciatella—broth with Parmesan cheese and egg

zuppa di cipolle—onion soup

zuppa pavese—hot broth poured over a piece of toast with an egg on top

Pasta and Sauces—Pasta e Sugo

agliata—sauce of pounded garlic, oil and crustless bread

agnolotti—square pasta folded and filled with meat or vegetables, served in broth or sauce all' amatriciana—sauce made with fats, white wine, tomato and chili peppers

al burro—with butter

al dente—pasta cooked till just firm or chewy

cannelloni—cylindrical rolls of pasta filled with meat, cheese and/or vegetables

capelli d'angelo—very thin spaghetti also called angel's hair

cappelletti—small hat-shaped pasta filled with meat or cheese and egg

alla carbonara—a sauce made of browned bacon, egg yolks, Parmesan cheese and cream

dolceforte—sauce with mustard and sugar

fusilli—short, twisted spiral pasta

gnocchi—potato or semolina dumplings

maccheroni—short, tubular pasta

manicotti—large, flat noodles rolled and stuffed with cheese or meat and baked in tomato sauce

marinara—spicy, meatless tomato sauce

perciatelli—long macaroni

pesto—sauce made of basil, Parmesan, pine nuts, olive oil and garlic

piccata—veal scaloppina pan-sautéed with butter and lemon juice

alla pizzaiola—stews and sauces made with tomatoes, capers, oregano and anchovies

polenta—corn meal cooked with water, seasonings and parmesan cheese

alla puttanesca—sauce made from tomatoes, black olives, anchovies, capers, chili peppers and basil

ragu—a sauce made from tomatoes, herbs and ground meat

tortellini—stuffed pasta shaped into a closed ring

tortelloni—large ravioli stuffed with vegetables or cheese

ziti—long hollow tubes of pasta

Seafood/Fish—Frutti di mare e Pesce

acciughe—anchovy

anguilla—eel

astaco—Maine lobster

branzino o spigola—bass

calamari—squid

cernia—grouper

cozze—mussels

dentice—red snapper

filetto di sogliole—fillet of sole

gamberi—shrimp

impepata de cozzi—mussels steamed and seasoned with lemon juice, parsley and freshly ground pepper

merluzzo—cod

pescespada—swordfish

rombo— turbot

scampi—large shrimp

scungilli—conch

soglia—sole

tonno—tuna

troto—trout

vongole—clams

Meat and Poultry—Carne e Pollo

abbachio—baby lamb

agnello arrosta—roast lamb

animelle—sweetbreads

anitra—duck

bistecca—steak

bollito misto—various boiled meats

bue—beef

cacciagione—game

cappone—capon

carpaccio—very thin slices of lean raw beef seasoned with olive oil, lemon, salt and pepper

cima—stuffed breast of veal, served cold

coniglio—rabbit

cotoletta—a boneless pork or veal cutlet, pounded flat

fegato—liver

fegato alla venezia—calves' liver with onions

lingua—tongue

maiale—pork

manzo—beef

oca—goose

osso bucco—braised veal shanks

pancetta—salt-cured pork belly similar to bacon

pollo—chicken

polpetta—meat ball

punta di petto—brisket of beef

quaglia—quail

scaloppina—thinly sliced veal pounded flat

spezzatino di vitello—veal stew

tacchino—turkey

valdostana—veal chop sliced and stuffed with fontina cheese, then breaded and fried

vitello—veal

vitello tonnato—cold veal with tuna, anchovy and caper sauce

Fruits and Vegetables—Frutta e Verdure, Insalate e Legumes

aspargi—asparagus

broccoli di rape—bitter broccoli

cannellini—small white beans

caprese—salad of tomatoes, basil, olive oil and mozzarella

carciofi—artichokes

ceci—chickpeas

ciliege—cherries

fagiolini—green beans

fragola—strawberry

al funghetto—cooked vegetables thinly sliced and diced, then sautéed with parsley and garlic

funghi—mushrooms

insalata mista—mixed green salad

lattuga—lettuce

limone—lemon

mela—apple

melanzana—eggplant

peperoncino—chili pepper

pesca—peach

piselli—peas

pomodoro—tomato

pompelmo—grapefruit

porcini—wild mushrooms

radicchio—red chicory with white veins; slightly bitter taste

riso—rice

risotto—long grain rice cooked with onions, butter, broth and Parmesan; often has other vegetables, meat, fish, or shellfish added

tartufi—truffles

uva—grapes

Desserts—Dolce

amaretto—cookie made of almonds, sugar and egg white

baba—dessert made from yeasted dough, soaked in liqueur and syrup, topped with fruit

bacio—two cookies stuck together with cream or chocolate

baicoli—Venetian biscuit used to dip in wine or hot chocolate

focaccia—cake or pie

gelato—ice cream

granita—sherbert, frozen ice drink

mascarpone—a rich, vaguely sweet cheese used both in desserts and savory dishes

miele—honey

panettone—Milanese Christmas cake studded with dried fruit

semifreddo—chilled blend of custard and whipped cream

sfogliatelle—puff pastry filled with ricotta and candied fruit and resembling a seashell

sorbetto—sherbert

tiramisu—cold dessert made of coffee-soaked layers of sponge cake covered with mascarpone cream

zabaglione—warm, fluffy dessert made from egg yolks, Marsala and sugar

zuppa inglese—cake soaked with liquor or rum and layered with custard, chocolate and fruit preserves, served with whipped cream

The Spanish Menu

Soups and Potages—Sopas Y Potajes

cocido madrileño—chickpea stew Madrid style

fabada asturiana—white bean stew

gazpacho—cold spicy tomato based soup

sopa de ajo—garlic soup

sopa de cebolla—French onion soup

sopa de fideos—noodle soup

sopa de pescado—fish and shellfish soup

sopa de verduras—vegetable soup

Meat and Poultry—Carnes Y Aves

alitas al ajillo—fried chicken wings in garlic sauce

chuletillas de cordero—rack of baby lamb

cochinillo—roast suckling pig

cordero asado—roast lamb

entrecote—sirloin steak

filete empanado—steak, Milanese style

pollo asado—roasted chicken

pollo al ajillo—fried chicken in garlic sauce

solomillo—filet mignon

Seafood and Fish—Marisco Y Pescados

almejas a la marinera—sautéed clams in garlic and parsley

angulas—baby eels

atun—tuna

bacalao—cod

boquerones—anchovies

calamares in su tinta—squid cooked in its own ink

calamares rebozados—fried squid

chipirones—baby squid

gambas—shrimp

gambas al ajillo—sautéed shrimp in garlic sauce

gambas a la plancha—grilled shrimp

langosta—lobster

langostinos—prawns

lenguado—sole

mejillones—mussels

merluza—hake

mero—grouper

necora—swimming crab

ostras—oysters

parrillada de mariscos—mixed seafood grill

pez espada—swordfish

pulpo a la gallega—octopus, Galician style

salmonetes—red mullet

vieiras—scallops

Rice—Arroz

arroz a la Cubana—rice Cuban style

paella de marisco—shellfish paella

paella mixta—chicken and shellfish paella

Vegetables and Fruit— Verduras Y Frutas

alcachofas—artichokes

ensalada mixta—mixed salad

guisantes—green peas

judias verdes—green beans

manzanas—apples

menestra—sautéed fresh mixed vegetables

naranjas—oranges

peras—pears

platanos—bananas

Desserts—Postres

arroz con leche—rice pudding

flan de la casa—caramel custard of the house

fruta del tiempo—fruits in season

helados—ice cream

natillas—custard

tartas heladas—ice cream cakes

Tapas and Miscellaneous—Tapas Y Varios

aceitunas—olives

champiñones al ajillo—stuffed mushrooms

croquetas—croquettes

ensaladilla rusa—potato salad

huevos fritos—fried eggs

jamon serrano—cured ham

pan y mantequilla—bread and butter

panecillos—coffee cakes

patatas fritas—French fries

patatas fritas a la inglesa—potato chips

pimienta—pepper

queso—cheese

sal—salt

tostada—toast

tortilla francesa—plain omelet

tortilla de papas—Spanish potato omelet

Beverages—Bebidas

agua minerale—mineral water

cafe con leche—coffee with milk

cafe solo—espresso

caña—draft beer

cerveza—beer

jugo de manzanas—apple juice

refrescos—soda

rosado—rosé wine

vino blanco—white wine

vino tinto—red wine

zumo de naranja—orange juice

zumo de tomate—tomato juice

FOODS TO AVOID

It is difficult to concentrate on business negotiations when trying to negotiate foods that are awkward, difficult or messy to eat. Avoid them whenever possible. If they are served to you at a prearranged meal, deal with them as best you can, but remember that the focus of the meal is business, and the conversation takes precedence over the food. If in doubt or in trouble, leave the food and concentrate on business.

A young woman who was a prime candidate for a job was taken out for lunch by the prospective employer who purposely ordered difficult-to-eat foods to gauge her response. The woman was so overwhelmed trying to eat the food without creating havoc that she neglected the conversation. The employer felt she did not have the management savvy to handle complicated situations, and she did not get the job after all.

Here are some of the foods that may be tricky at a business meal. Practice whenever possible on your own time.

Vegetables

ARTICHOKES are eaten with the fingers. Remove one leaf at a time, dip the soft end into the sauce and pull it through your teeth to remove the edible part. Discard the rest. Scrape the fuzzy part off the heart with a knife, then eat the heart with a knife and fork.

ASPARAGUS is eaten with the fingers in Europe. Here a bite-sized piece is cut from the stem and eaten with a fork.

BAKED POTATOES are eaten out of the skin with a fork. If you wish to add butter, take it from your bread and butter plate with a knife and pat it onto the potato. The skin can be eaten afterwards with a knife and fork.

CELERY, OLIVES, PICKLES and RADISHES are taken from the serving dish with your fingers and placed on your bread plate or on the side of your dinner plate. They are eaten with the fingers. If the olive is pitted, eat it whole. If the olive has a pit, hold it in your fingers and eat it in several bites. Then lay the pit on the side of your plate.

CORN ON THE COB is only eaten at casual meals, and never in Europe where it is considered fodder for the animals. Butter only a few rows at a time and eat them, holding the corn firmly with your fingers. Never butter the whole corn at once.

FRENCH FRIED POTATOES are cut in half and eaten with a fork, not fingers, unless you're at a fast food establishment.

Fish

CAVIAR is spread on toast and eaten with the fingers.

CLAMS and OYSTERS served on the half shell are held in one hand, and the clam or oyster is removed whole with a fork. Dip it into the sauce and eat it whole. Fried clams are eaten with a fork.

LOBSTER is either cracked in the kitchen before being served or it is served with a nutcracker-like tool. Crack the two big claws, then break them apart with your hands. Dig the meat out with the seafood fork and put it on your plate. Eat it with a knife and fork, dipping it into the butter sauce if you wish. Break the small claws with your fingers and either dig out the meat with the seafood fork or suck it out as if it were a straw. The coral colored roe and the green liver are eaten with your fork. They are considered delicacies. Stuffed lobster is eaten with a knife and fork.

SHRIMP with the tail still on are held by the tail if they are cold, dipped into the sauce, bitten off and the tail is discarded. When hot, cut the tail off with the knife and eat the shrimp with a fork.

SHRIMP COCKTAIL is eaten with the seafood fork provided. If possible, eat the shrimp in one bite. If it is too large, eat it in two. When you're finished, the seafood fork is put on the plate under the dish.

SNAILS are served hot in their shell. Pick up the snail in the metal tongs provided and use the seafood fork, held in the other hand, to dig out the snail. Eat it in one bite. You may dip small pieces of bread into the garlic butter with your fork.

SOFT SHELL CRABS are cut with a knife, and the entire crab is eaten with a fork. When eating hard-shelled crabs, only the meat is eaten with a knife and fork.

Meat

BACON is eaten with a knife and fork unless it is very crisp, and may then be eaten with the fingers.

BONES from small birds and frog's legs may be held with one hand to eat the meat, but never gnaw on them. Lay the bones back on the side of the plate.

CHICKEN, DUCK and TURKEY are eaten with a knife and fork. Steady the piece of poultry with the fork and cut away one bite at a time with the knife. Fried chicken is eaten with the fingers only at a picnic.

PATÉ DE FOIE GRAS is spread on a piece of toast with a knife and eaten with the fingers.

SPARERIBS, while best avoided at a business meal, are eaten with a knife and fork. Use your fingers only at a family gathering. Never gnaw on the bones.

Fruit

APRICOTS are eaten with the fingers in several bites. Put the stone on the side of the plate.

AVOCADOS are eaten with a spoon when served in the shell, with a fork when served peeled and sliced.

BANANAS served at a table are peeled and eaten with a knife and fork.

BERRIES are eaten with a spoon. Strawberries served with the stem are held by the stem and dipped into the sugar or sour cream and eaten in one or two bites. Discard the stem at the side of the plate.

GRAPES are eaten by cutting a small stem off the bunch with the scissors or a knife, then consumed one at a time. Drop the seeds or inedible skin into a cupped hand and deposit them on the side of your plate.

GRAPEFRUIT halves should be served with the sections loosened. Otherwise, leave it. Trying to loosen the sections yourself is too hazardous because you risk spraying someone. Eat the sections with a spoon. Don't squeeze out the remaining juice.

LEMONS are served as garnish with the food. Pick a wedge of lemon up with your fingers and squeeze, covering it with your other hand to prevent spraying anyone. A slice of lemon may be held down with the fork and squeezed by pressing with the knife.

MANGOES are cut in half, the pits are removed and the mango is quartered. Turn the sections over and pull the skin away while holding the piece with a fork.

ORANGES and TANGERINES are peeled with the fingers or a sharp knife, then eaten with the fingers one segment at a time in one or two bites.

PEACHES are quartered and eaten with a fork after the skin has been pulled away.

PINEAPPLE served in slices or quarters is eaten with a fork. When it is cubed, it is eaten with a spoon.

WATERMELON is eaten with a spoon if it is cut up; otherwise, it is eaten with a fork. Drop the pits into a cupped hand and place them on the side of the plate.

Miscellaneous

BREAD and ROLLS are broken, never cut, one bite-sized piece at a time, then buttered on the plate and eaten.

CONDIMENTS should be put on the dinner plate to the side.

EGGS are eaten with a fork when hard-boiled. Soft-boiled eggs are eaten from the shell with a spoon after the cap has been sliced off with a knife.

PASTA is eaten with a fork. When it is long-stranded like spaghetti, fettucine or angel hair, pull a few strands aside with the fork and break them against the edge of the plate if necessary. Don't stir.

SALAD is eaten with a fork. Use a knife to cut large pieces and wedges. Salad is eaten with a knife and fork when eaten as a separate course.

SANDWICHES that are open-faced are eaten with a knife and fork. Club sandwiches can be eaten with a knife and fork or quartered and eaten with the fingers. Canape type sandwiches are eaten with the fingers.

WATER and WINE should never be sipped if you still have food in your mouth. Blot the mouth before taking a drink. If you've eaten something that is too hot, take a sip of water, but don't act as if you're trying to douse a fire.

THE FAST TRACK

Table Manners:

1. Keep briefcases and handbags off the table.

2. Let the host determine the seating arrangements.

3. Seat the guest of honor on the host's right.

4. Sit up.

5. Don't order foods that are unfamiliar, difficult to eat or messy.

6. Don't smoke before or during a meal. Wait till everyone has finished and coffee is served.

7. Keep elbows off the table.

8. Keep your hands down. Don't wave your cutlery in the air like a conductor.

9. Use flatware from outside in. Spoons and knives are on the right, forks are on the left. Dessert is across the top.

10. Liquids are on the right. Solids, like salad or a bread plate, are on the left.

11. Don't wipe dirty flatware or glasses. Ask the waiter to bring you clean ones.

12. Cut one piece of food at a time.

13. Bring the food up to your mouth.

14. Don't chew with your mouth open.

15. Don't talk with food in your mouth.

16. Scoop soup away from you. Don't crumble crackers into the soup.

17. Break, then butter, one bite-sized piece of bread or roll at a time.

18. Hold tumblers by the bottom of the glass, small stem glasses by the stem and large goblets at the bottom of the bowl.

19. Pass food to the right. Turn the handles so the next person can pick them up easily. Pass salt and pepper together.

20. Don't reach.

21. Blot, don't wipe, your mouth on the napkin. Don't blot lipstick on a linen napkin.

22. If you spill something, blot it up without fuss, and let the victims of your mishap blot themselves.

23. Don't thank the waitstaff repeatedly. Let your tip do the talking.

24. Keep your end of the conversation up.

25. Keep your alcohol intake down.

26. Comb your hair, straighten your tie, apply lipstick or use a toothpick in the washroom, not at the table.

Entertaining:

1. Always extend the invitations personally.

2. Decide which meal best suits your purposes:

   —Breakfast has a sense of urgency and should be kept to an hour.

   —Lunch is more relaxed, and the ideal male/female business meal. Allow two hours.

   —Tea is a good time to get to know someone better.

   —Dinner should be saved for special occasions or out-of-town clients. Never entertain someone for the first time over dinner.

3. Let your guests know the purpose of the get-together.

4. Don't place the burden of where to eat on your guest.

5. Make reservations as far in advance as possible in your name and specify where you want to sit.

6. Reconfirm the arrangements with both the restaurant and the guest the day before.

7. Arrive early. If you and your guest are going to be late, call or you may lose your table.

8. Wait for your guest in the lobby. If there is none, wait at the table, but don't order a drink or open your napkin.

9. Never table hop.

10. Don't take calls at your table.

11. Make two recommendations from the menu to give your guest an idea of an acceptable price range.

12. Let the guest order first.

13. Be firm, polite and businesslike about the service, but never chastise a waitperson in front of others.

14. Don't jump into a business discussion. Begin with small talk.

15. Begin the business conversation when your guest appears to be ready, and by the time you start on the main course.

16. If you have to cancel a business meal, do it personally. Try to re-schedule at that time.

17. If your secretary has to cancel on your behalf, follow up with a personal call and a note of apology as soon as possible.

18. When making a toast, don't roast. Keep it short and simple.

19. Stay seated and don't drink when being toasted.

20. Always respond to a toast.

21. Pay the check if you've extended the invitations or if you're the one benefitting from the business arrangement.

22. Never comment on the total. Add up the bill and calculate the tip silently if the bill is brought to the table.

23. Arrange for the bill not to be brought to the table if at all possible.

24. Write a thank you note to your host within twenty-four hours.

At Large Events:

1. Find out as much as possible beforehand about the event and the other guests so you'll be well prepared.

2. Don't wait to be introduced, introduce yourself.

3. Never park yourself at the bar or at the hors d'oeuvres table. Give others a chance, too.

4. Control your alcohol intake so you retain control of your professional demeanor.

5. Keep the drink in your left hand so you don't give anyone a cold, wet handshake.

Theater Etiquette:

1. Be punctual.

2. Stay for the whole performance, including the applause.

3. Be quiet. Don't talk, rustle programs, jewelry or candy wrappers.

4. Learn the appropriate times to applaud.

5. Don't sing along, squeal with delight, sigh with boredom or snore.

Sporting Etiquette:

1. Don't name call or yell insulting epithets.

2. Cheer for the home team.

3. Dress appropriately whether as a spectator or a participant.

4. Every sport has its own rules and etiquette. Learn them before you start to play.

Private Clubs:

1. Never entertain for business at a club that discriminates.

2. Don't entertain at a private club if you want press coverage.

3. Deal with the staff the way you would at a first class restaurant or banquet facility.

4. Tip according to club policy.

5. Respect the rules! Remember that your host is responsible for your behavior.

6. Obey the club's dress code.

7. Don't wander around unescorted.

8. Don't offer to pay. Return the hospitality in kind.

Entertaining At Home:

1. Hire a caterer or trained servers if you don't have household help. Book them well in advance.

2. Make sure you have adequate seating and place settings.

3. Make sure that the caterer or someone else is handling coat check, valet parking, cocktail service and cleanup in addition to the dinner.

4. Order flowers for the centerpiece.

5. Make sure your home is immaculate.

6. Keep pets and children out of sight.

7. Give accurate directions and parking instructions.

8. Keep the cocktail hour short.

9. Plan the timing so that everyone will be able to get home at a reasonable hour.

10. Don't invite your boss unless it is a large function or you've been invited to the boss's house several times first.

11. Do your best to make everyone feel welcome and wanted.

12. Have a cohost, either a spouse or a fellow executive of the same gender, for a large affair.

GIFT-GIVING

Give. That is one of the world's greatest messages.

John Loring

Do not do unto others as you would that they should do unto you. Their tastes may not be the same.

George Bernard Shaw

The purpose of gift-giving, whether by an individual or a corporation, is to please the recipient. Your reasons for doing so may vary from showing appreciation to cementing a friendship or business relationship, to apologizing, to congratulating someone for an achievement like graduation or promotion, to currying favor for yourself or your company. Whatever the reason, the focus must remain on the recipient if you want to elevate your gift-giving to an art.

CHAPTER

10

Routine, careless or improper gift-giving, with no thought for the recipient, can do your cause or relationship more harm than good. Gifts are never a substitute for a caring attitude, good business practices, good will or company manners. Nor should a gift ever be given as a bribe or when it could be misconstrued as one, for instance when you're in the middle of negotiations.

Giving a gift that is just right is really a fairly simple process that involves three steps: the research, the shopping and the presentation.

RESEARCH AND PLANNING

Keep a file on your clients and anyone else who might be on your gift list. Note any interests, hobbies and other personal information that arise in conversation throughout the year, such as the person's alma mater or the purchase of a new home, that may be a source of inspiration. Don't forget to list birthdays. The file does double duty because it is also a source for casual conversation or reasons to stay in touch, like calling a sports fan to discuss his team's victory over a major opponent. Often the clues might be visible in the person's office. If the office walls are covered in Ansel Adams photographs or paintings of vintage automobiles, a comment about them may lead to a valuable source of inspiration.

If you've never been able to get any information from the person, or if you've mined a vein of ideas to exhaustion, call the person's secretary. Aside from the immediate family, who knows that person better? If you are acquainted with the person's spouse, you might even want to call him or her. Never call a spouse you've never met, though.

Should you not be able to come up with any information about hobbies or interests, then consider a gift for the office like a leather business card case, good desk accessories, a crystal paperweight or a crystal and sterling inkwell for someone who uses a fountain pen. Gifts for the home are another option, provided they are not too personal or stylized. A good crystal vase filled with seasonal flowers, for example amaryllis during the holidays, is appropriate for men and women. Food always makes an excellent gift, whether it is a case of Florida citrus fruit, a wheel of Vermont cheese or a crystal jar filled with candy.

In your research, don't forget to note any dislikes too. A gift should not focus on someone's shortcomings. Someone with a skin problem may misinterpret a gift certificate for a facial. And, while a sense of humor is wonderful, a gift should not be used to play a joke on someone. Avoid liquor and wine unless you know the people well because they or their company might have ambivalent attitudes toward alcohol.

BUDGETING

First consider your budget and the acceptable price range. Currently, the Internal Revenue Service allows a deduction of $25 per recipient per year for gifts. However, if the gift has a logo, it falls under promotion and does not have the same deductibility constraints. But check with your accountant to see how this fits your personal circumstances. Many people, especially at a senior executive level, consider the allowable amounts too low and deem the additional nondeductible expenditure a wise business investment.

Beware of excessive spending. It is as much a faux pas as miserly gift-giving and may force the recipient to return your lavish gift. A gift from a junior executive to a client need not exceed $25. Mid to upper management should consider spending up to $50, while a senior executive may want to spend up to $100 for the best customers. A gift costing more than $100 would only be given in very special circumstances.

Most major stores have corporate gift accounts that entitle the company to benefit from store discounts on quantity purchases.

SHOPPING

Specialty stores that cater to the person's interests are probably the best source of ideas within your budget. Don't be afraid to consult the sales staff, especially if you know nothing about the hobby. Friends and acquaintances with similar interests can also be a source of inspiration. While I know nothing about golf, many of my friends and business associates are avid golfers. Not only do I use them as resources, I make note of their suggestions as possible future gifts for them.

Don't forget catalogs, especially if you don't live near a prime shopping area. Most major department and specialty stores throughout the country as well as catalog houses will gladly add a potential customer to their mailing lists if you write them a note or call them.

Most large stores have an in-store shopping service that will make selections at little or no extra charge. Specialized gift services and personal shoppers can also be found in your local Yellow Pages.

Many executives depend on their support staff to take on the task of gift shopping for people they don't even know. If your secretary has excellent taste, he or she may be the person to do your legwork, with several stipulations. Never expect the secretary to shop on personal time; the shopping should be on company time. The secretary should only be enlisted if shopping will not entail working overtime or require other back-up to complete regular work assignments.

PRESENTATION

Always wrap a gift before giving it. Not wrapping a present implies carelessness and undermines the impact of your gift. If you are all thumbs trying to tie a bow, have the store where you purchased the gift wrap it for you. Or, have a wrapping service or a friend do it for you. In selecting the wrapping, consider the recipient just as you did in buying the gift. A pink and blue bow on flowery paper will probably cause the executive who receives it to raise an eyebrow.

Remember to enclose a gift card with a personal comment and your signature. A correspondence card is an ideal enclosure card. A business card is adequate, but only if you put a slash through your name, write a brief message on the back and sign it.

If possible, give the gift in person. Taking the time to share the moment adds immensely to the occasion. More important, make sure the gift is timely. The impact of the gift diminishes with every passing day. Just think how thrilled you would be to receive your birthday presents three or four months after the day has passed. Unless you are attending a celebration at which everyone else is giving gifts too, give your gift in private. Singling the person out with a gift in front of others can be embarrassing to the recipient and to the people who neglected to give a gift. When giving a gift, don't insist the person open it immediately; some people might prefer to open gifts in private where they don't have to worry about making the appropriate responses. Don't disparage the gift with remarks like "Oh, it's nothing!" because the recipient might believe you. I'll always remember a vendor who got hundreds of thousands of dollars in business from me annually and told me that she had found my Christmas present in a close-out store around the corner.

RECEIVING GIFTS

Always accept a gift gracefully, regardless of how you feel about the gift or the giver. Even if a gift appears to be a hostile act, like a health club membership for someone who is overweight, it may have been well-intentioned, albeit misguided. A simple "thank you" is always an appropriate expression of appreciation. Never diminish the giver's generosity with a statement like "you shouldn't have" even if you wish they hadn't. How would you feel if someone did that to you after you had invested your time, effort and money?

Although a telephone call may be easier and more convenient, a thank you note is compulsory. The note should be written immediately. Putting it off makes it an increasingly onerous task and diminishes the impact of your gratitude.

REFUSING GIFTS

It is perfectly acceptable to refuse a gift and, under certain circumstances, it becomes obligatory. **Always return a gift that is extravagant, too personal, has sexual implications or can be misconstrued as bribery.** Although you may be furious about the gift, venting your anger can put you at a disadvantage. Enclosing a note that because of the nature of the gift you are unable to accept it is more than sufficient. Be sure to keep a copy of the note and return it in a way that ensures you have receipt of the return.

Company policy occasionally dictates that an employee is not allowed to receive a gift. It takes a great deal of the pressure off the employee if the company publicizes this beforehand. Corporations like Wal-Mart send out letters to all vendors notifying them of its policy. If your company doesn't send out notification, you may want to make business associates who might give you a gift aware of company policy well in advance of the occasion. Politely letting others know either beforehand or at the time the gift is offered that you appreciate the gesture but are prohibited by policy from accepting is always acceptable and should never create hard feelings.

CORPORATE GIFT-GIVING

Most companies feel that corporate gift-giving enhances the company's image and improves customer relations, especially if the gift is reflective of the giver. A gift can convey many messages like power, sophistication, knowledge or interest. Most importantly, it must reflect the image of the company, be it conservative or cutting edge, while still considering the recipient.

The ideal corporate gift is the company's product, imaginatively packaged with a twist to make it interesting, like adding the latest gadget that can be used with the product. For instance, a publisher might want to give a selection of paperbacks with one of those book covers that has a battery operated reading light. If the company's products are targeted toward a particular market based on sex, age or interest, don't give the product as a generic gift. Women may not appreciate the latest electric drill from a tool manufacturer any more than men would appreciate a set of electric hair rollers from a small appliance manufacturer; however, the latest travelling hair dryer would be appropriate for everyone.

Tickets to company sponsored events or exhibitions are also appreciated gifts, particularly if you've discovered in your research that the recipient is interested in that sport or cultural activity. A balletomane may not be particularly thrilled with tickets to the basketball game.

Some suggestions for corporate gifts are: pens, small calculators, clocks, watches, glassware, desk sets or baskets of fruit. Diaries and desk calendars can also be good gifts, but they must be spectacular and of the highest quality to be appreciated because executives usually receive a number of them. Don't send the same gift every year, or it will be taken for granted.

A gift that is useful or practical will always be valued as long as it is appropriate to the intended receiver. A female traffic manager received a pewter beer stein from a trucking firm she deals with. Although she does not drink beer, she considered using it as a vase or pencil holder, except for the large three dimensional corporate logo soldered on to the side of the mug.

LOGOS

Logos should always be used with discretion on any gift. Don't put a logo on just anything. Logo gifts, in fact all gifts, must be of the highest quality and in good taste. Always keep the logo small so it doesn't look as though the gift is really a corporate advertisement.

CLIENT GIFTS

To those clients with whom you've developed a closer relationship, the gift should be much more personal than the standard logo item or the generic gift purchased by the corporation. There is no excuse for being unable to come up with an appropriate gift for someone with whom you have an established association. Yet it happens all the time. A classic example of thoughtless gift-giving is the wine an owner of one of the finest wine shops in Manhattan regularly receives...purchased from other stores! I can appreciate her perplexity at these gifts and admire her ability to receive them gracefully none the less. If you expect the client to make the effort to give you his or her company's business, you had better make the effort to buy a gift that shows you care. **"It's the thought that counts," does not mean remembering to buy a present, it means thinking about buying a gift that is appropriate to the recipient.**

SPECIAL CLIENTS—SPECIAL OCCASIONS

If you deal with clients long enough, invariably special occasions, whether marriage, children, bar/bat mitzvahs, graduations or grandchildren, occur in their lives. If you are invited to attend one of these occasions, a gift is required and is sent to the address on the invitation. More often, though, you will hear about the event and the person's joy in it. In these circumstances, to give or not to give is your choice because a gift is not necessary. The savvy or caring executive often finds it beneficial to go beyond the basic requirements.

Even if you don't give a present, it is always advisable to write a personal note of felicitation.

GIFTS FOR COLLEAGUES

Colleagues exchange gifts because they care about one another or because a special occasion arises. These gifts should not be extravagant or too personal; rather, they should show you care. Office gifts should never be so extravagant that they strain anyone's budget. Many offices use a holiday grab-bag with price limits to control the rampant spread of the holiday gift-giving mania. In this case, a gift that could be appropriate to anyone in the office, male or female, young or old, is the rule of thumb. At one company, the staff of an entire office had been relocated to the bowels of the building, and the lack of windows was a constant source of complaints. One staff member, as his contribution to the grab-bag with a $10 limit, focused on the one thing absolutely anyone in the office could enjoy. He gave an unframed $4 poster of a window opened to look out on puffy white clouds in a blue sky. It was the most appreciated gift in the entire grab-bag.

Other occasions like birthdays or showers for weddings or babies also tend to incite a flurry of gift-giving. Acknowledge the birthday with a verbal wish, the weddings and births with a personal note. Any further celebration is a social event that does not belong in the office. Save the cake and gifts for after hours. No one should ever feel compelled to contribute to a collection for this type of event. It is quite acceptable to decline politely. It is not necessary to give a reason. However, it is not appropriate to vent your disapproval of the gift-giving. An executive should not participate in this type of occasion either, unless there is a close working relationship with the staff member.

Some companies do have a corporate fund that automatically sends a gift on specific occasions to help foster company morale and loyalty. Other companies have an office pool that everyone contributes to on a regular basis. Whatever the policy, it is a good idea to appoint someone with excellent taste and investigative skills to be responsible for gift purchasing. There is nothing surprising about the "automatic" present. Not only does it become expected, it is mundane and dull, with no thought given to the recipient. Keeping notes on everyone's interests and hobbies makes it a great deal easier to come up with a gift suggestion when the time comes.

Because group gifts are seldom opened in private, unwrapping the gift is part of the ceremony. Make the wrapping an occasion by putting some thought and effort into it. If no one is capable of tying even the simplest bow, have the gift professionally wrapped.

GIFTS TO THE STAFF

Companies are social organizations with certain social customs and obligations. These include mandatory gift-giving to everyone that you have a valid reason to bestow a gift upon unless company policy prohibits it. It is advisable for all companies to have an established policy on gift-giving because it is a factor in employee morale and can be read as an indication of how the company is doing.

The policy could range from a stated "no policy, anything goes" to a total ban on gift-giving within the organization. Most companies have a more traditional policy to deal with any occasion from holiday giving to retirement.

HOLIDAY GIFTS TO EMPLOYEES

Bonuses should never be considered a gift, even if they are given at year's end. A bonus is an earned reward for good performance on the job. A written company policy on bonuses will avoid misunderstandings and morale problems.

During the holiday season, corporate gifts to employees tend to run along traditional lines like a turkey or a store gift certificate. Other companies make donations on behalf of the employees to the needy in the community. A card with a personal message from and signed by the CEO sometimes substitutes as the corporate gift. In lieu of a gift, some firms hold an annual holiday party. When I was a child, I always looked forward to the holiday party staged by my parents' employer.

In addition to the company's gift to the employee, an executive should give his secretary and assistants a gift based on the length of time they have worked together, the boss's position or importance within the organization, the amount of responsibility that person has and whether that employee does a lot of favors for the boss, like running personal errands, handling personal appointments and balancing checkbooks.

Within these parameters, the standard amount spent on a gift ranges from $25–$100. While this value need not increase annually, it should never decrease from one year to the next. The gift should reflect the employee's interests, but should never be too personal nor have any sexual connotation whatsoever. A sterling pen, a museum membership, a pocket electronic appointment/telephone book, or all-purpose wine glasses make excellent gifts. For the employee who travels a great deal, a travel alarm clock or an electronic multilanguage dictionary would also be appreciated.

The savvy executive also remembers the people he may not work with directly, but who make his life run smoothly, like the mailroom clerk, the elevator operator or the switchboard operator, if they haven't been eclipsed by modernization. Small tokens of appreciation to these employees make a significant impression and are received with pride because the gift was not obligatory.

SERVICE AWARDS

Service awards, whether they commemorate length of employment or achievement, should always reflect the employee's pride in himself, his work and his employer. The awards are recognition for a job well done.

Incentive gifts like these can range from televisions to trips to a crystal bowl or sterling silver tray. There are premium and incentive trade shows that are a valuable source of gift ideas; you may want to check with your nearest convention center for dates. Whatever the gift may be, it should reflect the company and the occasion for which it was given. It should not reflect the company's logo; this is not a promotion of the corporation.

RETIREMENT GIFTS

Many companies have a standard retirement gift like the proverbial gold watch. If there is a standard gift, be sure to personalize the gift and the occasion with a letter from the employee's boss and, if possible, the CEO. Since retirement is such an abrupt severance of a large part of the retiree's life and relationships, mementos like an album filled with photographs, a chronology of the person's years in the organization and reminiscences by fellow employees are an excellent idea because they will give the employee years of pleasure. One major corporation in Westchester hires a well-known cartoonist, who himself had retired from the company years earlier, to compose a caricature of the person based on stories told by fellow employees.

If corporate guidelines are more flexible, a gift that is appropriate to the individual's interests, like golf clubs, a tennis racquet or season tickets to the ballet or opera may be far more appreciated than that gold watch. Asking the person's secretary or spouse will usually reveal at least one or two constructive ideas.

GIFTS TO THE BOSS

A gift from an employee to the boss is usually not expected and can be misconstrued as "apple polishing." A thoughtful personal note of appreciation would probably be more meaningful than any gift. If you have worked quite closely under someone's direct supervision for a long time, you may want to give that person a token gift like a batch of cookies, a desk thermos, a plant, a picture frame or an addition to a collection (like records or toy soldiers, but not fine art). The gift should be meaningful and in good taste. An expensive gift is inappropriate. Remember, your boss knows how much you earn and what could be construed as reasonable. Extravagance could be interpreted as poor money management and bad business judgment.

INTERNATIONAL GIFT-GIVING

Many cultures have some form of gift-giving during the winter solstice. Giving your international associate a gift at this time conveys your warm feelings and enhances business ties. Before embarking on a shopping excursion, though, it is necessary to understand the customs and traditions of that person's culture so that you don't give unintentional offense. The taboos of international gift-giving can range from not giving leather in India where the cow is sacred, to not giving a clock in China because the word for clock sounds like the word for death.

Colors and the way a gift is wrapped can also hold a great deal of significance. **If you cannot do your homework, contact the corporate gift department of a major store because someone on staff is usually well-versed in the intricacies of international gift-giving.**

Don't forget that the recipient may be required to pay duty on your gift. This could affect the joy with which it is received. If in doubt, check with the nearest consulate of that country. Avoid this by placing an order via telex or FAX with a major store in the recipient's country.

SENDING FLOWERS

Flowers are an ideal solution to certain gift-giving situations because they are easy to send through your local florist anywhere in the world. Again, certain cultures attribute meaning to certain colors or types of flowers. In Japan, for instance, white flowers and chrysanthemums are symbols of death; in Germany, red roses have serious romantic connotations. It is always a good idea to have the florist specify the occasion for sending the flowers to guide the florist in the other country.

Flowers can be sent almost anywhere on very short notice. As a rule of thumb, send arrangements to someone's office and cut flowers to someone's home. Always send flowers before or after a meal at which you are an honored guest. Never bring flowers because the host or hostess will have to fiddle with them rather than attend to the guests or the last minute food preparations. The flowers will be enjoyed more if they arrive after a party because they convey a message of appreciation.

Although flowers brighten up a hospital room, a plant that requires little maintenance is usually much more appreciated. Many people are also bothered by something dying, as flowers tend to do, when they are in less than optimum health.

THE FAST TRACK

1. If a gift is worth giving, it is worth doing your homework to make sure it will please the recipient.

2. International gift-giving demands additional research into the occasions and types of gifts that are appropriate.

3. By starting your shopping well in advance, you won't be rushed into an inappropriate choice.

4. The cost of the gift is determined by your position and your relationship to the recipient.

5. A tip is given to someone in the basic service industries; a gift is given to a fellow professional.

6. If the gift is worth giving, it is worth giving well. Make sure it is attractively wrapped with a personalized gift card enclosed. If at all possible, give it in person.

7. Keeping a computerized record of your gift-giving, cards and tips avoids omissions and duplications. Good record keeping also helps in dealing with the IRS.

8. Return gifts immediately that are inappropriate or contrary to corporate policy.

9. Always accept a gift gracefully with a "thank you."

10. Always, always write a thank you note immediately for any gift you have received.

A gift given solely for the joy of giving is the most wonderful gift to receive. Enjoying the process of gift-giving elevates the act to an art.

ON THE ROAD

Travel is only glamorous in retrospect.

Paul Theroux

All travel becomes dull in exact proportion to its rapidity.

John Ruskin

When you travel, you are the representative of your company. As such, you are under scrutiny twenty-four hours a day. Anything that you do reflects on the company. Never behave in a manner that would besmirch its reputation.

Business travel produces additional stress and strain. You must take even better care of yourself on the road than when you are at home. Getting enough rest, eating properly, watching what you drink, making detailed preparations before your trip, staying in touch with the home base and, above all, retaining your composure will help you be as effective as possible.

CHAPTER

11

CARS, CABS AND LIMOUSINES

The person who owns the car drives the car unless the owner requests that someone else do the driving. Signalling discomfort about someone's driving or insisting on driving another's car could be misconstrued as a power play and a deliberate attempt to demean the person's position. Should someone offer to drive, expressing appreciation for the offer but regretting that your insurance policy does not permit someone else to drive your car allows everyone to save face without surrendering control or creating a confrontational situation. If, however, you dislike driving and are grateful for the offer, simply smile, express thanks and hand over the keys.

As frustrating as traffic jams or the poor skills of other drivers may be, never lose your composure or start cursing. That type of behavior will only make you appear unable to handle pressure or stressful situations and can cost you a promotion.

When you are one of several passengers in the car, always ask the driver where you should sit, especially if you hold a junior position to the others. Never hog the best seat unless you're intent on making enemies or putting your job in jeopardy.

Studies claim that the cars we drive are directly related to our egos. **Keep your ego in check in any business situation and treat the vehicle only as a means of travel.** Don't be like the hotshot young executive who met a client at the airport in a brand new Rolls Royce and asked the man if this was his first time in one of these cars. "My first time in the front seat," replied the client with amusement. Touché!

Limousines lend an air of importance and sophistication to business travel, but don't abuse them. I'm reminded of the executive in New York whose company was in serious financial straits, and who insisted on being driven two crosstown blocks and one uptown block, just over a quarter mile in total, to a board meeting. Because of gridlock and New York's one-way system, the trip took forty-five minutes when he could have walked in ten minutes at most. His ego delayed the board meeting over half an hour. Do you think the board members were particularly responsive to his plight? Look upon limos as a convenience that can help you be relaxed and more effective, not as a symbol of prestige.

In both cabs and limousines, the best seat is passenger side, rear. If you are travelling alone, this is the seat you should take. If, however, you are travelling with others, pay attention to the rank and hierarchy of your fellow passengers and seat yourself accordingly, regardless of gender. Junior executives should always wait until the senior executives are seated and then take the jump seats or ask, "Where do you want me to sit?" In limousines, the jump seats and the middle back are the most uncomfortable. In a cab, it is the middle back seat. If two senior and three junior executives were to travel in a limousine, the most senior would sit passenger side rear, the next senior would sit driver side rear, the junior executive with the longest legs would take the front seat and the other two junior executives would sit on the jump seat. While the front seat is much more comfortable than the jump seats, it can leave a person feeling cut off from the group. It is always a courtesy to keep the partition open if one person is sitting with the driver.

When two people are travelling in a limousine or cab, the more junior person enters the limousine first from the curbside and slides across. In metropolitan areas like New York with major one-way thoroughfares, the cab may pull up to the left side of the street and complicate the situation. The senior executive might go around to enter from the passenger side, or he might slide across. Don't assume you're being respectful by sliding across and taking the best seat; ask where the executive wants you to sit.

Clients are the most important persons in the group, regardless of title, and are treated as though they were the most senior executives.

In social situations, a man defers to the woman and gives her the seat of honor that he would give to a more senior executive in a business situation.

Airplanes

Problems caused by air travel are more stressful than traffic jams. A missed or delayed airplane may lead to a missed meeting which may result in missed contracts. Planning a business trip with care eliminates much of the stress caused by unexpected problems.

Make your reservations as soon as you have confirmation of the trip. Ask the reservations clerk for the on-time rating of the flight to give you some warning of potential delays. Many cautious executives doublebook themselves with another carrier as a back-up. **Since doublebooking is a major cause of overbooked flights, the courteous executive also has his secretary cancel unused reserva-**

tions. Consider how you would feel if your clients booked orders with you as a hedge against nondelivery by other suppliers and then refused your delivery because they didn't need the goods. Always attend to your commitments or you have no reason to expect that type of consideration from others.

While making your reservations, also request your seat selection and boarding pass as well as any special meals. The booking agent has a layout of the plane and should be able to tell you which seats have the most leg room. Space is a major factor in stress. The more space you have, the more relaxed you will be during your trip. Travel first class whenever possible. While most corporations have restrictions against first class travel these days and while that savings may look good on a financial statement, a tired, stressed executive who is not operating at peak performance can be more costly than the additional fare. Use your accumulated mileage awards for upgrades if the company won't pay for them. You might even consider paying for the upgrade to insure a comfortable flight.

Also worth the cost of memberships for frequent flyers are the airline clubs that offer a haven from the hustle and bustle of the terminal. The lounge staff can help solve many scheduling problems that can arise. Many of the clubs also provide meeting rooms that you can book if you are on a very tight schedule and have to meet someone at the airport. Some have FAX machines, copiers and PCs to help you work more effectively.

The best insurance against last minute delays and jet lag is to arrive the night before. **If you can't and your flight is cancelled, don't risk offending a client by waiting for the airline staff to rebook you.** They'll be surrounded by upset, stranded passengers. **Head for the nearest phone and call your travel agent or another airline**. You might want to carry your own copy of *The Official Airline Pocket Flight Guide* to calculate your own rerouting. Whatever happens, stay calm and you'll be able to think a lot more clearly and effectively. More importantly, you won't offend the people from whom you require assistance. Always be polite and friendly, but persistent, when trying to get your needs met.

Once aboard, remember to smile, say "excuse me" in the aisles, "please" when you make a request of the flight attendant and "thank you" when you get it. If you're not sitting in the aisle, ask the attendants to get you something rather than disturbing other passengers. **Don't try to tip the flight attendants.**

The attendants are not on board to chat with you, nor are fellow passengers. Good etiquette does not demand that you talk to strangers. To dissuade others from talking with you, put on a headset or immerse yourself in a book, a magazine or your work. If fellow passengers insist on chatting with you, simply say, "I would like to talk with you, but I must finish this work," or "I'm very tired. Please excuse me while I try to get some sleep." Should you want to chat with your fellow passengers, be careful what you say. Travellers often tell total strangers personal things they wouldn't even share with close friends and family. Loose lips can make you look juvenile and can compromise your security.

Telephoning from a plane also can compromise security because passengers often speak so loudly that a large section of the plane is privy to the conversation. On a flight I took recently, an executive got on the telephone and started barking orders, frequently dropping names and interspersing the conversation with curses. No one was impressed. Equally irritating was the unsophisticated firstclass passenger who shouted into the phone, "You'll never guess where I'm calling you from! No, guess, guess!" and then gossiped loudly for ten minutes to the annoyance of the passengers near him.

While much of this book was written on a notebook computer on planes, trains and other modes of transportation, laptops and notebooks can annoy fellow passengers. If the people next to you are trying to sleep, the clicking of your keyboard could keep them awake. Also consider the confidentiality of the material you are working on and whether you want the person beside you to read everything on your screen. **Be considerate and ask fellow passengers if they would mind you using the computer.** Otherwise, see if the flight attendant can find you a seat in a less crowded area of the plane. A word of warning: if your screen isn't center hinged, it could get squashed if the person in front of you reclines the seat.

Female travellers often complain that male travellers are seat hogs. Men unconsciously take more physical, psychological and conversational space than women. If seat hogs annoy you, try to book an aisle seat so you don't feel hemmed in. If your fellow passenger does hog the armrest, though, politely ask if he would mind sharing it. If that does not work, insist that he restrict his person to his seat.

If the plane is running late and you must make a connection or get to a scheduled appointment, let the attendant know of your predicament before landing so he or she can make sure you're one of the first to deplane. Trying to push your way to the front will not necessarily get you there, but it will annoy the other passengers and raise your stress and anxiety level.

As you leave, thank the attendants and say goodbye. A simple courtesy can be a wonderful boost for the flight attendants and keep them bright and smiling for the next passenger. One airline would not allow their attendants to work the New York—Miami route more than three months at a time because of the negative effect the passengers had on the attitudes of the flight attendants.

CORPORATE JETS

Many corporations are cutting back on private jets and resorting to commercial carriers. Yet, a corporate jet can be the fastest, most convenient means of travel. Statistics show it has become the safest. If you are offered a ride on a corporate jet, your company's or another's, consider it a special privilege and exercise the utmost courtesy.

Be early! Extra time allows the flight crew to be ready to taxi down the runway well in advance. Even a few minutes' delay can mean losing the departure slot and having to wait for an hour or more for another to take-off. **Travel light and be prepared to carry your own baggage**.

The senior executive boards the plane first and takes his choice of seats. An astute and sophisticated Florida businesswoman was travelling with her CEO and a group of fellow executives, all male. The chivalrous CEO indicated that the businesswoman should precede him aboard, but she demurred. She was surprised when one of the male executives complimented her on the handling of the situation. After all, the man was her boss and she was well aware of corporate hierarchy; nor would she have known where to sit if she had boarded first. **Ask where you are to sit. Take the refreshments that are offered, and don't ask for something special**. Be neat; pick up and deposit your own litter. The crew is not there to clean up after you.

Treat the crew with respect. Not only are they fellow employees, but they are responsible for your safety. Thank them and compliment them on their skill when deplaning. **Write a thank you note within twenty-four hours to the executive responsible for getting you the seat on the plane**. Mention the crew favorably in your note.

Entertaining in Unfamiliar Ballparks

Doing your homework and making preparations before you ever depart helps you appear as knowledgeable and savvy as you would on your home turf. Call the newspaper in the city you'll be visiting and speak to the food, lifestyle or business editor and ask for recommendations of restaurants and what types of food they are known for. Or, call the executive's assistant and ask for the executive's preferences or local recommendations. **Make the reservations by phone before you leave on your trip.** Entertaining is often a topic of safe conversation in first class on a plane. Fellow passengers often share the best restaurants, the names of maîtres d'hotel, house specialties and the best tables to request.

When you arrive, confirm the reservation in person so you can check the facilities and develop a rapport with the maître d'hotel. If you can't, call the restaurant during an off hour and speak to the maître d'. Ask for food and wine recommendations. And, ask for that special table. **Make credit arrangements in advance so that the check is not presented at the table.** Any good restaurant responds to this level of customer concern with commensurate service.

Glance at the food section of the local newspaper to see what foods are in season in that area. But be flexible when entertaining in restaurants you don't know. Become aware of the smells as you enter, look at people's faces as they are eating, gauge the reaction of the captain or waiter as suggestions are made. Then, you can guide your guests through a menu as you would in any dining situation on your home turf.

Expense Accounts

Not only is it bad manners, it is downright unethical to pad an expense account. If you're caught, it may cost you your job and the loss of unemployment benefits. Inquire discreetly to learn what is acceptable; if in doubt, err on the side of caution. If the expense is essential to the business at hand, the expense is acceptable. If it is done for your own pleasure, and that includes experimenting with five star restaurants when business meals at home would be three star at most, the cost is yours to bear.

Clients are not necessarily impressed by your ability to spend the company's money freely. It may cost you business if the expenditure is perceived as fiscal irresponsibility. Some clients will try to get fancy freebies on your company. **Curb unreasonable demands by offering a selection of two restaurants rather than letting the client choose carte blanche.** If the client does make a suggestion that is out of line with corporate policy or what you consider reasonable, suggest another restaurant and give a reason for doing so such as, "It's quieter and less hectic, so we'll be able to talk more easily." Never make your company look cheap by saying the company doesn't allow such extravagances. Don't undermine your own authority and credibility by saying you don't think your boss would ever allow so extravagant an expense on your part.

When travelling with a more senior executive, the junior executive is responsible for paying the drivers, tipping, checking in and out of hotels and paying the tab in restaurants. Your skill in handling expenses and the efficiency with which you keep records will be noticed.

Making daily notes of expenses, including the names of the people you saw, their company and the reason for the get-together makes it easier to reconstruct your trip days and weeks later, and the accounting department will be ever appreciative of your thoroughness.

HOTELS

Take a room alone and use the privacy to unwind or stay on top of the work. Adapting to other peoples' habits, or expecting them to adapt to yours, can strain even the most established business relationships. The memory of you dealing with your daily toilette or strolling around the room in flannel pajamas can undermine the respect you've earned. **Under no circumstances should male and female business associates share a room, regardless of how platonic the situation may be.** Your credibility will be undermined, the gossip will spread and, worst, you will make your business associates uncomfortable.

How you handle yourself on the road will enhance or detract from your credibility with both colleagues and clients. Never turn your room into the party room. It will rob you of your privacy and make you look juvenile or like a spoilsport when you try to reclaim the room from revellers with greater stamina. Arrange to meet in the lobby and celebrate in the cocktail lounge.

Never conduct business in your hotel room. It is not a business environment and can make any client feel uncomfortable. Have the concierge at the hotel reserve a suite, a conference room or meeting space for you, either within the hotel or at a nearby temporary office facility. If such space is not available, meet with clients at their offices.

The hotel's concierge can contribute to a smooth stay. A good concierge has the inside knowledge and clout to obtain impossible to get restaurant reservations and tickets to sold-out events. The concierge also will advise you on how to dress for local functions, how to get around town, where to entertain, where to buy business gifts and, if you're a jogger, where to run safely. Turn the concierge into your ally by treating him or her like a skilled professional.

While the housekeeping staff of the hotel often has appliances for guest use, it is always wise to take your own if you think you'll need them. Being late because the hotel hairdryer wasn't as powerful as the one you're used to or because you had to wait for an iron to get the creases out of your suit jacket will only make you look like a novice to the clients you're trying to impress. Always take a travel alarm; never rely on the hotel staff to get you up for an important meeting.

If you feel compelled to take home a souvenir of your trip, go to the gift shop in the hotel or have the concierge advise you. Don't help yourself to hotel property; that constitutes theft. Taking something as insignificant as the little samples in the hotel bathrooms can undermine your credibility. Several years ago I travelled with an executive of a cosmetics company who would immediately, upon arrival, call housekeeping and demand extra samples because "they were so great for travelling." The impression she gave me is that her company's products weren't as good as the ones the hotel offered.

PRIVATE HOMES

Avoid staying at the home of a client or business associate because it puts you on show round the clock. Even the most proper executive feels the additional stress of always being on guard for possible faux pas.

If being a houseguest is impossible to avoid, be on your best behavior. Start by determining beforehand if any activities have been scheduled and pack accordingly.

Arrange your own transportation and arrive at the scheduled time. **If the host has not specified a time, let the host know when you expect to arrive. Upon arrival, let the host know your expected departure time, unless it was specified in the invitation.** It is totally inconsiderate to expect others to adapt to your time schedule.

Take an appropriate gift that is not too personal and that compliments the lifestyle of the host. Specialty foods, books, candles, potpourri, guest soaps and towels or gadgets are all appropriate. Gifts an entire family can share, like candy, are also appropriate. If there are children in the household, you may want to bring each child a small gift. Try to return the hospitality by taking your hosts out to dinner while you are their guest.

Ask about the household rules and routines and abide by them. **Be punctual for meals and any other planned activities. Don't infringe on your hosts' routines.** If activities are planned, join in; otherwise, get a book to entertain yourself. The only thing more unnerving to a host than the guest who treats another's home like a hotel is the guest who has to be led by the land through the entire day.

Restrict your use of your host's phone. If you must make a call, keep it short. Use your telephone credit card to place any long distance call.

Look after yourself and keep your room and the bathroom tidy, even if there is household help. Unless your host tells you not to make your bed, do so. At the end of your stay, ask if you can put fresh sheets on the bed and where to put the towels you've used. Don't burden your host by leaving belongings behind that have to be forwarded to you.

If your host has household help, don't request special favors unless it is absolutely necessary. You're creating extra work for them just by being there. **It is customary to tip the household help unless your host instructs you otherwise.** A standard tip is ten dollars per night, which you would put into an envelope with the person's name. Include a note of thanks and give it to the person or leave it on a visible surface in the room you occupied.

Always, always write your host a thank you note, preferably accompanied by flowers, within twenty-four hours after your departure.

USING ANOTHER'S OFFICE

If someone extends the use of an office to you, either at a branch office, a client's office or at a friend's, be sure to take a token of appreciation, like some chocolates. When you arrive, ask about the office procedure so that you don't upset anyone else's business routine. Keep your eyes open for the culture within that corporation, as you would if you were starting a new job in a new office.

Don't abuse the phone, FAX or copier privileges; use a credit card to place long distance calls. Keep your use of someone else's equipment to a minimum.

Never make excessive demands of someone else's secretary or support staff. **Always check with the secretary's boss before requesting any work of the secretary.** Treat the secretary with courtesy and be sensitive to any burden you're placing on the secretary's workload.

STAYING IN TOUCH

Your trip will have fewer interruptions and distractions if you arrange to have your office function smoothly in your absence. Before you leave, name the persons responsible for your daily operations, explain their positions to them and to any staff who will have to deal with them. Your secretary could coordinate the people, but should not be left in charge. You should never cause someone to report to a person whose job title is of lower rank than theirs. Specify to everyone the one person to contact you if it becomes necessary so that you are not inundated with a constant stream of phone calls. Your secretary might be the best person to act as telephone coordinator since the secretary should have your itinerary and your contact numbers. Clarify also what should not be done in your absence.

You need not inform everyone about your trip, but do let people know in advance that you may be in touch by phone. By being indefinite, you signal your interest without implying concern about their abilities. **When checking in, speak to the individuals personally. Don't relay messages through others.** This becomes especially important if it is a client or a superior whose problem can't await your return. Never create the impression that a matter is too unimportant for your consideration by passing it on to others.

In your absence, some situation may not be handled as effectively as if you had attended to it yourself. **Don't discipline an**

employee over the phone. Nor should you imply a lack of trust or make someone feel ineffectual because he or she couldn't handle a predicament without you. Never attempt to resolve interpersonal disputes over the phone. Negotiate a truce between the parties until your return.

NAME TAGS

At conferences, trade shows, conventions and other meetings, you'll often be given a badge or a name tag. The tendency is to place it on the left side because most of us are right-handed and it's easier to pin it on that way and because it looks better in the mirror. **The name tag belongs on the right-hand side**. When you shake hands, the eye follows the line of the arm and focuses first on the other person's right shoulder. A properly placed name tag can be read quickly and easily without having to scan another person's body and refocus. Too often, the tag has one of those swivel clips that are designed to attach to a left breast pocket. Carry your own generic pin-on badge and slip the name tag into it so you can pin it on the proper side.

TRADE SHOWS

You're at a trade show to represent your company, to meet clients and to promote the company and its products, not to catch up with old cronies and gossip or behave as if you were at a fraternity party. Take yourself seriously as a businessperson, and others will too. First dress the part. **Even if the show is being held in a resort area, you're there to work and that means business attire,** seasonally adjusted to the locale, unless everyone in the booth is wearing a costume or a uniform.

       Stand. Sitting in a booth implies fatigue or disinterest, so prospective clients are much less likely to enter your display area. Because standing for long periods does get tiring, keep the shifts in the booth short, under three hours if possible, so the fatigue doesn't show on everyone's face.

       Look alive, alert and approachable to attract visitors. Invariably, you'll be asked a string of potentially irritating questions for directions to the facilities, the water fountain, the snack bar, the information booth or the exits. Before the show starts, learn the answers and you'll be able to respond to the questions knowledgeably and helpfully. Rather than considering these requests as annoyances or intrusions, look upon them as opportunities to make a favorable impression, possibly even to start a conversation that may lead to you qualifying a prospect.

Attendance in a booth always seems to come in waves. **Although you must focus on one customer at a time, never ignore additional customers.** Think of dealing with a stream of people the way you would field a rapid series of telephone calls at the office. Ask the persons with whom you're dealing to excuse you for just a moment and put them on hold, in effect. Then, ask the newcomers if they want information or if they want to place an order and if they would prefer to wait or to book definite appointments for later in the day. Get their business cards, especially if you are just giving out information, and make notes on them after they've left. Finally, return to the first customer and thank him or her for waiting. Making your booth as attractive, comfortable and hospitable as possible with chairs, coffee or water and cups, some cookies or candies and a private area to sit and discuss business makes it easier to keep prospects in the booth.

After hours, no one should feel obligated to take part in any festivities, but no one should feel left out, either. Any events that your organization stages should be planned months in advance with the help of a party planner, preferably one who knows the local caterers and florists and any interesting sights like stately homes, museums, concert halls or boats on which to entertain. Make sure that the function matches your company's image and ties in with the theme of your booth and your product. By sending "hold the date" cards and invitations well before the event, the turnout is likely to be much greater. Any important clients you want to entertain privately should be invited well before the event. Their schedules get booked quickly by competitors, and good entertainment facilities are booked weeks and months beforehand. Don't jeopardize a valuable client relationship by adopting a cavalier "come what may" attitude.

CONVENTIONS AND SEMINARS

While trade shows focus on expanding and solidifying a client base and making sales, conventions are intra-company or industry with a focus on information, development and problem solving within the organization. It pays to be prepared. Know your needs and the contributions you are expected to make, know who the other players are and know how to conduct yourself.

If you make a presentation, credit those people who have helped you. Such magnanimity only makes you look good because it indicates you are a team player who is secure enough to share the kudos. When attending someone else's presentation, give thought beforehand to what you want to gain from the presenter and what you need to ask or do to get that information. Establishing a relationship with the speaker by asking perceptive questions broadens your base of resources and sends the signal that you are a corporate player on the move.

Background on other participants and on the speakers provides entrée to a discussion, makes you look informed and interested and flatters the people you're addressing. Through your homework, you can map out the key players you will need to meet. Keep your eyes open, too, for the unexpected shining stars who make major contributions with their questions and conversation.

Knowing how to make the introductions, how to handle small talk, how to mingle effectively and how to entertain and be entertained will give you the confidence to approach anyone and the skills to do so effectively. Social/business occasions are the ideal times to expand your horizons by mingling with others rather than remaining with your usual clique. And that's the stuff success is made of.

THE FAST TRACK

Travelling:

1. On the road you are representing your company twenty-four hours a day.

2. The person who owns the car drives the car.

3. Don't lose your composure or curse at other drivers.

4. Always ask the driver where you should sit.

5. Regard a car as a means of travel, not an ego statement.

6. Consider limos a convenience, not a symbol of prestige.

7. The most prestigious seat is passenger side, rear.

8. Pay attention to the hierarchy of your fellow passengers and seat yourself accordingly.

9. The more junior executive enters curbside and slides across to sit behind the driver.

10. Cancel airline reservations you're not planning to use.

11. If there are problems with your flight, stay calm and deal with airline personnel in a polite, friendly but persistent manner.

12. On board an airplane, remember to smile and say "please," "excuse me," "thank you" and "good-bye."

13. Don't tip flight attendants.

14. Don't be a seat hog.

15. If you want to use a portable computer, ask your fellow passengers if they mind.

16. Be early when travelling on a corporate jet.

17. Travel light and carry your own bags.

18. The senior executive boards the corporate jet first and takes his choice of seats.

19. On a corporate jet, ask where you should sit, take the refreshments that are offered and don't ask for anything special.

20. Thank the crew.

21. Write a note within twenty-four hours to the person who got you a seat on the corporate jet.

22. When using someone's office, don't abuse phone, FAX and copier privileges or make demands of support staff.

23. When checking in with your office, don't relay messages through others.

24. Don't resolve disputes or exercise discipline over the phone.

Trade Shows and Conventions:

1. Wear your name tag on the right hand side near the shoulder.

2. Dress in business attire at a trade show.

3. Stand, don't sit, in your booth at a trade show.

4. Focus on one customer at a time, but don't ignore additional customers at a trade show.

5. You need not take part in after hours activities.

6. Give credit to anyone who has helped you prepare a presentation.

Entertaining:

1. Make dining reservations by phone before leaving for a trip.

2. Confirm dining reservations in person when you arrive.

3. Make credit arrangements in advance so the bill is not presented at the table.

4. Offer clients a selection of two restaurants.

5. The most junior executive handles tipping and checking in and out of hotels.

Lodging:

1. Male and female business associates should never share a room.

2. Never conduct business in your hotel room.

3. When staying in a private home, let the host know when you will be arriving and departing.

4. Take an appropriate house gift.

5. Abide by house rules and routines and be punctual for meals and activities.

6. Look after yourself, keep the bathroom clean and make your own bed.

7. Tip any household help.

8. Always write your host a thank you note within twenty-four hours.

International Travel

Differences in culture can cause as many fluctuations in international business ventures as the foreign exchange rate.

Dorthea Johnson
Washington Trade Report

We're running a $170 billion trade deficit essentially because the captains of American industry don't know how to deal with people who are different.

Andrew Young
Former Ambassador to the United Nations

It is not to culture that one must adapt, but to culture as manifest and encountered in the behavior of individual foreigners.

Craig Stolti
The Art of Crossing Cultures

The born traveller—the man who is without prejudices, who sets out wanting to learn rather than to criticize, who is stimu-

CHAPTER

12

lated by oddity, who recognizes that every man is his brother, however strange and ludicrous he may be in dress and appearance—has always been comparatively rare.

Hugh & Pauline Massingham
The Englishman Abroad

THINK GLOBAL, ACT LOCAL

Business has become global, and corporate executives are finding themselves on international flights with increasing frequency. As you travel the globe, the one conclusion you can draw with certainty about other cultures is that the people don't think and act like Americans. No two countries are exactly alike; even neighboring countries like France and Germany can be polar opposites in their attitudes and behaviors. Canada, the United States' largest trading partner and the world's second largest country, shares a common language and many cultural influences like movies, music, television and magazines with the United States. Yet, there are many cultural nuances that cause conflict, especially because they are unexpected from a neighbor that appears, at a superficial level, to be so similar. One culture isn't right, the other wrong; they are simply different.

Culture is the system that enables human beings to establish and maintain relationships with one another. In *Culture's Consequences*, Geert Hofstede described research into the effect of different cultures on a multinational company that had its own strong corporate culture. Hofstede discovered that the culture of the country took precedence over the culture of the corporation. Americans act like Americans, Japanese act like Japanese, French act like french and so on around the world. To deal effectively in the international arena you can't paraphrase Henry Higgins in *My Fair Lady* and ask, "Why can't they be more like us?" The question to ask yourself is, "What adjustments do I have to make to elicit the desired response?"

We all tend to interpret other cultures in terms of our own. But, withhold judgment. To succeed internationally, you must learn to see another culture without being blinded by your own conditioning. **Acknowledge that there may be other ways of doing things that could be valid, even if you don't like them or feel comfortable with them.**

PREPARATION

Japanese sometimes describe the attitude of American businessmen as "ready, fire, aim." Unfortunately, it is too often true. But, there is no longer any excuse for cultural ignorance when you travel to another country. Seek out other executives within your firm or in professional associations who have been to the country. They are excellent sources of information. Find out what they did to prepare, what worked and where problems arose. International protocol consultants, courses, books, video tapes and cassettes are all available to help you. As Vince Lombardi said, "Confidence increases in direct proportion to preparation."

Whether you are travelling to another country or you are hosting international visitors on your home turf, find out who you will be dealing with. Get as much information as you can about the people, their positions, titles and degrees of responsibility. If possible, get a picture to make it easier to recognize people you'll be meeting for the first time. Put names to faces, and learn to say everyone's name correctly.

Provide your international associates with a packet of background information about yourself and the people who will be travelling with you. This becomes especially important if you are a woman or if women will be traveling in your group. Women are not as prevalent in business in other countries, and the automatic assumption will be that your entire party is male. By preparing your international associates, you'll allow them time to familiarize themselves with everyone in your group and prepare themselves accordingly.

Any information you can glean about interests or hobbies is also beneficial for small talk and for gifts. When gifts are an important factor in establishing business relationships in a country, do your shopping before you leave.

Have business cards printed in English on one side and translated on the other side. Invest in the services of a good translator for your business correspondence as well. It is pompous and presumptuous to expect the person you hope to deal with to read and speak your language.

No one expects you to learn another language in a few days or even months. **Before you board the plane, though, learn at least a few key words like "hello," "please," "thank you" and terms**

that might be useful when entertaining or dining. It is a gracious gesture toward the other person's culture and language that will be greatly appreciated.

Then, learn about the culture of the person with whom you plan to do business. Remember that people are individuals, even in the most group-oriented societies like Japan. Always pay attention to nuances in their response and retain a degree of flexibility in what you've learned. Don't be surprised if your international business associates start to behave like Americans rather than according to the book. They've been doing their homework, too.

Master your own culture. It is much more difficult to understand cultural differences and the adjustments you have to make without that awareness of how you, as an American, behave. And, it is positively embarrassing when people from another country are better versed in your culture's nuances of good behavior than you are.

CROSS-CULTURAL AWARENESS

While a potpourri of different cultural behaviors is fun to read through, it doesn't prepare anyone for the possible sources of culture clash. I'll review some of the main concepts of cultural diversity and sources of misunderstanding based on personal experience and the research of interculturalists like Geert Hofstede and Edward T. Hall and Mildred Reed Hall, whose books are essential reading for anyone interested in greater cross-cultural awareness.

Individual vs. Group

When you ask people from another country to tell you the first thing that comes to mind about the United States, they very often say "cowboys & Indians." This country is known for its pioneering heritage and rugged individualism. Research shows that the United States is the most individualistic society in the world. Every culture you come in contact with will be at least mildly more group oriented than yours.

Business and social structures in other countries require getting to know the other person and forming networks first. Americans, however, want to get down to business without taking the time to make small talk or to build relationships. Even Northern Europeans, who also do not relate strongly to group affiliation, will take more time to get to know one another. Relationships are an important component of the culture and should be nourished, especially when dealing with Asians, Arabs and Latins. The Japanese have a term for their system of loyal and dependent relationships, *amae*, and it is the glue that holds Japanese society together.

Group orientation or individualism affects the decision-making process in other countries. **You may find that the people you're dealing with will have to go off and caucus regularly to arrive at a consensus. Don't get insulted and assume they're gossiping behind your back.** By the way, the spokesperson for the group is not necessarily the most important person; he may only be the person with the best command of the language. Study the business cards and watch for the nuances in the group interaction that indicate respect.

Although individualistic Americans thrive on praise, a group-oriented culture deals with compliments and criticism much differently. **To be singled out, whether for praise or criticism, can be very embarrassing because it sets the individual apart from the group. Be careful to compliment the group, and do it privately.** Instead of, "Mr. Ishikawa, you did a great job getting that order shipped promptly," say "Mr. Ishikawa, we're very pleased with the way your company shipped our order so promptly."

American companies look to the quarterly bottom line and want to see immediate results. Whether you're the CEO or the sales and marketing manager, make sure you allow your employees the time to build long term relationships. Otherwise, any hasty attempts to venture overseas will be in vain. As costly as efforts to penetrate overseas markets are, the cost in ill-will and distrust of all American companies is even greater. The more important the relationship and the more group-oriented the culture, the more time has to be allowed.

Rank and Status

Without realizing the hostility that is aroused, Americans tend to barge into foreign situations with a take charge attitude and total ignorance of the local nuances of power to which other cultures are extremely sensitive. Americans believe strongly in the concept of equality; yet, efforts to treat everyone in other countries as equals can be counterproductive.

The Japanese value hierarchical relationships. They place tremendous emphasis on occupying one's proper place and performing a role corresponding to one's position or status. In Latin America, the distance between those with power and those without is vast, with great respect and ceremony shown to the power brokers. **Learn the power structure in your host country and don't try to circumvent it.**

In a youth oriented culture such as ours, age is seldom treated with deference. Especially in Asian countries, age can be venerated more than education. **If in doubt about someone's rank, age can be a good indicator of status, as can gender.** With the possible exception of a few northern European countries, women have seldom attained the same level of success in foreign business arenas that they have here. You can assume that the man holds the greater power, and an American woman must learn to temper her annoyance when an international associate ignores her and addresses her male assistant.

Forms of Address

Virtually every country is more formal in the way individuals address one another and use titles than the United States. The Japanese always introduce themselves by their surnames and their company affiliation, "I am Tanaka from Fuji." Once a relationship has been established, they will address you by attaching -*san* as a form of respect. Never attach it to your own name just as you would never refer to yourself as "the Honorable" in this country.

To omit even one in the string of German or Italian titles can give serious offense. Mr. Dr. Director Smith might sound strange to you, but Herr Doktor Direktor Schmidt sounds perfectly fine to a German's ear. **Treat all titles with respect and use the surname or family name.** Never use first names unless you have been asked to do so.

Introductions and Greetings

Learn to pronounce names correctly. If in doubt, ask and ask again until you get it right. While names are only a person's individual label in this country, elsewhere hundreds of years of history and family pride could be attached to the name. Find out which is the family name and which is the given name, especially in Asian cultures which often treat names differently. The Chinese, for instance, give the one syllable family name first, followed by a one or two syllable given name. However, if they deal with Americans frequently, they might reverse the order and put the family name last to accommodate you.

Be prepared to shake hands endlessly, both at the beginning and end of an encounter. The handshake is the universal form of greeting; the open hand means "I come in peace." The type and strength of a handshake differs from culture to culture. The Japanese, for instance, offer a much weaker handshake because they don't like to touch. In some cultures you may only pump once or twice, in others you will pump more vigorously. Be cautious about touching women, even with a handshake, because of possible religious taboos. Let them initiate the shake.

If you have not learned the intricacies of the bow in Asian cultures, stick to the handshake to avoid giving offense because how you bow is an indication of status. Remember, too, the bow is used differently in China, Korea and Japan.

Play your business cards right. **Use a formal style of card and have the translation printed on the back. Never write notes on a business card in the person's presence.** If your memory needs assistance, wait till the person has gone. In Japan, there is a ritual to the exchange of cards, or *meiji*, that is important to learn for those positive initial impressions. Always have plenty of cards with you. Invariably, you will need many more than you can ever imagine.

"Hi" and "bye" are never sufficient in greeting. Most other countries have much more formal and elaborate rituals to welcome guests. **At the very least, use "hello" or "how do you do?"**

Deal in small talk when first meeting someone to establish those relationships. Don't jump immediately into a business discussion. And beware of topics that may be taboo in that particular culture.

Eye Contact

While Americans make eye contact about 40-60 percent of the time, people from cultures founded on a more rigid system of hierarchy may consider that a brazen affront. Gender and status determine acceptable eye contact in most non-European cultures.

Business Dress

Dress up rather than for comfort. The way you present yourself is not only a sign of self-respect, it also indicates the respect you have for your international business associate. Fashion as an expression of individualism will most probably be misunderstood, possibly even perceived as an insult.

If you are conducting business in a tropical climate, you can adopt a less formal style, usually a short-sleeved white overshirt for men and a short-sleeved silk or linen dress for women, that coincides with the business dress of the country. Otherwise, dealing with a country's dress code is somewhat similar to dressing for IBM or Wall Street, only the repercussions can be more severe.

Information Flow

How you communicate will determine if you come across as rude, abrupt, impatient and pushy or as boring as a professor of dead languages. In communicating with anyone, several factors come into play.

The speed at which people give and receive information can determine whether your attitude will be perceived as dictatorial or condescending. In some cultures, information is disseminated in staccato shorthand like newspaper headlines, in others it resembles elaborate prose. Americans are very direct in their presentation; they like to get to the point. Asians, Latins and Arabs are much more circular in their presentation. We perceive that as beating around the bush, going around in circles; in other words, we have a very negative reaction to that type of communication.

When people communicate, they take for granted how much the listener knows about the subject under discussion. In cultures like that of the U.S., Switzerland, the Scandinavian countries and Germany, which compartmentalize everything, a great deal of background information is required. In cultures with extensive networks among family, friends and colleagues like Japanese, Arab or Mediterranean cultures there is little need for in-depth background information because it flows so freely. **How warmly your business presentation will be received depends a great deal on whether or not you insult someone by giving too much or too little information.**

Space and Distance

Space is an invisible boundary that defines a person's territory and, very often, power. By the amount of space we assume, we can be perceived as aggressive and pushy or cold and distant. In the U.S., personal space in conversation is approximately an arm's length. Elsewhere, as in Japan, it can be greater. In some Arab and Latin cultures it is much less. It is a temptation to back away when someone stands too close or assaults your olfactory or auditory space with strange smells or loud noise. You may also be tempted to move in when they keep their distance. Resist the impulse to do either.

Don't touch another person, except to shake hands. It is a serious insult to touch in many cultures. And, even if it is acceptable to touch or hold hands with someone of the same gender, it may be totally inappropriate for a man and woman to touch, even platonically. In some Asian cultures, the head is considered sacred and touching it is taboo.

The way space and distance are handled in a business environment can affect the way a meeting is conducted. That private corner office, so cherished by Americans ascending the corporate ladder, is unheard of except in Germany and Switzerland where closed doors and privacy are even more valued. Americans, Canadians, Germans, Scandinavians, the Swiss and the British will all give you that private meeting, with all calls held. But in France and Japan, offices are open plan. Even the heads of major Japanese firms are seldom found in their private offices; they often use them only for meetings with foreigners. If your company is planning to do business in an Arab land, don't be surprised to find yourself sitting in a large room, possibly even with your competitors, while the Arab works his way around the room. If you want privacy, an Arab will just lean closer.

Time Systems
The way time is perceived in a culture affects attitudes towards punctuality, task orientation and scheduling.

In monochronic cultures like ours, where the focus is on one task at a time, time is almost tangible—it can be spent, wasted, saved or lost—and priorities are a major consideration. It is highly unlikely that a monochronic German will keep you waiting, and you better not be even a minute late if you want your transactions to be successful. In contrast, Arab and Latin cultures are extremely polychronic, which means they do many things at once with little regard for schedules. For a South American, dealing with a chance encounter on the way to a meeting will take priority over getting to the appointment punctually. If you schedule a meeting with an Arab, bring a book and enough work to keep you discreetly occupied because, if something more important arises, you will be kept waiting for hours, possibly days.

In scheduling appointments, always consider the lead time involved. In the U.S. and Germany, a long lead time indicates the importance of the business to be conducted and/or of the people involved. Arabs require a lead time of only a few days; otherwise, the meeting may have slipped their minds as unimportant. After all, had it been important, you would have attended to it immediately. The Japanese also have a much shorter lead time than Americans, so Japanese of much higher rank than their American counterparts often attend meetings because they were able to rearrange their schedules.

When scheduling appointments, remember to consider different sabbaths and religious holidays. Whether it's the Chinese New Year, Carnival in Rio, Ramadan or Yom Kippur, holidays are plentiful, and they are treated much more seriously elsewhere than in the United States. While Americans, for the most part, take off Christmas Day and Easter Sunday, in most European countries December 26 and Easter Monday are also holidays. Canada, too, observes a holiday on December 26, Boxing Day.

The Faux Pas Factor

Cultural differences can often be a source of the most grievous offense and insensitivity. Religion plays an important part in most Eastern, Middle Eastern and Latin countries. Buddhists believe that suffering is caused by the desire for possessions and selfish enjoyment. Wearing white in Hong Kong signifies mourning. Beef and leather are taboo for the Hindu. Moslems and most Jews do not eat pork. Moslems are also forbidden by religious law to drink alcohol and to smoke. Nor will they predict the future because only God knows what will happen. By the way, the religion Moslems practice is Islam, not Mohamedanism.

Never comment on government, culture or technology, even if your host invites your comments. Don't even complain about the difficulty of placing a telephone call. In Third World countries, enthusiasm about the quaintness of the region is usually interpreted as an insult by people trying to advance into the twentieth century.

Americans have very few inhibitions to saying "no." But, the Japanese and, to a lesser extent, many Latins go to great length to avoid a direct negative that might create a loss of face. Japanese or Indochinese often reply in the affirmative to indicate that they heard the question, not necessarily that they agree. If they do say no, they do it indirectly. There is even a book by Masaaki Imai entitled *16 Ways to Avoid Saying No.*

One geographical gaffe can create frostbite in a budding relationship. Here are a few typical errors:

- Taiwan is the Republic of China and should never be confused with the People's Republic of China.
- South Korea is the Republic of Korea; North Korea is the People's Democratic Republic of Korea. Relations are strained.
- Indochinese refers to Vietnamese, Laotians, Cambodians and the Hmong.
- Belgium has two distinct groups. The Flemish live in the north and speak a language related to German and Dutch. The Walloons live in the south and southeast, and speak French. The two groups are culturally and temperamentally different.
- Scandinavian and Nordic are not synonymous. Only Sweden, Norway and Denmark are Scandinavian countries. Nordic refers to one of the three main divisions of the Caucasian race that includes Scandinavians as well as the people from Finland and Iceland.
- United Kingdom refers to England, Scotland, Wales and Northern Ireland. Great Britain doesn't include Northern Ireland.
- There are two Irelands: the Republic of Ireland, capital Dublin, and Northern Ireland, part of the United Kingdom, capital Belfast.
- Don't confuse Australia and New Zealand.
- Canadians dislike being referred to as Americans; Latin Americans consider themselves American, too, and resent the term being applied only to those from the United States of America.
- The correct name for Mexico is the United States of Mexico.

DEALING WITH AN INTERPRETER

Americans are not known for their linguistic skills and are notorious for speaking English wherever they go. Making the person from another culture speak in your language can put that person at a decided disadvantage. **Rather than fumble to make yourself understood, hire an interpreter.** Even if you speak the language of the country you are visiting, it is wise to get an interpreter, who usually has a better command of the nuances of the language than you do. Always get your own translator rather than using the services of your host's translator, whose loyalties might be divided.

Prepare your interpreter in advance for optimum effectiveness. Give detailed background information on your company or product. Explain the purpose of the meeting and with whom you'll be dealing. Explain the circumstances of the meeting, whether it is on a golf course, at a trade show or at a formal banquet, and what the appropriate attire would be.

Review any technical jargon to make sure that the interpreter understands it. An interpreter is paid for what he or she knows, so be careful of a tendency to admit to a greater understanding than actually exists.

Once the conversation begins, speak to the client rather than the interpreter. Watch the person's reaction to your interpreter's words to make sure you are not losing him.

Remember that a translation won't be the same length as the original; don't question your interpreter's use of words. Avoid slang or contractions that might give the interpreter trouble. Be careful of your phrasing and the placement of your words so you don't send confusing messages.

Never deal with more than one thought at a time. Speak slowly and clearly. Give the interpreter a chance to do the work without trying to remember volumes. Ask frequently for clarification to make sure you are being understood, and don't go on to another point until the first is perfectly clear.

The interpreter is speaking twice as much as you are, so make sure there is a glass of water on hand for the person. Remember to provide the interpreter with breaks and meals during long sessions.

EFFECTIVE INTERNATIONAL ENTERTAINING

Entertaining and being entertained are obligatory aspects of doing business overseas. Guests are treated with lavish care and attention in most cultures, but guests also have a responsibility to fulfill their role so they don't embarrass themselves, their company and their host. **Styles of dining, attitudes toward dining and the time meals are eaten can be as different from what you are accustomed to as the food you'll be served. Prepare yourself as much as possible before you leave,** and you'll feel much more confident handling any situation that may arise.

Once you arrive in Japan or China, it is too late to learn to use chopsticks. Get someone to teach you before you go, and practice. Executives who cannot master two little sticks cast doubt on their ability to handle more important aspects of business. If you are travelling to Europe, on the other hand, learn to wield a knife and fork in the Continental style as described in the chapter on entertaining. While eating in the American style may not cast doubts upon your capabilities, the strange way you handle the silverware may amaze your European hosts to such an extent that they will stare at what you are doing rather than focus on what you are saying. Learn a few phrases like "This is delicious," or "what a delightful aroma," to compliment your host. Don't learn "what is it?" because you may not want to know. Studying menu terms of the host country may avoid some of the problems you may encounter.

The power breakfasts and power lunches that are a staple of American business seldom go over well in other countries. Customary dining hours and conversation vary from culture to culture. **Meals are usually a time to enjoy yourself and socialize with your associates rather than negotiate.** Be wary of discussing business. It is inappropriate in social settings unless your host initiates the conversation.

Breakfast is seldom popular as a business meal, especially among the French and the Japanese. Lunch in Spain, Italy and Latin America is the biggest meal of the day, and can last two or three hours; dinner is eaten very late in the evening. In Africa, you may be invited to supper between three and six in the afternoon. In Arabia, coffee and fruit are served upon arrival, followed by conversation; dinner is served at the end of the evening. Nightlife is an obligatory part of doing business in Japan.

Never refuse food. As Roger Axtell writes in *Do's and Taboos Around the World*, "Acceptance of what is on your plate is tantamount to acceptance of host, country and company. So, no matter how tough things may be to swallow, swallow." To facilitate that process, he further advises that you slice everything very thin, don't ask what it is and swallow quickly. Small portions also help, even if you do know what you're eating. Those large Latin lunches can finish you for the remainder of the day if you don't pace yourself and eat small amounts. Never help yourself to food unless it was specifically offered to you. **And learn how to say "no," especially in China and Arab countries, in a manner that will not offend the host.**

Hosting involves toasting, and every culture does it differently. Learn how to respond to your host's toast appropriately, and how and when to make toasts.

While drinking is taboo in Islamic countries, elsewhere it is seen as a sign of hospitality. Just as you have to eat the food, you have to take a few sips. In France and Italy, food is paramount, so the cocktail hour is regarded with disdain as a boorish American custom. Only one aperitif before dinner is acceptable so you don't dull your tastebuds. In Russia, vodka is the only thing guaranteed to appear on your table. In Japan, you don't pour your own drink. It is the responsibility of the person seated to the right to keep the neighbor's glass or sake cup full at all times. The American awareness of alcoholism as a disease is not as prevalent in the rest of the world. **If you have a problem, blame doctor's orders for preventing you from drinking.** Just begging off by saying you've had enough, you don't drink or you have to get up in the morning won't do. You'll only be perceived as an ungracious guest.

Smoking, at least for men, is often considered very macho and seldom has the same negative connotations it does in this country. That does not give you carte blanche to light up, though. If you don't see an ashtray, don't smoke. Otherwise, follow the lead of your hosts. Smoking at mealtime in France is a grave insult because it affects the way the food will taste. In England, never light up at a formal function until after the Queen has been toasted. When you do, it is courteous to offer a cigarette to everyone.

Entertaining is seldom done in the home. A person's home and family are private. **If you are invited out by a business associate, don't assume that your spouse is included.** Because home entertaining is not the spontaneous affair it can be in the United States and because invitations are seldom casual, consider it an honor to be invited. **Bring the appropriate gift or flowers and remember to thank the host and hostess.**

When you wish to entertain your international associates, don't try to go native or to show the guests what American hospitality is all about. **Entertain using a combination of your usual style with some accommodation to local traditions, cuisine and taste.**

Schedule your event to coincide with the local customary hours and regard for time. Pay attention to local traditions relating to color, flowers and decor. A black and white ball is not appropriate to the Japanese; red roses are not a good choice as centerpieces for Germans and French. Flags look very festive, but they can cause as much insult as an improper seating order if current protocols are not correctly observed. It is always a good idea to call the local American Embassy or Consulate for guidance.

Tipping

Do not tip in some countries of the world, like Iceland and China. Tip most everywhere else, though, but not always to the extent you tip in America. While excessive overtipping is perceived as a crass capitalist gesture, undertipping can be equally insulting. **It is best to check with the concierge at your hotel to find out the current acceptable amounts to tip to whom because rules change.** If you are staying in a private home, check with your host, especially on the acceptable amounts to leave his household staff.

In restaurants and hotels, a tip of between 10-20 percent is often included, a *servis compris* as they say in France. Ask the maître d'hotel if you don't see it on the check. It is standard to leave an additional 5 percent to reward good service. In Germany, the change to the nearest Mark is usually left as *Trinkgeld* when the service is included.

Gift-Giving

Giving gifts is a normal part of business in many parts of the world. While a gift can reinforce a relationship and act as a tangible memory of you and your company, it also can sever it if the type of present, its value or the way it is given carry negative connotations. **The gift must be appropriate to the relationship, the culture and the occasion.**

Consider the amount you spend on a gift. It is the thought, not the price tag that counts. However, that does not mean the gift should be cheap. Regardless of what you give, it must always be of the best quality. The gift should not be so extravagant, though, that it can be construed as a bribe. Nor should it burden the recipient with obligation, as could easily happen in certain Asian cultures where duty obliges one to reciprocate.

The ideal gift is one that relates to the United States and/ or your company. Avoid logos. Buy the gifts here before you leave on your travels. The most ordinary of gifts to us will seem as exotic to the recipients as anything from their country might be to us. You may want to wait until you arrive and have passed through customs before wrapping your gifts, but take the necessary supplies.

In Arabian countries, give your gifts in front of others so they cannot be misconstrued as a bribe. In all other cultures, give your gifts in private. Wait till after business negotiations are completed before giving a gift so no one will take it to be a bribe. Don't apologize, act awkward or embarrassed when giving, unless that is the custom of the country, because you spoil the impact of the gift.

Receive gifts graciously. Learn to accept them in the accepted style of the country. Don't, for example, immediately tear the wrapping and dive into the box to see what goodies you got in Japan. Wait till you are alone before unwrapping your gift. **Always, always put your thanks on paper, and do it immediately.** Pack plenty of personal stationery so you can attend to those details at once rather than trying to deal with a long list of obligations after you get back home where a mountain of paper is probably waiting to distract you. The impact will have been lost on a gesture that may have already been forgotten. If you have had photos taken, include one as a token of remembrance.

HOSTING INTERNATIONAL VISITORS

When your international associates come to the United States, it is your turn to fulfill the role of host. Just because you are on your home turf, you can't revert to a lackadaisical attitude toward guests and expect them to look after themselves. You must do everything in your power to make them feel as warm and cherished as they would have made you feel in their country. Anything less is an insult.

Although you may never have seen their spouses when you were visiting them, cultural taboos are lifted to a certain extent when coming to America. Take extra care to attend to the needs of the spouses to make them feel welcome in a foreign situation. The presence of spouses on the trip does not mean cultural taboos, such as touching, have been left at home. Observe their traditions, and prepare those who may come in contact with your guests, and you will be thought as gracious an international host as you were a guest.

Globalization of markets means more than economics and trade agreements. Sometimes entire deals can turn on the most minor points of etiquette. The international Golden Rule is, "Do unto others as they would do unto themselves." So, learn to play by local rules. Then, practice, practice, practice. As Shakespeare wrote in *Hamlet*, "The readiness is all!"

THE FAST TRACK

1. New Golden Rule: Do unto others as they would do unto themselves.

2. Find out the names, titles and spheres of responsibility of the people with whom you'll be interacting. Get a picture if possible.

3. Provide your international associates with background information and pictures of all the people in your group.

4. Have your correspondence translated.

5. Have conservative business cards printed in English on one side and translated on the other side.

6. Shop for any gifts before you leave.

7. Learn a few key phrases like "hello," "My name is . . .," "please" and "thank you."

8. Get to know people and establish relationships before getting down to business.

9. Compliment the group rather than the individual.

10. Respect the local hierarchical structures and nuances of power.

11. Respect local attitudes to age, gender and family.

12. Treat all titles with respect and use surnames until invited to use given names.

13. Shake hands at the beginning and end of every encounter.

14. Don't use the casual "hi" and "bye." Stick to a more formal "hello" or "how do you do?"

15. Avoid topics that are taboo to that particular culture.

16. Dress up rather than for comfort as a sign of self respect and respect for your business associate.

17. Adjust the speed at which you communicate to a level that is comfortable for your international associate.

18. If someone gets too close, don't back away. If the person keeps a distance, don't close in.

19. Don't touch another person except to shake hands.

20. Be punctual, but don't be surprised or insulted if you're kept waiting. Not everyone has the same concept of punctuality.

21. Be aware of religious taboos.

22. Never comment on government, culture or technology, even if your host invites comment.

23. A direct "no" can cause a loss of face. Learn to be more tactful.

24. Avoid geographical gaffes.

25. Hire your own interpreter, and prepare him or her in advance on the topic, technical jargon and appropriate dress.

26. Speak clearly, grammatically and on one topic at a time.

27. Address your business associate, not the interpreter.

28. Learn to eat in the Continental style or with chopsticks, depending on where you're going.

29. Adjust to the dining hours of the culture.

30. Don't discuss business over a meal unless your host initiates it.

31. Never refuse food, but learn the appropriate signal for when you've had enough.

32. If drinks are served, accept. Blame doctor's orders if you can't drink.

33. When invited out, don't assume the spouse is included.

34. If invited to a home, bring a gift or flowers.

35. When entertaining, adjust your usual style to accommodate local traditions, cuisine, taste and timing.

36. Give gifts that are appropriate to the relationship, the occasion and the culture.

37. Give a gift that reflects your country or your company. Avoid logos.

38. Give gifts in private except in Arab countries where they should be given in front of others.

39. Wait until after business negotiations are complete before giving a gift.

40. Give and receive gifts graciously.

41. Always put your thanks on paper and send it out immediately.

TIPPING

Gratitude is the most exquisite form of courtesy.

Unknown

Most people working in basic service industries receive very low base pay; tips are an integral part of their income. You should fail to tip only for extremely bad service.

Although who to tip, when and how much can be confusing at times, there are several rules of thumb that can help when you're in doubt. One, give a present to a fellow professional and a tip to someone in the basic service industry. Two, if the person owns the establishment, you are not expected to give a tip. Three, 15 percent is usually safe; if the service is less than average, settle for 10 percent and increase it to 20 percent for excellent service.

Money folded into a Christmas or holiday greeting card, with a few handwritten words of appreciation, is the most tasteful way to give your holiday gift.

CHAPTER

13

GROOMING SERVICES

Tipping the people who look after your body is not only courteous, it is a matter of self-protection! When the same person attends to you on a regular basis, a gift of cash in addition to the standard tip is expected during the holiday season.

Hairdresser/ Barber/Colorist	15-20% per service. One week's fee in the holiday season.
Shampooist	$1-$2 for a basic shampoo, with an additional dollar for each additional treatment.
Manicurist	15-20%, with a minimum tip of $1. One week's fee during the holidays.
Masseuse	15% of the bill. At holiday time, half the maximum of a single visit.
Personal Trainer	For the holidays, $50-$100 and a gift. No tips after individual sessions.
Shoe Shine	$1 per shine and $5-$10 for the holidays if you use the same person regularly.

BUILDING SERVICES

Traditionally, building service and maintenance staff receive presents or tips each holiday season. This is your way of acknowledging their work and their contribution to your living environment. The tip varies according to the quality of the building, the neighborhood, the size of the staff and the amount of work each person has done, but you should always tip something. Old clothing or furniture, used appliances or leftover food are not substitutes for a tip.

Doorman	$10-$100 for the holidays, depending on how much service they give you during the course of the year, how often you see them and how tony the building. $35 is a good tip in a decent building in a moderate neighborhood.

Handyman/ Elevator Operator	$5-$15 as a holiday token. You should be tipping for services given throughout the year. Routine tips are $1 for replacing a faucet washer to $5-$10 for lugging a heavy appliance.
Superintendent/ Manager	Supers do not receive tips during the year unless they are also the handymen, in which case you may elect to tip when the services are performed and give only a token tip at holiday time. Otherwise, tip $30-$100 for the holidays, depending on the luxuriousness of the building and the location.
Maid/Butler/ Chauffeur	One week's pay for the holidays.
Nanny	One week's pay for the holidays.
Babysitter	An extra night's pay for the holidays.
Dog walker	Gift or cash equal to one week's service for the holidays.

DELIVERY PERSONNEL

It is not necessary to tip many regular delivery services like express mail carriers or other U.S. government employees. Nor is it necessary to tip a package service or messenger if you are receiving business-related material from a client who is paying for the delivery. However, it is customary to tip at holiday time for services that you receive regularly.

Newspaper Delivery	$10-$15
Mailman	$5
UPS Driver	$10-$15
Garbage Collector	$5-$15 per person

Other infrequent delivery services would be tipped at the time of delivery.

Food Delivery	15% of the bill, as you would a waiter.
Groceries	$1-$2 in addition to the store charge depending on the number and weight of the bags and the distance from the store.
Furniture	$5-$15 depending on the weight and whether you have stairs or an elevator.

ENTERTAINMENT/RESTAURANT SERVICES

Caterer	15-20% of total bill.
Private Clubs	Contribute $100 to annual employees' Christmas fund.
Maîtres d'hotel	$5-$10 occasionally at frequently used establishments. Tipping to get a good table is considered a serious affront at better establishments, although it seems to be par for the course at the trendy, hot new places. Professionals consider it unethical, none the less, because they are the masters of the dining room and there to serve you. A gift for the holidays, like a good silk tie, is appropriate at an establishment you frequent a great deal.
Captain	5% of the bill. If you're combining the tip with that of the wait staff, put a bracket around the two lines on the bill for the captain and tip and fill in the one amount.
Wait Staff	15-20% is standard, depending on the quality of your service. Don't hesitate to reduce the tip if lack of good service warrants it.
Sommelier	15% of the wine bill handed directly to the sommelier as you leave.

Hotel Services

You represent your company every time you travel on business. Throwing money around will create as negative an impression as not tipping adequately.

If any of the service is truly outstanding, in addition to tipping the employee, write a note to the hotel management praising that person. In a business built on customer service with a transient patronage, this helps the management assess the staff and maintain the standards of the establishment.

Door Attendant	$1 for taking your bags out of the car. $1-$2 to hail a cab, depending on the difficulty in obtaining one.
Bellman	$1 for each bag carried to your room, more if the bags are heavy. It is not courteous to try to save on the tip by carrying your own bags; consider it part of the cost of staying at the hotel.
Parking Attendant	$1 each time your car is brought out.
Room Service	15% of the bill. Sometimes the charge is on the bill, but most of it usually goes to the hotel, so include an additional 10%.
Housekeeping	Every time you request a special service like cleaning, extra towels or a hairdryer, tip the person bringing it to you $1.
Maid	$1 per person per day in an envelope somewhere in the room where it is easily visible. Write a brief note, even if it is only "Thanks!", on the hotel stationery and include it with the tip.

Other Situations

Country Clubs	Contribute $100 to annual employees' Christmas fund.

Sporting Events

When shown to your seat, give the usher $1. It is unlikely that an usher will be able to give you better seats than you already have at a sold-out event. If you have mediocre tickets and the event is only half full, you can try entering the expensive section through the regular doors and handing the usher your old tickets with $2-$5 per ticket folded under them. Don't come down from your own section or he won't be able to help you because you've been too obvious. And, don't argue with the usher if he says no. A good usher knows what seats are available; or he may be under management surveillance.

WOMEN AT WORK

Once a woman travels into the world of big business, she is in an all-male preserve. She is judged according to the customs and standards of that male society, not by those she was taught to apply to a different society.

Betty Lehan Harrigan

The only real drawback to being a woman in the business world is you have to deal with men.

Alex Thien

In previous appearances at women's colleges, my solemn remarks were addressed to women specifically—about the place of educated women in our society; about bringing up children

CHAPTER

14

in a neurotic world; about the conflict between the office desk and the kitchen sink.

After listening to my highly instructive address, I came to the enlightened conclusion that women would not be truly emancipated until commencement speakers ignored the fact that they were women.

Adlai Stevenson

CHIVALRY VS. HIERARCHY

The emergence of women at all levels of the corporate ranks in the last twenty years has had a great influence on acceptable business behavior. Yet, not everything has changed. Courtesy is still basic and it has no gender. **Unlike social etiquette, which is based on a concept of chivalry that cossets and protects the woman, business etiquette treats men and women as equals according to their position.** It is based on hierarchy and power. Business etiquette makes the workplace less discriminatory.

People who work together have always been treated as colleagues or fellow professionals, and that doesn't change now that they may be either male or female. In a business environment, they are not men or women first and professionals by happenstance.

A subtle unease in dealing with women who are peers still pervades many executive suites. Most male chief executives grew up in the 1930s through the early 1960s with the television image of women as mothers, girlfriends, corporate wives and daughters rather than as professionals. These executives, who usually have a much better grounding in social etiquette than the latest crop of MBA whiz kids, would be shocked to be told that their behavior is insulting or discriminatory. Unfortunately, you can't change them; you can only deal with the chain of command. One acerbic female executive reminds herself that you can't teach an old dog new tricks so she might as well make his remaining years as comfortable as possible. Meanwhile, she learns everything she can from him with polish and a professional attitude.

GENDER DIVERSITY

Very often what is construed as a lack of etiquette is really a disparity in styles of behavior between the two sexes. Although gender diversity specialists do not know if that dissimilarity is caused by innate genetic differences or by gender conditioning, they tell us that men and women listen, speak, make small talk and deal with humor and banter differently. Neither style is right or wrong, simply dissimilar. Gender diversity is very much like the cultural diversity discussed in chapter 12, because of the differences in the way males and females are raised. A woman in business is entering what was traditionally a man's world.

Since women are the latecomers to the business world, they are the ones who will have to set the stage for how they want to be treated. They can't communicate in a prim and proper, ladylike fashion, and then get upset at being overlooked for promotion to an aggressive new technical marketing division. **Women must let go of ladies' manners if they expect peer treatment.**

Don't go native and act like one of the boys. The rules of etiquette described in this book are, for the most part, gender neutral. But, while gender neutrality is ideal behavior in the business arena, this isn't an ideal world. Learning the differences in male, female and neutral styles of communication gives you the flexibility to use whatever style will be most effectively received by the person with whom you're dealing.

Women often nod and make murmuring "uh-huh" type noises while other people are speaking as a way to signal they are attentive to the speaker, not necessarily that they agree, much as the Japanese do. Men interpret this style of listening as agreement and, as with the Japanese, it leads to misunderstandings. A man, on the other hand, may do a variety of things while listening, like sort through mail or sign papers, which women misconstrue as rude and inattentive although he is listening to every word. Men interrupt without waiting for a long pause, the way women usually do. Nor do men apologize for making an interruption.

These gender specific behaviors can be misinterpreted as insults by someone who uses a different style of discussion. Taking umbrage only leads to further misunderstandings and breakdowns in communication that widen the gap between the sexes in the business arena.

Dealing with Co-workers

If you're often in conflict with co-workers of the opposite sex, re-read the first chapter for a better grasp on gender neutral behavior in the business arena. **Greet clients and colleagues with a smile and a handshake, no kissing.** Otherwise, keep your hands to yourself to avoid any possibility that touching will be misconstrued by others as harassment. Let your boss determine the formality or informality of the office. **If a co-worker of the opposite sex is friendly toward you, don't automatically assume that it is a romantic overture. Keep one-on-one meetings to daytime hours unless you include the spouses. And, don't call a co-worker at home** except with specific work-related questions, especially if the person is married or involved in a relationship.

Treat female executives with the same respect you treat male employers; they earned their position the same way a man would have, through hard work. **Women are women in the business arena, never girls, gals or ladies, regardless of the position they hold in the office.** If a man is condescending in the way he addresses you, you can ignore it and continue on with the business conversation, you can correct him by saying "my name is. . ." in a pleasant tone of voice, or you can revert to pointedly calling him "Mr." to re-establish a more formal exchange. Losing your composure won't correct his attitude; if anything, he'll gain satisfaction from rattling you.

No one is sweetie, honey or dear, regardless of age or gender, yours or theirs. However, if a person calls you by an endearment, it may be a bad habit rather than a sign of disrespect. Don't make an issue of it. Smile and correct the person gently by saying, "Peter, I would appreciate you calling me Hilka."

Women in management are often in a lonely position, isolated from the camaraderie of fellow male executives and from the support of other women in the office by rank. **Just because you've succeeded to a higher position, don't be condescending to the other women in the office.** Secretaries and receptionists can make your life miserable if they don't like you. **Nor should you appoint yourself as role model and preach to the other women to seek greater power and achievement.** That's patronizing. Treat the junior and support staff with respect, but don't try to turn them into your pals. You can cause a lot of resentment and bruise egos when you suddenly revert to a management role. If you need to confide your business problems to someone, find a mentor or a peer outside your office. Personal problems are best shared with a therapist. **Intimate details of your personal life are inappropriate in a business setting,** especially if the person is a subordinate or a superior, regardless of gender.

PROFESSIONAL, BUT PREGNANT

It is courteous to inform your superior first of your pregnancy. Alleviate any worries by explaining your plans, and especially the action plan you've formulated so that the office can continue to function smoothly in your absence, though these plans may change later.

Being pregnant is somewhat like being in a cast or on crutches because everyone, even strangers, approaches you and gets familiar. They make comments, crack jokes, ask personal details and recount their own stories...all unsolicited and all bad mannered. Pregnancy can become an exercise in patience when dealing with these situations. **Remember these comments are usually well meant, so maintain your sense of humor.** Even people you've dealt with for a long time in a professional setting suddenly see you differently and may feel uncomfortable. It is a good idea to keep the news to yourself until just before the pregnancy becomes obvious and speculation starts.

If a colleague is pregnant, wish her well and continue with business as usual. **Don't assume a woman who is pregnant needs help or a chair at all times.** If you want to be helpful, ask if there is anything you can do. Most female professionals feel much more comfortable discussing business related subjects than talking about the personal details of child-bearing and motherhood. Let the woman initiate any discussions about her pregnancy and be sensitive to her not wanting to discuss it. Don't venture your own war stories. It is mean to cause anxiety with any gory stories about childbirth.

Keep your hands off her belly! It is amazing how many people feel free to touch a pregnant woman's stomach when they would never have considered touching even her arm under other circumstances. If the woman wants to let you feel the baby kick, she'll offer, although that, too, is unprofessional. Never feel you have to touch her belly. It is perfectly acceptable and much more professional to decline.

Babies and children do not belong in an office. Leave them at home even if you are asked to stop by with the infant. Whether your visit is planned or impromptu, co-workers seldom know what to do with you once you're there. Even if the baby doesn't scream, cry or throw up, it distracts people from their work, and that is unprofessional. Worse, the situation is often awkward and embarrassing because you suddenly seem out of place in the environment in which your colleagues are used to seeing you and to which you'll eventually return. Bring a picture when you start back to work and let everyone admire it.

If you want to see a co-worker's new baby, arrange to meet her for a visit outside the office. Then you won't be the cause of a disruption to those who are not interested in the baby. Nor will you inadvertently place the woman in the awkward situation of being a misfit in her place of employment.

OFFICE ROMANCES

Although it is wiser to keep business and romance separate, wisdom often goes out the window when love rears its head. Women and men interact the most in the business environment, and dating a person you know beats picking up a stranger at a bar, in the supermarket or through the personals.

Here are some don'ts to office romances. If you ignore them, start scouring the classifieds for a new position immediately. **Never accept advances from anyone who is married, regardless of how sad a state the marriage is supposedly in. Don't get involved with someone with whom you work side by side.** The rest of the office will see it as an unholy alliance that threatens them, and it will be difficult to keep the relationship out of the office. One of you would be wise to transfer to another department. **Don't date your boss; it is awkward and inappropriate.** Your credibility will be questioned because colleagues will assume that you are trying to short-circuit the corporate ladder. At the same time, the boss's authority and impartiality will be undermined. **Dating clients is dangerous and unprofessional.** Wait until the business relationship has ended before you pursue a romantic relationship.

If you do get involved with someone in your company, don't flaunt it. No one has ever been accused of being too discreet. Don't talk about your relationship and don't let it become a topic of conversation by public displays of affection. Just as you should never involve yourself in someone else's office romance, don't involve your colleagues. It puts an unfair burden on them, especially if the relationship sours.

When a relationship ends, don't bore or burden co-workers with your pain. **Don't make disparaging remarks about your former lover**, no matter how justified you may feel them to be. Other people still must work with that person. **Don't dignify deprecating remarks about you by your former lover with a response or you will only destroy your professional image.** Smile and ignore the comments. If the person persists, speak to him or her in private about the threat to both your reputations.

SEXUAL OVERTURES

While both men and women are culprits these days, it has always taken two to start a relationship. **Don't give any suggestion of interest to an obvious overture unless you want to fan the flames.** If a person stares at you with longing, break eye contact. When someone won't let go of your hand, step back and your hand will be sure to follow.

When the overture is verbal, humor still works best. If you're too flustered by a pass to come up with the appropriate *bon mot*, at least be polite. Turning someone down with a compliment like, "I'm flattered, but..." doesn't strain a business relationship. If the person persists, get firm. Insist that you are not interested and would appreciate dropping the matter at once.

SEXIST REMARKS AND BEHAVIOR

Whether the source of a sexist remark or behavior is a man or a woman, the action is exploitative. Don't let it pass. **Deal with it immediately to keep the situation under control, but do so lightly to keep the business relationship functional.** If you seethe about the behavior, you are more likely to explode later. It is more professional and effective not to overreact.

Ask the person to explain what was meant by the remark in a neutral tone. "I don't understand what you mean by that. Would you please clarify it for me?" When called upon to elaborate, the culprit often withdraws and begins to learn behavior modification. The person will usually get the message with humor and remember it more. An unpleasant situation well handled can turn a potential foe into a business ally, so allow the person to save face if possible.

Don't chastise a person in front of others or you'll only cause further hostilities. Nor should you adopt a missionary zeal and try to change and enlighten the person. It doesn't work. Acting as a model of female professionalism will be more effective in the long run.

HARASSMENT

There is no such thing as "The Etiquette of Sexual Harassment," there is only prompt and decisive action. **If the sexist behavior is severe, warn the person that you will simply not tolerate that type of behavior and that you will report it if it continues. After the first occurrence, start diarizing the incidents in the event that further action is necessary.** Because of the seriousness of sexual harassment charges, you do not want to come across as a whiner whose accusations have no substance. If the person doesn't stop bothering you, notify the boss. Few companies deal with harassment lightly. If you feel you are not getting fair treatment, consult a lawyer.

ENTERTAINING CLIENTS

Regardless of gender, whoever extends an invitation picks up the tab, unless the person being invited is the one who benefits from the business association. **In other words, if you invite others to lunch or if your client asks to meet you for lunch, you pay.**

Some men in the business arena are still uncomfortable being invited to lunch by a woman. **It helps to state explicitly that you would like to discuss XYZ business over lunch.** Adding that you are extending the invitation on behalf of your company further clarifies that you aren't picking up the tab, your company is.

Make the reservation in your name, preferably at a restaurant or club where you are known. Arrange to pay the bill ahead of time so it is not brought to your table. If, for some reason, the restaurant cannot comply with your request, tell the waiter to bring you the check, and pay with a credit card, never cash.

If you feel that your business associate may have ulterior motives in seeing you outside the office, don't go. Insist on meeting him at your office, where you have all the files and information more readily available. It is always your prerogative to refuse an invitation.

Recently, a female executive in her family's advertising agency invited two female small business owners to dinner to meet one another, although neither stood to gain any new business in the foreseeable future. The hostess insisted on ordering lavishly for the group, including a bottle of expensive champagne and after-dinner drinks, despite the fact that one woman did not drink and the other did not like champagne. Even if she had not extended the original invitation, after usurping the role of hostess this woman should have picked up the check. When the bill came, though, she asked her guests if either one of them wanted to put the dinner on her expense account or if they should split the bill in three. For the price of a bottle of champagne, she did her reputation immense harm.

When you do get together informally with colleagues or peers, decide before the check arrives how it is to be paid. Anyone haggling over who had what, whether they are men or women, looks unprofessional. Many restaurants will take a credit card from each person and divide the bill for you. It is much better to divide the bill in equal parts even if it may cost you a few dollars more. If you order drinks or a lavish meal when others are eating salads, it is courteous to pay a more generous share rather than to be subsidized by your associates. Even when the bill is split evenly on credit cards, you can still pay the entire tip to redress the balance of payments. When you are regularly the beneficiary of this equitable division, it is a courteous gesture to pick up the entire check occasionally or alter your eating habits.

BUSINESS TRAVEL

When you travel as a representative of your company, make sure the way you dress says "business" even at a black tie affair; in other words, no jeans, no mini-skirts, no strapless dresses and no decolletage. You represent your company twenty-four hours a day.

Although many women do use their hotel rooms to conduct business, it isn't professional. Speak to the concierge or the manager about hiring a conference room. If none is available, upgrade to a suite, where you can at least close the door to the bedroom. Temporary office rentals, airline clubs, private dining rooms in restaurants or private clubs affiliated with a club you belong to are all possible facilities in which to conduct business professionally. If the town is overbooked with conventions or if you are in some small out-of-the-way place, try to meet at your client's place of business. If you have no choice but to use your hotel room, clear away all personal belongings and make the room look as businesslike as possible.

You need not hide in your hotel room every night. Don't be afraid to have a drink in the bar or to eat alone. Carry a slim briefcase to signal that you are businesswoman rather than someone looking for action. Just because you are alone, don't settle for a second class table or service. You don't get a discount for accepting anything less than first class treatment. Be polite but firm about where you wish to sit. Speak to the captain or the maître d' if the waiter ignores you. If the service still does not improve, leave or let your gratuity speak for you.

If you do feel as if the eyes of the world are focused upon you for eating alone, carry a small book to read. Forget newspapers; not only do they take too much room, they're dirty. Keep address books for major cities with the names and numbers of people you've met who live there. Dropping them a brief note or placing a call before your trip to let them know you'll be in town and would like to get together is the best way to avoid sitting at a table for one. You'll also improve your network of contacts.

At a convention or trade show, visit hospitality suites briefly to make contacts with people in a more informal setting, but avoid hanging out in them. Otherwise, you may pick up a reputation for being a party girl rather than a businesswoman.

THE GLOBAL BUSINESSWOMAN

Businessmen in other countries are getting used to the idea of American businesswomen, and will deal with you in a very professional manner, although it becomes more difficult the further east you travel. Outside the business environment, your reception may be less than professional because the man on the street may not be as comfortable with the concept of women in business.

Although you may be "Ms." at home, when you board that international flight, become a "Mrs." even if you've been divorced longer than you care to admit. Reference to family is always a good protective gesture, especially in societies that place great emphasis on familial relationships. Never date anyone you do business with overseas. The act will definitely be misunderstood by everyone and it will erode your prestige.

Remember Moslem and Buddhist societies have strict restrictions on the social intermingling of the sexes. Cover up in Moslem countries and don't drive in Saudi Arabia. Take care not to flirt in Latin countries, even if it means issuing a stern "no." **Err on the side of caution everywhere when giving gifts so that they will not be misconstrued as overtures.**

While dining alone is no problem in Canada and Western Europe, it can make you look suspect elsewhere. Stick to room service or invite some of the women from the local office to be your guests. Don't be surprised if you are seated with the wives when you are invited to dinner. Rather than take it as an insult, use it to your advantage to learn aspects of a culture unavailable to a man. An American executive and her male assistants were invited to dine at the home of her Saudi Arabian business associate, a rare honor. Much to her shock and dismay, she was shown to the kitchen to eat with the wives while her assistants were to dine with the host. The woman threw a temper tantrum and walked out on the dinner. She insulted her host who was only acting according to his religious and social dictates. Had she been as savvy as she professed to be, she would have realized beforehand that this could happen, and would have met with her staff to prep them on the objective of the dinner and how they were to behave. Then, if she felt the possibility of being segregated would undermine her position, she should have feigned a headache, stayed at the hotel and debriefed her assistants upon their return.

Whatever you do, don't start proselytizing to anyone about women's rights and the changes that should be made to correct their position within that society. It is none of your business, even if you think you know the culture well. Even if you are asked for a comment, abstain.

While international business travel may make more demands and impose more restrictions on a woman, don't let that block you from seeking a world of opportunity. Do the homework, be prepared to make the required adjustments, and you stand to be enriched personally and professionally.

THE FAST TRACK

1. Realize that differences in style between men and women are often mistaken for breaches in etiquette.

2. Drop the ladies' manners, but don't act like one of the boys. Adopt a gender neutral style of behavior.

3. Greet clients and colleagues with a smile and a handshake, not kisses.

4. Keep your hands to yourself.

5. Don't assume friendliness is a romantic overture.

6. Keep one-on-one meetings to daytime hours.

7. Don't call co-workers at home except with specific work-related questions.

8. Never call a woman girl, gal or lady.

9. Don't call anyone sweetie, honey or dear, regardless of age or gender.

10. Don't be condescending to other women because you've achieved a higher position.

11. Don't try to turn your staff into your pals.

12. Intimate details of your personal life are not topics of conversation in a business setting.

13. Inform your boss first of your pregnancy, but wait until it's necessary to do so.

14. Exercise patience and retain your sense of humor in handling uninvited comments and advice.

15. Don't assume a pregnant woman is in need of your help. Ask.

16. Confine conversations to business topics. Let the mother-to-be initiate conversations about the pregnancy.

17. Don't touch a pregnant woman's belly.

18. Don't offer to let business associates touch your belly.

19. Babies and children do not belong in an office.

20. Keep business and romance separate.

21. Never accept advances from a married man.

22. Don't get involved with someone in your department.

23. Don't date the boss or clients.

24. Be discreet about an office romance.

25. Don't get your colleagues involved in your romance or vice versa.

26. When a romance ends, don't make disparaging remarks about your former lover.

27. Don't dignify your ex's nasty remarks with a response.

28. Give no indication of interest to an obvious sexual overture.

29. Turn someone down with a compliment to soften the blow.

30. Deal with sexist remarks immediately, but lightly, so the business relationship remains functional and the person is allowed to save face.

31. Deal with sexual harassment promptly and decisively.

32. Specify that you would like to discuss business when extending an invitation to a man who is uncomfortable with a woman paying the bill.

33. Whoever extends the invitation or benefits from the association picks up the tab.

34. Extend an invitation on behalf of your company to ease the blow of you picking up the tab.

35. If you suspect someone has ulterior motives, refuse that person's invitations.

36. Make sure the way you dress says "business!"

37. Don't use hotel rooms to do business.

38. Don't hang out in hospitality suites.

39. When travelling internationally, use "Mrs." Refer to family and children often.

40. Never date anyone with whom you do business overseas.

41. Err on the side of caution when giving gifts.

42. If you're segregated from the men, don't take offense. Use it.

43. Don't proselytize about women's rights.

DISABILITY ETIQUETTE

Etiquette imposes consideration for others. It demands willingness to discipline oneself for the sake of others, or for a principle. It acknowledges high standards of behavior and is valuable to the community because, by acknowledging them, it strengthens them.

Millicent Fenwick

The only ones who have a handicap are those who can't get along with others.

Bill Veeck

Passage of the Americans with Disabilities Act opens the way for many persons with a mental or physical impairment to enter the workforce. Consequently, many people will be dealing regularly with co-workers with disabilities whom they may have avoided pre-

CHAPTER

15

viously. The disabilities of others often discomfit us because they remind us of our own vulnerability.

A disability is simply another condition that a person must cope with. Unfortunately, persons with disabilities also have to cope with restrictions imposed by physical structures and the attitudes of the non-disabled. Some simple rules of etiquette and a large dose of common sense can go a long way in making everyone more comfortable.

COMMON COURTESIES

A person with a disability deserves the same respect you would extend to any other adult. Never act as though the person doesn't exist by using a third party as a go-between when you can address the person directly. The disabled are not inanimate objects.

Persons who have disabilities also may have families, pets, jobs, hobbies, cultural interests and sports that they play. Get to know them and their interests the same way you would anyone else, by making conversation. You may be surprised at all the activities that appeal to them. **Focus on those abilities rather than the disability.**

The disability is not taboo, though. Respect their privacy, as you would want yours protected, if the issue seems to be sensitive. Take your cue from them. But, if the disability comes up naturally in conversation, talk about it. However, if you are with several other people, don't turn the impairment into a topic for group discussion. Refrain from being reverential or patronizing toward a person with an impairment. Let them guide you if you don't know what to say or how to behave. Relax!

Don't be embarrassed if you happen to use a common expression that refers to the person's disability like "I hear you received a promotion" or "I ran into your boss" or "See you tomorrow."

Offer assistance, if you want to, but wait for the person to accept before you do anything. Many people with impairments are very capable of functioning independently. Be considerate of the extra time it might take to say or do something. Don't appeal to others to help, and don't respond to someone with an impairment with a "There, but for the grace of God..." attitude.

When you plan a meeting or function that includes someone with a disability, think about the needs of the person ahead of time. If an insurmountable barrier seems to exist, make that information available beforehand and discuss it. Perhaps the person with the impairment, through experience, can offer a solution you never considered, like having someone act as "translator" for a slide presentation.

How persons with disabilities are portrayed causes much stereotyping and misconception. A disabling condition may or may not be handicapping, so use the term "disability" and save "handicap" for golf. **Out of respect for the individual, focus on the person before the disability.** Say, "the person with the disability" rather than "the disabled person." Nor is the person a condition, so never say "the epileptic"; rather, if it is necessary to add a qualifier, saying "the person who has epilepsy" is much more considerate and accurate.

The National Easter Seal Society advises choosing words that carry positive, non-judgmental connotations. Here are some of their recommendations:

Eliminate:	Replace with:
victim	person with/person who has/ person who experienced
cripple(d)	person with a disability/individual who has a disability caused by
afflicted with or by	the person has
invalid (= not valid)	the person who has a disability from or caused by
wheelchair bound	uses a wheelchair
homebound employment	employed in the home
unfortunate, pitiful, poor, deaf and dumb, deformed, crip, blind as a bat, or any other cliché that is judgmental or stereotypical	NO REPLACEMENT

To that list, I would add "handicap," which is particularly offensive in the workplace because of its negative historical references. In the past, people who had any kind of disability were unable to find work and were reduced to being beggars with "a cap in hand," hence "handicap." Now, people with disabilities are able to contribute in the business arena according to their individual capabilities.

WHEELCHAIR ETIQUETTE

The wheelchair is an extension of the body of the person who uses it. **Don't lean, hold on to or sit on it.** Nor should you patronize people in wheelchairs by invading their personal space with a pat on the head just because it is at a similar height to a child's. **For an extended conversation, position yourself at their eye level since it is much lower than yours;** it prevents a lot of neck strain for both of you.

Allow a person who uses a wheelchair or crutches to keep them within reach unless you are specifically requested to move them. Offer help, but wait for the person to accept it. **Push a wheelchair only after asking the occupant if you may do so.**

If you're planning any kind of function, give thought to the location and whether or not it has wheelchair access. In giving directions, take into consideration obstacles like steep hills, stairs and weather. The time it takes them to get from place to place may also differ from yours, especially if it is necessary to take a circuitous route.

Handicap parking is specially designed and located to meet the needs of persons who have disabilities. Understand the need for this handicap parking and don't use it. Leave it for those who truly need it.

All the considerations mentioned should also be extended to persons who rely on crutches, canes or walkers for assistance.

VISUAL IMPAIRMENT ETIQUETTE

Vision loss can vary in degree. Persons with visual impairments may see some things, but not others. Regardless of the extent of the impairment, they should always be treated with the same respect you would give a sighted person.

Guide dogs are working animals, not pets. **Do not distract a guide dog by trying to get its attention or pet it.** Allow guide dogs to accompany their owners into all stores and buildings. Because they are highly trained animals, they will require no special attention other than that given by the owners.

When offering assistance, ask if it would be helpful; sometimes a person who is blind prefers to get along unaided. **If the person wants your help, offer your elbow.** You will then be walking half a step ahead, and the movements of your body will indicate when to change direction, when to stop and start and when to step up or down. Watch out for half-open doors; they're a hazard to everyone, but especially to the person who is blind.

Give directions with the person who is blind as the reference point, not yourself. For instance, "You are facing Broadway and you will have to cross it to go east on Wall Street."

When helping people who are blind into a car or taxi, place their hands on the inside door handle and let them get in alone. If the door is closed, open it for them or guide their hands to the car door just above the handle, and let them open the door for themselves.

When entering an unfamiliar office or a restaurant, offer your arm to guide the person with the visual impairment. **Always use specifics like "right" or "left."** Then, place his or her hand on the back of the chair so he or she can be seated without further assistance.

When accompanying people who are blind, offer to describe the surroundings. In describing the placement of food when dining, use an imaginary clock as reference. For example, mashed potatoes are at one o'clock, broccoli is at four o'clock and the chicken breast is at seven o'clock.

If you enter a room in which a person with a visual impairment is alone, make your presence known by speaking. Always identify yourself when greeting a person with severe vision loss. If others are with you, be sure to introduce them, too, and specify who is where. Say, for example, "On my left is Bill Smith and on my right is Mary Jones." When offering a handshake, say something like, "Allow me to shake your hand." If the person extends a hand first, be sure to take it or explain why. "I'd like to shake your hand, but I'm afraid I may drop all these files."

Talk to a person without sight as you would to a person who can see. **In a group, use the people's names as a clue to whom you're talking and be sure to address those who can't see by name if they are expected to reply.** Speak directly to the person in a normal tone of voice. Raising your voice never helps anyone see better, whether they are sighted or not. **While you should always excuse yourself when you are leaving, it is more important to do so when ending a conversation with a person without sight so the person isn't left talking to thin air.**

When a person with visual impairments has to sign a document, providing a guiding device such as a ruler or card helps a great deal. In handing money to a person who is blind, separate all the bills into denominations and specify if they are ones, fives, tens, etc. Coins will be identified by touch.

HEARING LOSS ETIQUETTE

Hearing losses range from mild to severe and can influence the way a person communicates or responds to the speech of others.

Never talk from another room. When people who are hearing impaired can't see you, they may not be aware that you are speaking. **Be sure you have the person's attention before you start speaking;** if necessary, wave a hand, give a tap on the shoulder or make some other signal. Turn off the television or radio and reduce background noises so you can be heard.

Place yourself facing the light rather than letting it shine in the face of the person with the hearing loss. Keep your hands away from your face and don't eat, chew or smoke while speaking. A moustache may hide your mouth and make it more difficult to understand you, so don't get frustrated if you have to repeat yourself, write it down or get a translator.

Speak slowly and clearly, without exaggerated lip movements or shouting. Face the other person, preferably on the same eye level. Do not turn away until you've finished talking. The person who has a severe hearing loss will rely on your facial expressions, gestures and body language for help in understanding. **Speaking directly into a person's ear won't help, and may even be harmful.**

If a person has difficulty understanding you, don't keep repeating the same phrases; be flexible. Switch the words and rephrase the sentence. If difficulty persists, write it down or use a sign language interpreter. Speak directly to the person rather than the interpreter.

Fatigue, stress, illness or fright affect those with hearing impairments as they affect us all. Be aware of external factors like jet lag or a common cold that can increase difficulty in communicating and adjust your behavior accordingly.

SPEECH IMPAIRMENT ETIQUETTE

Give your complete, unhurried attention to those who have difficulty speaking. Allow them the time to express themselves. Don't correct their pronunciation, complete their sentences or try to speak for them. Encourage them to speak for themselves, but give help when they indicate they need it.

Ask questions that require short answers or a nod or shake of the head, and the person with the speech impairment will have less trouble communicating. However, don't pretend to understand when you don't. Repeat what you thought you understood. The person's reactions will guide you.

DEVELOPMENTAL DISABILITY ETIQUETTE

Don't infantilize people who are developmentally disabled. Treat them as normally as possible and set the same standards for them as you would for others. If, for example, the person tries to get very affectionate, explain that such behavior is not appropriate in a business setting. Be careful of touching the person. It signals such behavior, often used by a person with developmental disabilities to curry favor, is OK.

Persons with developmental disabilities tend to be very sensitive to body language and tone of voice, so make sure your silent messages are non-threatening. **Be firm but pleasant; try to address them with a smile on your face and in your voice. Don't demoralize the person by using accusatory language** like, "You made a mistake." Instead, ask, "How about doing it like this?" Remember the tact you should be using to address all employees.

If the person has a job coach, don't make the person feel inconsequential by dealing only with the job coach. Speak to the person directly. If the person has difficulty in understanding your needs or instructions, then say, "I'll let coach work on that with you," and the coach can take over.

Repetition is very important in teaching a person with developmental disabilities, so be patient. If patience is not your strong suit, delegate the supervisory task to someone else. Check regularly to verify that they still understand how to perform their job.

MANAGING EMPLOYEES WITH DISABILITIES

Disability is not synonymous with inability. When interviewing a potential employee, focus on the abilities rather than the disability. Think of hiring qualified individuals who may happen to have a disability. Ask questions about the person's abilities. Focus on those skills that are required to do the job. As Alfred E. Smith said of Franklin Delano Roosevelt during his campaign for governor, "The Governor of the State of New York does not have to be an acrobat."

Once people with disabilities start working for you, you must hold them as accountable as you would any other employee to meet the needs of your department. Don't be over-obliging or patronizing, but be sensitive and give both positive and negative feedback periodically.

THE FAST TRACK

1. Treat someone with a disability with the same respect you would extend to any other adult.

2. Deal with the person directly rather than through a third party.

3. Focus on the person's abilities, not the disability.

4. A disability is not a taboo topic, nor is it a topic for group discussion. Respect a person's privacy.

5. When offering assistance, wait for the person to accept.

6. Put the person before the disability.

7. Choose words that are positive and non-judgmental.

8. Don't lean, sit on or hold on to someone's wheelchair.

9. Position yourself at eye level to converse with a person in a wheelchair.

10. Keep a wheelchair or crutches within reach of the person.

11. Push a wheelchair only if the occupant wants you to.

Visual Impairments:

1. Do not distract or pet a guide dog.

2. Don't take a person who is blind by the arm; let that person take your elbow.

3. Give directions from the reference point of the person who is blind, and use specifics like "right" or "left."

4. Offer to describe the surroundings to a person who cannot see.

5. Always make your presence known and identify yourself when greeting someone who is visually impaired, and excuse yourself when you are leaving.

6. Use names to let the person who is blind know who you are speaking to.

Hearing Impairments:

1. Get the attention of a person with a hearing loss before you start speaking.

2. Place yourself in the light so the person who is hearing impaired can watch your face.

3. Don't eat, chew or smoke while speaking to a person with a hearing impairment.

4. Speak slowly, without exaggerated lip movements.

5. Never speak into the ear of someone with a hearing impairment.

Speech Impairments:

1. Give your complete, unhurried attention to those who have difficulty speaking. Allow them time to express themselves.

2. Don't correct the pronunciation of someone with a speech impairment.

3. Ask questions that require short answers.

4. Don't pretend to understand someone with a speech impairment if you don't.

Developmental Disabilities:

1. Don't infantilize someone who is developmentally disabled.

2. Don't touch someone with developmental disabilities because you may be sending the wrong signals.

3. Be firm, but remain pleasant when you deal with someone who is developmentally disabled. Keep a smile on your face and in your voice.

4. Don't demoralize a person with developmental disabilities by using accusatory language.

5. Exercise patience with a person with developmental disabilities.

JOB SEARCHES AND SWITCHES

Suit the action to the word; the word to the action.

Shakespeare

Most people who fail to get the job they really want fail not because they are not qualified but because they failed in the interview. And most failures occur because they aren't prepared.

David W. Crawley, Jr.

Etiquette alone will not get you the job of your dreams, but a lack of etiquette will certainly prevent you from being hired. Bad manners will turn an interviewer off faster than a lack of experience because skilled interviewers are trained to pick up all the nuances of behavior. Be astute, and demonstrate that you know how to behave among civilized company and in the business arena.

CHAPTER

16

NETWORKING

The wider a base of connections you have when you start your job search, the greater your chance of success. While you obviously cannot enlist the help of your colleagues, it is acceptable to contact other business associates and let them know you are planning a career move. **However, if you haven't spoken to someone in years, it is presumptuous to call and expect help.**

Keep in touch with acquaintances with an occasional telephone call or a note. A successful management consultant I know makes a point of contacting five people a day just to stay in touch. She claims it takes a year to work her way through her Rolodex once, but she can always call on someone with confidence when she does need them.

When you do spread the word that you are shopping for new career opportunities, remain low key. **It is not polite to try to press someone into giving referrals or taking a copy of your resumé.** Once you've made your position known, let the other person extend the offer of assistance.

If you've been given a referral, don't take that as a carte blanche invitation to monopolize the person's time. **After you've introduced yourself, ask if the person has the time to talk with you; if not, make an appointment to talk at that person's convenience.** After all, he or she is doing you a favor. If the person offers to give you five minutes, don't extend it to fifteen.

Recently a man who had been referred to me by a business associate called to ask how he, too, could become an etiquette and protocol consultant. Because I was working against a deadline, I explained I could speak to him for only ten minutes. For the next half hour he had "just one more" question about all aspects of my business, including my marketing plan, despite my constant attempts to terminate the call. I finally had to get firm and hang up on the man.

HANDLING THE HEADHUNTER

Headhunters are more properly known as executive search firms. These companies are several steps above personnel agencies. Contrary to the way personnel agencies function, executive search firms seek qualified people for the jobs they have listed.

When a headhunter calls to ask you for a referral for a certain job, he may actually be fishing to see if you are interested in the position. A meeting with a headhunter can be the fastest way to determine your true worth in the business arena.

Honesty is the best policy in dealing with a headhunter if you expect develop a successful relationship. Anything less will surely backfire. **Don't try to act blasé about finding another position and don't pretend to be anything other than who you are at your best.** Unless you're a member of Actor's Equity, no one will believe you and the headhunter will be insulted by your disrespect.

The Interview

Before you interview with a company, do your homework so you arrive prepared. Learn about the company because it displays an interest in the organization. A skilled interviewer will let you talk about what you know of the company rather than lecture you about it. All the information you give should be public knowledge, gleaned from publications and the annual report. If an acquaintance within the organization has made you privy to inside information, keep it under your hat. **It is bad form to divulge information given to you in confidence.**

Bring any support materials that have been requested. If you prefer to tailor your resumé to the requirements of the job, don't tell the interviewer you forgot; it implies that you didn't care enough to prepare it. Instead, tell the interviewer that you'll be happy to have it sent over by messenger the next morning.

Before you leave the house, check yourself over carefully in a full length mirror. The way you present yourself at the interview shows respect for yourself, the interviewer and the company you hope to be employed by. **Don't overdress, but dress in the best clothes that you would wear to your office.** Make sure that everything you have on is in good repair, clean and polished, and that you are well-groomed. If in doubt about what to do, refer to chapter 2. No one will give you a chance to present your impeccable credentials if your appearance doesn't match.

Be on time for the interview. **Punctuality is crucial in forming that initial impression of your businesslike mien.** Arrive at the appointment early, if possible, to scout out where you are to go.

Then, take a walk and reappear at the receptionist's desk five minutes before the appointed time.

If you are going to be late, call. Interviewers are human, and they do understand that crises can occur; but, like everyone else, they don't like to be left hanging. A comptroller with an unusual name who stood an interviewer up at one company, after the interviewer had agreed to stay after hours to accommodate him, was refused an interview several months later at another firm by that same interviewer who had herself changed jobs.

Treat everyone at the company where you are interviewing, from the security guard to the receptionist to the secretary, with respect. It is not unusual for the interviewer to solicit the opinion of the secretary about your suitability; nor is it unusual for the secretary to express an opinion even if none was asked. By treating that secretary well, you may have won an ally when you are called back for a second interview.

Extend your hand in greeting when you meet the interviewer, and use the person's name when thanking him or her for seeing you. Don't forget to smile; it creates a rapport more quickly than anything else you can do. Being too serious, stiff or formal will not make you look more mature; it will make you look ill at ease and nervous. Keeping a smile glued on your face throughout the interview will make you look inane, though.

Take your cue about whether to use the surname or first name from the interviewer. **Use first names only if the interviewer is your age or younger and has used your given name.** If in doubt, stick to surnames until you are invited to use the person's given name. Don't repeat the name over and over during the interview, only when you greet the interviewer and when you leave. Using the person's name over and over comes across as an affectation.

Sit where you are told to sit; it is the interviewer's office, not yours. If the interviewer hasn't shown you a chair, sit when he or she sits. It is a bad power play to remain standing. If there are several chairs, ask which to take. If you are given your choice, sit closest to the interviewer as long as you don't crowd the person. Three feet is the ideal distance so you neither invade the interviewer's personal space nor appear too distant. Don't dawdle over your decision or it will create needless tension and make you look indecisive in business, too. Sit up straight. Better still, lean slightly forward to indicate that you are interested and alert. Leaning back with your arms crossed can be misconstrued as a defensive posture.

Be friendly, but don't try to turn the interviewer into your buddy. Don't discuss personal matters, yours or theirs; keep the conversation and questions pertinent to the job. Don't be flip or phony, and don't joke; it implies a lack of seriousness.

Speak to be heard. **If you are asked about your former employer and colleagues, speak well of them.** Don't blame them for any failures on your part. It's bad form to speak negatively of someone who isn't there to defend himself. Instead, phrase your answers in a positive manner. Instead of saying, "My current boss is a misogynist who wouldn't promote a woman if he were in front of a firing squad," try "Opportunities for women are limited in upper management at my present place of employment, whereas your company has an excellent reputation for its support of women in management." And don't admit to personal faults that could create doubt about your suitability for the position. A job interview is not the time to state that your greatest life achievement is your victory over drug addiction.

Be forthcoming in your responses and answer fully, rather than with an uncommunicative yes or no. If thrown a trick question, give yourself a moment to think and impress the interviewer with your thoughtfulness by making a comment like, "That's an interesting question. Let me think," rather than making a comment or giving a look that implies the interviewer is lost in left field. Always take the time if you need to think about an answer.

Polish your listening skills. No one ever likes to be interrupted. And, by interrupting, you can't answer the question properly. If you have difficulty hearing what's being said, ask the interviewer to speak up. If you don't understand a question, ask to have it repeated. Let your body show that you are listening by your facial expression and your posture. Remember to make eye contact about 60 percent of the time to convey careful attention without staring the interviewer into submission. Anything less will make you look insecure and like you have something to hide.

Don't fidget, tap a pencil, drum your fingers, play with your hair, swing your foot, wring your hands or your handkerchief, bite your fingernails or chew gum unless you want the interviewer to shoot you or usher you out as quickly as possible. The most brilliant answers will be wasted if you talk with your hands in front of your mouth. **Remember that the interviewer's desk and anything on top of or behind it are off limits.** Don't touch or pick up anything, even out of nervousness. It will be misconstrued, as will trying to read anything that is lying on the interviewer's desk.

Don't discuss money or benefits until you are offered the job. It's putting the cart before the horse and implies your only concern is for your welfare rather than for your contribution to the company. Once you are at the negotiating stage, couch your demands for benefits in terms of benefits to the company. A country club membership should not be requested because the spouse plays tennis every day. Instead, it should be requested as a place to make new business contacts and to entertain clients.

Never ask to make notes. It looks juvenile and implies a bad memory. Write down only essentials like a telephone number or a follow-up appointment. Be sure to carry a good pen and a small notepad for that purpose.

Interviewers are not perfect and it is always possible that you may encounter one who is rude. However, you make no brownie points by responding with rudeness. By keeping your composure you demonstrate an ability to handle difficult people. The interviewer's behavior may be a test to measure your temper.

Although interviewers should be well aware of questions that overstep acceptable limits and invade your privacy, they may ask them anyway for a variety of reasons. The way you handle the answer can terminate your chances or show you to be a savvy individual who can handle anything thrown at you. **Don't give in and answer whatever is asked. You will come across as someone who has no backbone. Nor should you alienate and embarrass the interviewer by calling him or her to task for asking illegal questions.** Smile and say nothing. If that is not possible, phrase your answer in a way that will lay their worries about you to rest, "I feel that I am at that perfect age where I have the wisdom of experience and the energy to execute anything that is demanded of me." You might want to give some thought to potentially intrusive questions and how best to handle them before the interview so you will appear calm and won't react with hostility.

Be sensitive to signals in conversation and in body language that indicate the end of the interview. If you feel the interview has gone well, you may want to make a closing statement in one sentence that summarizes your desire to work for that organization. Never, ever, beg, plead or whine to try to cajole the interviewer into giving you the job. Nor should you express or imply that you expect to hear from the interviewer. Be sure to ask about the company's notification schedule if the interviewer hasn't told you. To leave without it is to imply that you feel you didn't get the job, and you leave a negative final impression that may make the interviewer reassess your potential. **Smile, shake hands, thank the interviewer for seeing you, remembering to use the person's name, then leave with the same strong, positive stride with which you entered.**

Post-Interview Etiquette

Always write a thank you note. While no one is ever hired on the basis of a thank you note, a well written note can give you an edge, especially if there is a follow-up interview for the job. Make sure your note isn't of the formula variety that begins, "It was a pleasure to meet you. Thank you for taking the time out of your busy schedule to see me." Make reference instead to the interview, to a shared moment, to an amusing exchange or to an interesting challenge that was presented.

If you want the note to be memorable, make sure it is a sincere expression of gratitude that makes the interviewer feel good about him- or herself. Reference to the person's skill in interviewing, generosity of spirit and sensitivity toward you, if justified, will make the note believable and win you an ally for the rest of the hiring process. Be careful not to go overboard in your praise, or you will undo all the good of sending it by appearing insincere.

The note may be typed, especially if your handwriting is illegible, because it has a more businesslike appearance. Keep the note short, or you'll impress the interviewer with your inability to get to the point.

Remember also to send a thank you note to anyone who helped you get the interview with a referral. You never know when you'll need them for future referrals. In the note, you may mention the outcome of the interview or how their assistance helped you.

Giving Notice

Always inform your superior in person when you've accepted another position. It is very bad form to have him find out from someone else, and will probably make it more difficult for you to get a referral from that employer in the future.

Request that your new employer give you the amount of time necessary to tie up loose ends at your present position and to transfer the work to someone else. Often your current employer will request you leave the premises immediately rather than prolong your stay. Be prepared for this eventuality by keeping your work and your files as up to date and as organized as possible during your job search. Pack your personal belongings as quickly and quietly as possible, tell those near you that you've enjoyed working with them and leave without a fuss.

GETTING THE AX

Even grown men cry when they get fired or downsized, and it does help to release the emotion. But, try to do it in private. **A public display of emotion will only embarrass you when you think back on the situation, and you may be too embarrassed to maintain contacts with people who may become friends and allies at a later date.**

Say little or nothing except a positive parting statement like, "I'm sorry to go. I've always enjoyed working for this organization. May I get a letter of recommendation and use you as a reference?" Losing your temper or spewing vitriol may make you feel better momentarily, but will alienate people you may need for references and justify their decision in firing you.

Don't write any letters that you may regret at a later date. If you feel the action is unjustified, let your lawyer or your union act on your behalf. Try to retain your self-respect. Remember that success is the best revenge, so pick yourself up, dust yourself off and get started on your next achievement.

DELIVERING THE BAD NEWS

One of the most difficult acts for any executive is to fire people. It never gets easier, but you can learn to do it with style. There is never a good time to lower the ax, so the sooner you deliver the blow, the better.

Never take a person to lunch to deliver the bad news. It is cruel to deliver such an emotional blow in public, and you can bet the employee will get emotional. **Always fire someone in the privacy of your office.** Keep the details confidential.

This is not a time for small talk. **Don't stall;** get to the point and deliver the bad news in as kind and constructive a manner as possible. Don't try to elicit any responses; of course the person is hurt, angry, scared and a whole range of other negative emotions. Tell the person of any special arrangements for outplacement services or severance. Offer a reference if possible. The less opportunity the person has to speak, the better for both of you. Never, ever get into personal issues.

Maintaining Contacts

Leaving a place of employment is a time to sever some relationships and to strengthen others you wish to continue, especially now that you are no longer peers competing for the same promotions. The onus is on you to keep those business and personal ties you value. Inviting those individuals to lunch or dinner is a good opening to a continued relationship.

Send your former boss a note of thanks when you leave, and make a point of keeping in touch over the years. The next time you change jobs, you'll have to call on that former employer for a reference. A person you haven't kept in touch with for years might have scant recollection of you and may not be inclined to give you more than a perfunctory reference.

The Interviewer's Role

The interviewer represents the company to the potential employee. The impression that interviewer makes will help to attract the best candidates for the job. Your manner should set a tone that is reflective of the company, be it conservative or cutting edge. If you act very conservatively, the interviewee will probably react accordingly, and if the company is very relaxed in its behavior, you may assume incorrectly that the person will not fit in.

Don't keep the interviewee waiting; it is a petty power play that won't facilitate a smooth meeting. Greet interviewees in the reception area or have your secretary escort them to your office. Shake hands and indicate where you would like them to sit. Let interviewees know if you would prefer to be addressed by your first name.

Don't fidget. It is distracting to the interviewee. Make good eye contact and give the interviewee your undivided attention. Have your secretary hold calls while you're interviewing. Keep your questions clear and to the point, and speak loudly enough so you can be heard easily.

When the interview is over, let the person know. Give some indication when he or she can expect to hear from you. Shake hands and show the interviewee out. **It is good manners to let everyone know the outcome of the interview within two weeks.**

If you've advertised for the position, you need only contact those applicants you wish to interview. However, it will enhance the reputation of your company if you extend the courtesy of acknowledging all the responses you're received.

To avoid unnecessary gossip and fears, you should let those who will be working with a new employee know that you are interviewing. Leaving them to guess what is going on will only turn everyone into nervous wrecks fearful for their own job security.

Once you've made the decision to hire an individual, introduce the new employee to his or her co-workers as soon as possible to establish a sense of belonging. Appoint one individual, preferably the one who will be working most closely with the new employee, either as a peer or as an immediate supervisor, to take the person to lunch at company expense so the two will have some time away from the distractions of the office to get acquainted. That individual can then make further introductions to others at the company and guide the person through the maze of the corporate culture.

THE FAST TRACK

1. Keep in touch with people to keep your network strong.

2. Don't ask someone you haven't spoken to in years to help you in your job search.

3. Don't try to press someone into giving you a referral.

4. Make an appointment to speak with a referral at that person's convenience, not yours.

6. Don't try to act blasé about finding another job.

7. Don't pretend to be anyone other than who you are when interviewing.

8. Never divulge information given you in confidence.

9. Be well-groomed and appropriately dressed for an interview.

10. Be punctual for interviews.

11. Treat everyone in the company at which you are interviewing respectfully.

12. Shake hands in greeting.

13. Thank the interviewer for seeing you.

14. Unless asked to, use first names only if the interviewer is your age or younger and has used your given name first.

15. Sit where you are told to sit.

16. Don't remain standing after the interviewer sits down.

17. Don't try to turn the interviewer into your buddy.

18. Speak up.

19. Speak well of former colleagues and employers.

20. Listen!

21. Don't touch anything on or behind the interviewer's desk.

22. Don't answer questions that are unethical or invade your privacy. Smile and say nothing.

23. Smile, shake hands and thank the interviewer, then exit with a positive stride.

24. Always write a thank you note to the interviewer immediately.

25. Write a thank you to those who helped you get the interview, and let them know the outcome.

26. Inform your boss personally when you've accepted another position. Stay in touch after you leave.

27. If you're fired, try not to break down in front of your co-workers. Say as little as possible.

28. Don't say or write in anger anything you may later regret.

29. Fire a person in the privacy of your office.

30. Deliver the bad news as quickly and kindly as possible.

31. Let others in the office know when you are interviewing.

32. When hiring, treat the interviewee with the same courtesies you would a client appointment.

33. Let people know the outcome of their interviews within two weeks.

34. Introduce the new employee to co-workers as soon as possible.

35. Appoint one individual to look after the new employee.

BEYOND ETIQUETTE

The great thing in this world is not so much where we are but where we are moving.

Oliver Wendell Holmes

Etiquette is a word coined in the reign of Louis XIV when he posted etiquettes, or notices, that outlined correct behavior at his court. Books on civility and table manners had been written as early as the thirteenth century. Even George Washington wrote a book on etiquette. While many rules are surprisingly the same, etiquette, unlike protocol, is flexible and changes as cultures evolve.

As egalitarian as American society is, a mastery of manners has always been and still is an arbiter of class and status in both the social and the business arenas. Dowagers were once able to discern a person's background by the way that person spooned the soup. Fortunately, etiquette has become much more accessible. A mastery of etiquette skills is within everyone's grasp. In America, even paupers can become princes, in act if not in fact. But knowledge without implementation is wasted. Dreams and aspirations are achievable only if you act upon the knowledge.

CHAPTER

17

By dedicating yourself to excellence, to pursuing your own vision of your personal ideal, and then taking the appropriate actions, you can achieve the confidence and polish necessary to success.

Cary Grant, the epitome of suave sophistication tempered with a sense of humor, is a perfect example. Mr. Grant was born Archie Leach, a Cockney vaudevillian. After the movie studios renamed him, he played the role of Cary Grant, molding himself into the type of gentleman he aspired to be. Late in life, Mr. Grant said that he lost track of when he stopped playing the part and actually became the character.

To become a businessperson who negotiates the corridors of power with ease and grace, manners must become an integral part of your daily behavior. If you do make a mistake in etiquette, let it go or, if necessary, apologize and go on. Many faux pas can even be comical in retrospect. Just remember to learn from them.

According to studies, it takes twenty-one consecutive days to make or break a pattern of behavior. After a hundred consecutive days, that behavior becomes automatic. However, it takes only thirty days to forget a new pattern of behavior. With only eight days of constant reinforcement, though, you'll remember 90 percent of what you learned. Spend a few minutes each morning giving thought to how you would like to be perceived and what adjustments you'll have to make in your conduct to be effective. Give thought at the end of the day to what actions could have been improved, and you'll be prepared when the situation next arises. Take the time before every meal at home to reflect on polite dining etiquette, and those manners will soon become automatic.

Some time ago I cut out the copy of an ad and framed it for my desk as a daily reminder. Unfortunately, I don't remember what product the ad was for to credit the clever copy writer. You might want to note these succinct words of advice too:

> look famous
> be legendary
> appear complex
> act easy
> radiate presence
> travel light
> seem a dream
> prove real

A mastery of business etiquette is a vital business skill, more important than an MBA, for those who want to get to the top and stay there. Diana McLellan once wrote in the *Washingtonian*, "Good manners will get you where you're going faster than a speeding BMW." As important as corporate etiquette is in determining how you will be perceived, it is not enough. Sales executives are often exhorted to sell the sizzle, not the steak. Etiquette is the sizzle. You cannot continue to sell sizzle to the same people without ever serving the steak. Learn to do your job well, to give more than you get. Business annals are filled with success stories of people who gave 150 percent and of losers who practiced the theory of entitlement.

Most important, be ethical in your dealings. Etiquette and ethics ideally go hand in hand, but the two are not synonymous. Etiquette is acceptable behavior and ethics is moral behavior. Many a person has been conned by a suave, silver-tongued rogue while giving short shrift to a concerned, caring bumpkin. Don't make the mistake of judging others only on the basis of their manners. Given my druthers, I'd take *mores* over *politesse* any day. And so would most companies. Business etiquette has to be considered within the guidelines of a corporation's code of ethics. Over half the Fortune 500 companies have taken some steps to implement an officially endorsed code of ethics.

Yet, a Gallup Poll shows that public confidence in the integrity of business people is on the decline. A reader survey report by *Working Woman* magazine shows that ethics have deteriorated alarmingly. Of particular concern is the frequency of unethical behavior in interpersonal relationships like taking credit for others' work (67 percent), violating confidentiality (64 percent), lying to employees (62 percent), discrimination (47 percent) and sexual harrassment (41 percent).

Ethics and the pursuit of profit often seem to work at cross-purposes in business. But, according to Dr. Kenneth Blanchard and Dr. Norman Vincent Peale in their book *The Power of Ethical Management*, being ethical is good business not just because it is the right thing to do, but also because it results in a more successful operation. Companies are more likely to be profitable when clearly stated corporate values are communicated to all employees. In fact, most American companies that have paid consecutive dividends for 100 years or more consider ethics a high priority.

While the leaders of an organization determine the ethical standards within a corporation's culture, ultimately each employee is responsible for adhering to ethical business practices. When codes of ethics are given more than lip service and it is clear that doing the wrong thing is hazardous to one's career, few employees will take ethical risks.

Loyalty to a friend does not excuse insider trading. Gift-giving is not acceptable when it is intended or perceived as bribery. Even something as seemingly innocuous as moving a golf ball "just a little" on a client outing can be a person's downfall. A lack of integrity in one area is perceived as indicative of behavior in all areas.

By adhering to standards of both etiquette and ethics in your personal and professional life, you will be at ease in any situation you find yourself, and you will set an exemplary standard for others to follow.

Rudyard Kipling's poem "If..." is addressed to a boy, but the moral is valid for all. Gender neutralize it if you must, but heed its message.

Enjoy the process!

IF-

If you can keep your head when all about you
Are losing theirs and blaming it on you,
If you can trust yourself when all men doubt you,
But make allowances for their doubting too;
If you can wait and not be tired by waiting,
Or being lied about, don't deal in lies,
Or being hated don't give way to hating,
And yet don't look too good nor talk too wise:

If you can dream—and not make dreams your master,
If you can think—and not make thoughts your aim,
If you can meet with Triumph and Disaster
And treat those two imposters just the same;
If you can bear to hear the truth you've spoken
Twisted by knaves to make a trap for fools,
Or watch the things you gave your life to, broken,
And stoop and build 'em up with worn out tools:

If you can make one heap of all your winnings;
And risk it on one turn of pitch-and-toss,
And lose, and start again at your beginnings
And never breathe a word about your loss;
If you can force your heart and nerve and sinew

To serve your turn long after they are gone,
And so hold on when there is nothing in you
Except the Will which says to them: "Hold on!"

If you can talk with crowds and keep your virtue,
Or walk with Kings—nor lose the common touch,
If neither foes nor loving friends can hurt you,
If all men count with you, but none too much;
If you can fill the unforgiving minute
With sixty seconds' worth of distance run,
Yours is the earth and everything that's in it,
And—which is more—you'll be a Man, my son!

Rudyard Kipling (1865-1936)

INDEX